HAIL TO THE
VICTORS

Greatest Moments in
Michigan Football History

Edited by
FRANCIS J. FITZGERALD

Research by
BOB ROSIEK

ACKNOWLEDGMENTS

Chapter 1 has previously been published in *The Chronicle*, the University of Michigan's student newspaper in that era.

Chapter 2 has previously been published in *The U. of M. Daily*, the University of Michigan's student newspaper in that era.

Chapters 31 and 32 have previously been published in *The Michigan Daily*, the University of Michigan's student newspaper. Reprinted by permission of *The Michigan Daily*.

Chapters 20, 24 and 53 have been previously published in *The New York Times*. Copyright © 1940/48/91 by The New York Times Company. Reprinted by permission.

"Crisler Says Best Team 'Played Greatest Game' Against Trojans" reprinted by permission of The Associated Press.

Chapters 3, 4, 5, 6, 7, 8, 9, 10, 11, 12, 13, 14, 15, 16, 17, 18, 19, 21, 22, 23, 26, 27, 28, 29, 30, 33, 34, 35, 36, 37, 38, 39, 40, 41, 42, 43, 44, 45, 46, 47, 48, 49, 50 and 54 have been previously published in *The Detroit Free Press*. Reprinted by permission of *The Detroit Free Press*.

Chapters 51, 52, 55 and 56 have been previously published in *The Detroit News*. Reprinted by permission of *The Detroit News*.

Research Assistance: Greg Kinney, Bentley Library, University of Michigan; Tara Preston, Jennifer Sutherland, Jim Schneider, B. J. Sohn and Bruce Madej, University of Michigan Sports Information Office, and Pat Harmon, College Football Hall of Fame.

First Printing, *October 1995*
Second Printing, *November 1995*

ISBN 1-887761-00-4
Library of Congress Catalog Card Number: 95-79346

Cover, Book Design and Box Cover by Shayne Bowman.
Typefaces: Village & Bureau Grotesque from Font Bureau.

PUBLISHED BY:
AdCraft Sports Marketing
Kaden Tower, 10th Floor
6100 Dutchmans Lane
Louisville, KY 40205
(502) 473-1124

CONTENTS

Introduction by Bo Schembechler

Contents

Contents

INTRODUCTION

WHEN football fans across the country are asked to describe Michigan football, the image they most always visualize is that of a halfback or receiver such as Tom Harmon, Rob Lytle, Anthony Carter or Desmond Howard in his winged helmet running for big yardage – and for glory.

This is the Michigan mystique. It has also been our tradition.

The University of Michigan has won more college football games than any team west of the Allegheny Mountains and more than any team in Division I-A in America. This is an awesome accomplishment.

Michigan's football and athletic tradition is based on this excellence, and excellence has to be achieved over a long period of time for it to be called tradition. The necessary ingredients that have allowed us to have this wonderful, successful tradition are leadership among coaches and administrators, great players, top-notch facilities and one of the best academic schools in the country.

Fritz Crisler, who preceded me as Michigan's football coach and athletic director and led the Wolverines to greatness on the gridiron in the late 1930's and 1940's, perhaps best described the Michigan tradition when he explained, "Tradition is something you can't bottle. You can't buy it at the corner store, but it is there to sustain you when you need it most. I've called upon it time and time again and so have countless other Michigan athletes and coaches. There's nothing like it. I hope it never dies."

One of the anchors in Michigan's tradition has been its stability in leadership for almost 100 years. Since 1898, we have had just eight athletic directors, and since 1901 there have been only ten football coaches – Fielding Yost, Tad Wieman, Harry Kipke, Fritz Crisler, Bennie Oosterbaan, Bump Elliott, Bo Schembechler, Gary Moeller and now, Lloyd Carr. None of these 10 coaches had a losing record and some established records that will be tough to break for a long, long time.

Yet regardless of who is coaching at Michigan, there will always be a great winning tradition.

And those who coach here and play here accept the responsibility of playing up to that level. We might not always have the best players and we might not always have the best coach, but I doubt if there is any place in America that has a stronger tradition for winning football than Michigan.

This book and video, *Hail to the Victors: Greatest Moments in Michigan Football History*, commemorates that tradition. When it was first planned last fall, the central theme of the project was to pick an all-time list of Michigan's 100 greatest football games and recount the stories of the the Top 50 from this list. And as one might expect, picking 100 of Michigan's greatest games can be a difficult chore.

Finally, however, the list of 100 was set and the book and video were headed for release in early September, soon after the beginning of the 1995 season.

Then an unexpected but very remarkable event took place – one that will be recounted by Michigan men and women to their sons and daughters for years.

Against Virginia in the Pigskin Classic, which featured Lloyd Carr's head-coaching debut, the Wolverines fought valiantly to earn the greatest comeback win in Michigan's long, storied history. Trailing 17-0, and with only 12 minutes remaining in the fourth quarter, Lloyd's gritty youngsters came back to win, 18-17, on the final play of the game when Scott Dreisbach lofted a pass to Mercury Hayes in the corner of the end zone.

I must admit, although Michigan has had many memorable comeback wins, never have we been down so far – by 17 points – and came back to win so big.

This victory was a big boost for Lloyd's new program. And another that added to the Michigan mystique and tradition.

And that finely-tuned list of 100 top Michigan games? As might be expected, a few hours after the win against Virginia it was expanded to 101 games. But these 101 games, which cover more than a century of college football at its best, are ones that will live on in the memories of Michigan fans.

These are a big part of the Michigan tradition.

That tradition, however, is only as rich as the people who have built it. Fortunately, through the years we've been blessed with a lot of special individuals who have contributed to its development. Here are just a few of the great ones:

• One of the first Michigan players to be mentioned should be Gerald Ford, our center who wore jersey number 48 on Harry Kipke's national championship teams of the early 1930's and was the only Michigan football player to become President of the United States.

• Going back to 1898 you have William Cunningham, who is recognized as Michigan's first all-America. He played in the win against Chicago that inspired Louis Elbel to write *The Victors*, the greatest of all college fight songs. Adding to Michigan's tradition is the fine Blue and Maize marching band that plays *The Victors* each fall.

• In the early 1900's you have Neil Snow, the star of the first Rose Bowl game; the great Willie Heston and Adolph (Germany) Schulz, the player credited with inventing the linebacker position.

Those are names that have lived forever in Michigan football history.

• Benny Friedman at quarterback and the "Benny to Bennie" passing combo in 1925 and 1926 with the guy who many think is the greatest player in Michigan football history – Bennie Oosterbaan, another player who became a great coach.

• Another all-America was end Paul Goebel, later a Big Ten official, the mayor of Grand Rapids and a Regent of the University of Michigan. He was a friend I frequently visited who told me stories of Yost's coaching prowess.

• The Wistert brothers - Francis (Whitey), Albert (The Ox) and Alvin (Moose) - what a great story with three brothers wearing the same number (11), and all three great football players. And all three were all-Americans who have been enshrined in the National Football Foundation Hall of Fame.

• Heisman Trophy winner Tom Harmon "Old 98" would have been a great running back in any era.

• Harry Newman at quarterback and Bobby Westfall at fullback; Julius Franks, the all-America guard from up in Grand Rapids; Merv Pregulman at tackle; and the two Elliott brothers, Chalmers (Bump) and Pete, both splendid football players.

• Bob Chappuis, the last of the great triple threat, single-wing backs; Lowell Perry from the more modern era in the early 1950's; and Ron Kramer, one of the greatest all-around athletes that ever played at Michigan and perhaps the greatest tight end we've ever had.

• Bob Timberlake at quarterback and Jack Clancy was a "clutch" receiver. Ron Johnson was one of the finest runners we've ever had here. Our leading interceptor, Tom Curtis, and Jim Mandich, a "big-play" end in the era in which I coached, with Dan Dierdorf at tackle, Henry Hill at middle guard and Reggie McKenzie at guard.

• Thom Darden and Randy Logan as defensive backs and Paul Seymour – three who went on to brilliant pro careers.

• Dave Gallagher, the last player in his recruiting class and an all-America in 1973. Dave Brown, a defensive back who played for at least 15 years in the National Football League, and Don Dufek Jr., one of the toughest guys we've ever had here.

• The best all-around back in my era: Rob Lytle, who played both fullback and tailback, Calvin O'Neal at linebacker and offensive guard Mark Donahue. Jim Smith, the great receiver for us, and the multi-talented Rick Leach at quarterback.

• Curtis Greer at defensive tackle, Ron Simpkins, the all-time leader in tackles; offensive linemen Kurt Becker and George Lilja, and Butch Woolfolk, who was the great ground gainer in my first Rose Bowl victory running behind tackles Ed Muransky and William (Bubba) Paris.

• Anthony Carter, the greatest wide receiver ever to play here and wearing the number 1 jersey.

• Stefan Humphries at guard and Tom Dixon at center, Mike Hammerstein at defensive tackle with Brad Cochran at defensive back.

• Jumbo Elliott at tackle and Jimmy Harbaugh, who won a lot of football games for us at quarterback. Four-time All-Big Ten defensive tackle Mark Messner and center John Vitale.

The list goes on and on...

But I must add Heisman Trophy winner Desmond Howard and Butkus Award-winning linebacker Erick Anderson, as well as offensive tackle Greg Skrepenak and defensive tackle Chris Hutchinson – all players that helped to build the Michigan mystique and tradition.

Once, shortly after my retirement, a sportswriter asked me what Michigan football had meant to me. I pondered the question for a moment because there were many emotions and special memories to draw from. Finally, I told him:

"When a football team takes the field in any stadium in America and sees those winged helmets, you know Michigan is there.

"And because of winning so often and leading the Big Ten in football championships and having the great tradition here, there is a lot of envy out there, but I don't think there is anybody out there – friend or foe – whether from Ohio State, Notre Dame, Michigan State or Penn State or anywhere else in the country that doesn't respect what has been done here at Michigan. Because THIS IS WHAT COLLEGE FOOTBALL IS ABOUT!"

The greatest tradition we have at Michigan is that the vast majority of our players – once they leave the football program – are highly successful in whatever endeavor they have chosen. They make an important contribution to our society. That's what football is all about and that is where Michigan has done an excellent job. THAT IS TRADITION.

Everyone of these players, no matter from what era, would tell you, if they could, that playing football was the greatest experience they had at Michigan.

What more could you ask?

GLENN E. (BO) SCHEMBECHLER
September 7, 1995

Michigan's first varsity football team in 1879. The Wolverines were undefeated in this inaugural season.

MICHIGAN DEFEATS RACINE IN FIRST GAME OF FOOTBALL

BY L. HALSEY
Special to The Chronicle

CHICAGO, May 30, 1879 - The day opened exceedingly warm and continued the entire afternoon. But despite the weather, about 500 Racine students and citizens of Chicago witnessed, what we may call, the finest game of Rugby football ever played this side of the Alleghenies. The White Stocking Ball Park grounds were not in the best condition, with half of the field being quite soft. At about 3:15 a bus took the Michigan team from The Clifton House to the Ball Park, and at 4:15 the game began.

A sharp wind was blowing from the south, which was sure to give the advantage to someone, as the goals were in a north and south line. Michigan won the toss and let Racine have the opening kick, which was caught by Charles Campbell.

Michigan then mixed some good runs and skilled passing to others on the team to move downfield. A scrummage occurred at midfield and the ball advanced toward the Racine goal. Racine eventually brought the ball back to midfield for another scrummage, which occurred but with no advantage to either team. Soon after, Michigan worked the ball slowly back toward the Racine goal. In a short time, Michigan made a touchdown. D. DeTarr, the team captain, added the point-after kick which, according to the referee's decision, missed; but the umpire and the whole team and the spectators declared the goal was safely made.

The ball was then brought out and kicked splendidly by Racine's A.L. Fulforth. Frank Reed fielded the ball for Michigan and attempted a field goal, but it failed. With the ball at midfield, Martin made a good run for his team, but was headed off by R.I. Edwards. Martin again made a good run, but carried the ball just a short distance. As the ball hovered back and forth at midfield the friends of both teams enthusiastly cheered when an inch was made by either team in hard scrummages.

A good kick by Edwards and a run by Irving Pond brought the ball near the Racine goal, but it was carried a short distance away from the Racine goal by Fulforth.

With the wind blowing briskly in Michigan's favor, the ball was worked back to midfield again by the splendid running and throwing of both teams. Racine's A.C. Torbet had the wind knocked out of him briefly, but was soon up again and plucky as ever.

At this point, the ball got out of bounds, near the goal line, and was thrown in by Michigan's W. W. Harman, but declared by the referee a foul, although the majority of the crowd thought differently. R.G. DePuy made a run in for a Michigan touchdown but it was not counted by the referee. Racine then made a safety. Edwards followed up with a good kick and was moving the ball towards the Racine goal when the first 45-minute inning was completed.

At this point, Michigan led by one touchdown.

A rest period of ten minutes was given both teams, during which time several Racine and Michi-gan graduates amused themselves with a few field-goal kicks. However, they only succeeded in covering themselves, not with glory, but with dirt.

The second inning was opened by a good kick-off by DeTarr, which was caught by Racine's George Roberts, who succeeded in bringing the ball to midfield. Michigan eventually got control of the ball and advanced it to within about ten feet of the Racine goal, and it remained there for at least twenty minutes, by drops and pickups. This was the best part of the game, and both teams fought like dogs of war.

John Chase of Michigan especially distinguished himself, and the shout "Chase is there" was made at least twenty times.

DeTarr, however, hung on like a bulldog, and the other men of the Michigan team played exceedingly well. Soon cheer after cheer went up, "Pond forever."

In the stands, it was often noted: "Racine tackles pretty well, but is not skillful at throwing."

Racine briefly gets control of the ball, but Edwards steals it and advances toward the Racine goal, where another *fight* for it occurs.

Again, the ball is thrown out and Pond carried it across the grounds, where he gives it to Harman, who throws it to DePuy. DePuy then carried it across the goal for a touchdown. But a foul was claimed and allowed. Again, the ball is thrown in and the fight is renewed.

Soon DeTarr put it down in a scrummage, where it was kicked by the Racine team and caught by Chase, close behind DeTarr.

Only two minutes more and the second inning would be over. But the gods gave Michigan time to make a field goal, which they did – a place kick by Capt. DeTarr.

The game closed with a score of one touchdown and one field goal for Michigan.

A banquet for the Michigan team this evening at the Palmer House was to be hosted by local alums.

SCORE BY PERIODS

MICHIGAN	0	1	—	1
RACINE	0	0	—	0

Football's first step West

BY WALLACE RICE
Special to The Chicagoan

CHICAGO, September 1930 - Prevailing uproar about college football, past, present and to come, had its modest beginnings in the first game played west of the Alleghenies fifty-one years ago last May, when I acted as an umpire. It was between Racine College, since moribund, and the University of Michigan. Michigan won by a goal and a touchdown, as well as six safeties against Racine – which were not counted in the score. Nor, for the matter of that, was the touchdown; the score was given as one goal to nothing (1-0). And that field goal was kicked in the last two minutes of play. It wasn't such a bad game, but it would hardly be recognized today as a game at all.

Nobody on either side had ever seen a game and Michigan did not have a coach.

I was home on a forced vacation from a prep school in Massachusetts, where I'd played through the fall of 1878 on an amateur eleven called the Newtons. I read in the morning paper that Racine was playing the University of Chicago at baseball that afternoon late in May.

Having been in the grammar school of Racine College for eight years, I went out to see the game. There I learned of the coming football match, Racine being the challenger, and my old schoolmates learned that I had played.

I was promptly invited to come and tell them something about it, and I went. For two afternoons I showed them how to snap the ball back out of a line-up. Nobody ever did tell the Michigan team, but they saw Racine do it after the game began, and did likewise.

In those days each side had an umpire, professedly partisan, and a referee to whom they made their protestations, and he did the deciding. A.J. Petit, at Ann Arbor, who had never seen a game, stood for the University; I came down with the Racine eleven and acted as umpire for them; and W.D. Van Dyke, a Princeton man from Milwaukee, was the referee. Both sides were as polite as football players ever were, and there were no disputes worth mentioning.

It was Friday, May 30, Decoration Day, and hotter than need be – 80° in the shade, and we were in the sun. The place was the old White Stocking Ball Park, on the lake front just across from where the public library now stands. There were side and goal lines marked out, but no yard lines to make a gridiron of the field, there being no penalty for downs in those days.

In fact, the game was played chiefly by brute strength and awkwardness, and it was customary for the heavier side to get the ball and force their way down the field a foot or an inch at a time until they made a touchdown, holding the ball for half an hour or more at a stretch in the process.

The rules were much closer to English Rugby than they are today, as may be seen by the 0-0 game Harvard played with Yale that autumn, with fifteen men on a side.

The wind was high from the southwest. Michigan won the coin toss and Racine kicked off. In those days, let it be said, they played two forty-five minute halves, with a fifteen minute recess between. The game began at 3:45, with about 500 spectators in the grandstand. Racine kicked off. A surprised Inter Ocean reporter would later describe this scene: "In a few minutes the greensward was heaped with the fallen bodies of stalwart students, rolling over a big brown spheroidal-shaped ball."

It should be noted that Racine had six players and Michigan seven in the rush line, the first being the usual disposition in those days. After the game began one of the Michigan men dropped back. There were no quarterbacks, so designated, but two of the halfbacks handled the duties.

The Michigan men were older and heavier, and they forced the play, keeping the ball near the Racine

goal and forced five safeties in the first half and one more in the second against the Wisconsin squad.

Michigan's touchdown was made midway in the first half. K. Green got the ball for Racine and started down the field. Irving Pond, just inches over six feet and weighing more than 200 pounds, caught Green by the neck of his jersey, sending him into a complete forward somersault. After Green dropped the ball, R.G. DePuy picked it up and ran it over for the touchdown, but Michigan missed the point-after goal.

The Racine men thought they were in better condition than Michigan but at the beginning of the second half Pond began performing a series of somersaults which shocked the Racine bench. In the second period, Racine got the ball into Michigan territory, but the game was not settled until almost the last minute of play, when John Chase made a fair catch of a Racine punt at the Racine 20. D. DeTarr, the Michigan team captain, then kicked the field goal.

After that initial contest between Michigan and Racine, it was years before the game really got a hold here in Chicago. Eleven years later, when I was a reporter, I was the only newspaper man in town who had any knowledge of the game whatever, and I reported all the earliest contests – and they were good ones – of the Chicago Athletic Club all-star team against the Boston Athletic Club and other occasional eastern college teams.

More than 50 years later the college football game has come a long way since one of its early contests in Chicago.

CHAPTER 2

An artist's drawing of Charlie Widman's touchdown run against Chicago.

CHAMPIONS OF THE WEST

BY T. R. WOODROW
Special to The U. of M. Daily

CHICAGO, Nov. 24, 1898 - The greatest game of football ever played on a Western gridiron was played on Marshall Field Thanksgiving Day; and Michigan won it, and with it the undisputed title to the Western championship. She won it because she had the best team and played the best game. By hard, consistent teamwork she wrung the prize of victory from Amos Alonzo Stagg's veteran giants.

The coin toss was won by Kennedy of Chicago and he chose the north goal, giving Michigan the kickoff. Bill Caley's kick of 29 yards was a poor one, but Chicago proved unable to advance the ball past Michigan's stonewall defense and Clarence Her-

schberger punted.

Following a pair of fumbles by both teams, Chicago began to move the ball downfield utilizing a series of trick plays. But Stagg reached into his bag of tricks one too many times and Chicago lost the ball on a fumble.

This set up Michigan for its march to a touchdown.

Using consistent, but small gains, Michigan advanced to Chicago's 8-yard line. Their drive was quickly halted by a fumble, which was recovered by Stagg's aggressive defense.

Herschberger then punted on first down. However, a strong Michigan rush caused him to hurry his kick and mis-hit the ball, which sent it directly towards the sidelines for no gain.

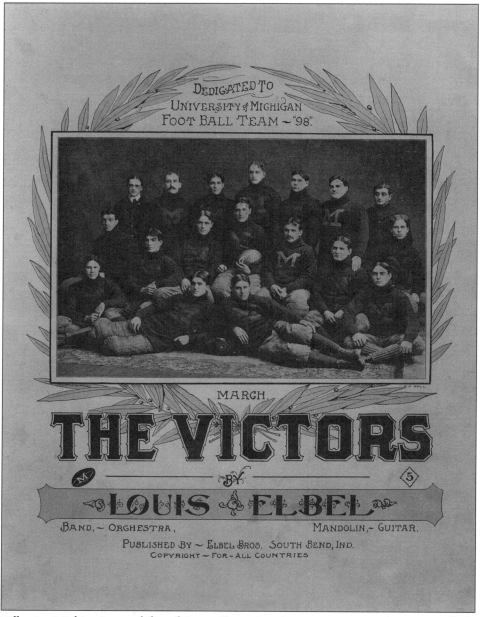

DEDICATED TO
UNIVERSITY of MICHIGAN
FOOT BALL TEAM ~ '98"

MARCH.

THE VICTORS

BY

LOUIS ELBEL

BAND, ~ ORCHESTRA,   MANDOLIN, ~ GUITAR.

PUBLISHED BY ~ ELBEL BROS. SOUTH BEND, IND.
COPYRIGHT ~ FOR ~ ALL COUNTRIES

Following Michigan's 12-11 defeat of Amos Alonzo Stagg's Maroon, U-M student Louis Elbel was inspired to write the famed "The Victors" fight song.

of the day for a field goal. From the Chicago 45, he sent the ball square between the goal posts, so high and far that it would have been an easy field goal if it needed to have gone another 5 or 10 yards. The first half ended with Michigan in control of the football at their own 17-yard line.

Herschberger started the second half with a 50-yard kickoff which Snow returned for 15 yards.

Neither squad was able to make much progress in the opening minutes of the new period. After an exchange of punts, Michigan recovered a Chicago fumble at midfield and then picked up a pair of first downs.

Following a pair of unsuccessful plunges into the line, Widman was called on for a mass on tackle. As the play began, Chicago's ends were drawn into the Michigan mass behind Widman, who was being pushed back. Then suddenly, Widman twisted sideways out of the mass and made a sensational sprint of 45 yards for a touchdown. Three of Chicago's fleetest tacklers were after Widman but neither could reach him or crowd him out of bounds.

As Widman continued toward the Chicago goal line only Ralph Hamill was able to catch up with him before he crossed over. Hamill then made a diving tackle in effort to bring Widman down. A determined Widman, however, managed to shake Hamill lose and in a twisting spin dove for the goal line.

Charles Widman went around end on the first play for a touchdown. Neil Snow easily added the point-after kick.

Henry Kennedy kicked off to Charles Street, who returned the pigskin 25 yards, to begin the new series. Chicago held for the first time in the game which required Caley to punt.

Following a 35-yard return, two Chicago backs hit the Michigan line without budging it.

Herschberger then made the most sensational kick

After several exchanges of punts, Chicago mounted a drive for a touchdown. With William Cavanaugh and Kennedy as his shields, Frank Slaker made most of Chicago's yardage on a series of desperate, diving rushes.

The game later ended with Michigan in possession at midfield.

The Michigan-Chicago contest will go down in the history of football as one of the most memorable ever played in the West. Both squads were in the prime of condition and played fast, clean aggressive football during the entire game.

The Chicago squad was composed almost entirely of veterans who had played in the biggest western games of the past few years. The few new players had played enough games this season to make them veterans. Michigan's team was made up mostly of new, unseasoned players.

The defensive play of Michigan was a sight to behold. Chicago hit the line and tried to sweep the ends again and again but rarely was able to manage a significant gain. Even Chicago's advantage in weight and their quick, aggressive play failed to penetrate the Michigan line. Only when they went to a trick play in the first half and later in the second half when the Michigan men began to let down was Chicago able to mount an offense.

Michigan's offense was nearly the equal of its defense. Led by Widman, it was seldom slowed down.

This afternoon, Widman had an opportunity that comes to few football players, and he took advantage of it. He always made yardage when called upon and followed his blockers closely; leaving them only when compelled to do so, and then would dodge and twist for a gain. It was in his long 45-yard run that Widman had his brightest moment.

He had already outrun three Chicago defenders as he had sailed down the sideline. Finally, when a fourth defender dove at his heels as he neared the Chicago goal line, the determined Widman managed to spin from the Chicago defender's grasp and lunged for the touchdown.

This one game when viewed along with the rest of the Michigan team's play proves why they are now the proud champions of the West.

SCORE BY PERIODS

MICHIGAN..........6   6 — 12
CHICAGO............5   6 — 11
* Time of halves: 35 minutes

Michigan's first all-Americans: Bill Cunningham holding for Neil Snow's kick.

CHAPTER 3

Michigan's vaunted offense en route to another touchdown in its 49-0 defeat of Stanford in the first Rose Bowl game.

MICHIGAN CRUSHES STANFORD IN ROSE BOWL

Special to The Detroit Free Press

PASADENA, Calif., Jan. 1, 1902 - Stanford was convincingly defeated, 49-0, by Fielding Yost's Midwest titans in the inaugural Tournament of Roses football game.

Michigan has now completed its wonderful season by vanquishing eleven great football teams, while scoring 550 points and holding their opponents to none.

For the first 20 minutes of the contest, Michigan showed little advantage over Stanford. On their first two series, Michigan failed to move the ball into

Cardinal territory. Later the Yostmen attempted a pair of field goals which weren't successful; the first from 45 yards wasn't long enough and the second from 25 yards was blocked.

Late in the first half, Stanford mounted the most magnificent defense ever seen on a far Western football field. Michigan's powerful offense had driven down to the Cardinal 3-yard line with little effort and appeared to have a touchdown score cinched up. But on the next four plays Stanford's defense began to dig in.

On first down, the Cardinal forward wall stopped

8

TOP: *Fielding Yost (far left) and his team at practice at Tournament Park prior to 1902 Rose Bowl game.*
BOTTOM: *The Michigan squad crowded into this wagon for the Tournament of Roses parade.*

Michigan just four inches from the goal line. The Yostmen charged into the Cardinal line on the next two plays but were hurled back on each occasion.

Then with the spectators all on their feet in expectation, Michigan rammed into the line once again but the Cardinal defense stiffened and denied the Maize and Blue offense any penetration. After the play, the umpire set the ball 6 inches from the goal line.

Suddenly, a roar and a thunderous applause went up for the California boys.

Three minutes later, Michigan was back battering at the Cardinal goal line once more but the Stanford defense stopped them at the 1-yard line.

The 70-minute match was 25 minutes old before Michigan could score a point. Stanford, however, had already missed two field goals by this point.

But Michigan was too powerful, too quick, too tricky and too immune from injury for Stanford to endure the awesome Michigan smashing attack.

Stanford's men played like demons, but they were sapped from the preparation of the last few days. Six of the original Cardinal squad limped to the sidelines and fresh troops replaced them, but Michigan

stormed on and redoubled the fury of its attack on Stanford's line.

Steadily, the score grew from 0-0 at the end of 25 minutes to 17-0 at the end of the half, and 49-0 at the end of the contest. When the game was finally over, Michigan's squad walked off the field singing and no one was injured.

Up until this contest, Iowa had been the most difficult game for Michigan.

During the game, Michigan rushed for 527 yards on 90 attempts, scored 8 touchdowns, kicked 4 field goals, and made one, for a total of 49 points. Willie Heston led Michigan with 170 yards rushing on 18 carries. Stanford picked up 57 yards on the ground on 24 carries, missed two field goals and failed to score.

Michigan punted 21 times, gaining 858 yards while Stanford punted 16 times for 508 yards.

As darkness began to fall late in the second peri-od, Stanford captain Ralph Fisher approached the Michigan bench offering to concede. This cut the final period short eight minutes, or surely Michigan would have put more points on the scoreboard against the Cardinal.

The 49-0 score speaks for itself. It caps a season that will be long remembered in college football history. Yost's Michigan squad won 11 straight games while outscoring its opponents, 550-0.

SCORE BY PERIODS

MICHIGAN	17	32	—	49
STANFORD	0	0	—	0

Difficult winter conditions forced Yost's squad to practice in the snow while on campus in December 1901.

CHAPTER 4

Willie Heston scored 2 touchdowns in Michigan's 23-6 victory over Minnesota at Regents Field.

MAIZE AND BLUE WAVES TRIUMPHANT IN WEST

Special to The Detroit Free Press

ANN ARBOR, Nov. 27, 1902 - Under a sullen sky that broke at midday, Michigan's eleven met Minnesota and established beyond question the right of the Ann Arbor warriors to take to themselves the title of football champions of the West. The score was 23-6.

It rested with today's game to assure Michigan the championship, though developments of the afternoon proved that the title was really won when Michigan defeated Wisconsin at Chicago.

Michigan played the game as its admirers had hoped that it would, beginning with a fierce onslaught that gave it a score in the first five minutes of play. From that point on, there was never any question as to the ultimate result.

An estimated crowd of more than 8,000 paying customers were in the stands and more then 1,000 people who love football, but didn't want to pay to see the game, viewed the contest from various vantage points around the field.

But the dominant note of the gathering was girls. They were there in every type and style, in every section of the stands and on every row. There were college girls and town girls, sweater girls and girls

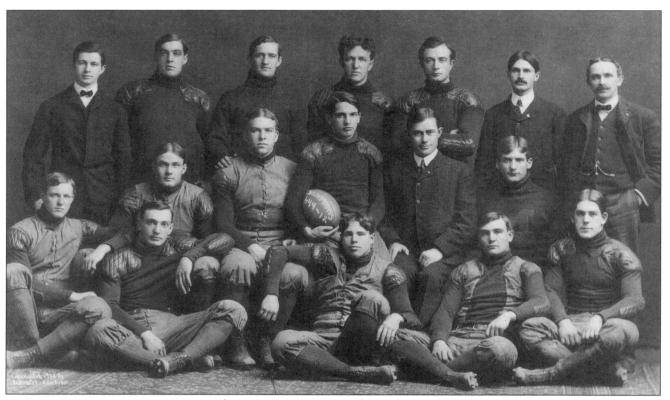

Yost's 1902 "Point-a-Minute" team outscored its opponents, 644-12, and posted an undefeated record of 11-0.

in gowns. And whatever type of girl she was, she was always a Michigan girl. Without her the game would undoubtedly have progressed but it would have lacked its inspiration. To her especially appealed the spectacle of the exhausted A.E. Herrnstein, fighting to get back into a game in which he was unable to continue, or valorous Everett Sweeley, struggling to get back to his feet time after time in the second half, after having been made the brunt of the Minnesota attack. It was her inspiration, more than the love of the applause, that propelled onward Michigan men who were tiring under the strain of a fiercely waged contest.

Prior to the opening kickoff, there were various formalities. Minnesota introduced its mascot, "Doc Knipe," the bulldog that has been announced before the contest, parading him at the head of its brass band, a uniformed organization of forty pieces. Michigan produced a rival mascot in the form of a live turkey, its wings dyed blue, its other plumage a bright yellow. It proved, ultimately, to be Turkey Day in a double sense.

For the first seven minutes of the game Yost's men

never loosened their grip on the pigskin until it had been forced over the goal line at the other end. The Minnesota line was hurled back again and again. Herb Graver and Joe Maddock led the attack downfield, with Maddock taking the ball over for the touchdown. Sweeley added the point-after kick.

Afterward, a punting contest developed. Sweeley punted no less than five times. Minnesota punted in return four times. The Gophers' last punt, however, was fatal. It went out of bounds near the 30-yard line. On the first play Willie Heston broke through the line, got by left end, and sprinted for a touchdown. Sweeley's extra-point conversion was successful.

The second half, from several standpoints, was not as pleasing as the opener. For one thing, while less than fifty minutes of actual time sufficed for the opening thirty-five-minute half, it required one hour and a quarter to play the second thirty-five minutes. Frequent injuries to players on both sides caused this. And each fleeting minute found the wind more biting. Minnesota's touchdown was the second touchdown that has been recorded against Michigan in two years.

It fell to John Flynn to achieve the honor of crossing the Michigan line – and to win for Minnesota partisans much money, based on whether or not the Ann Arbor boys would shut out their rivals. Flynn scored by recovering Harrison Weeks' fumble of a pass from center and running for the touchdown. The Gophers added the extra-point kick.

Minnesota, encouraged, now began to play fiercely.

After an injury to Herrnstein, Michigan moved the ball to the Minnesota 25. On fourth down, Weeks decided on a desperate play. The ball was way over towards the sideline, in front of the covered stand. It was a most difficult spot, but Sweeley was called on for a place kick. He was equal to the occasion, and as Weeks placed the ball Sweeley took careful aim and shot it between the goalposts for another five points. This play sent the rooters into a wild frenzy.

Sweeley's heroics were now in the center of the spotlight and the focus of the Minnesota squad, whose fierce hitting soon took its toll. After one play, Sweeley received an elbow in the stomach, knocking him out. The ball was picked up by a Minnesota runner (Flynn), who took it over the goal line, twenty yards away. On the next play Lawrence fumbled, but another Minnesota player picked it up and carried it over for a touchdown, but it was called back, too, after Laurie Bliss, the umpire, penalized Minnesota for hitting Sweeley's head after he was down. This, of course, was rough work and Minnesota would eventually tire under the fierceness of its own play.

Michigan's final score came when Heston broke through on the 35-yard line and only had to outrun one Minnesota player en route to the goal line. Heston hurdled him. Sweeley made the extra-point kick easily.

SCORE BY PERIODS

MICHIGAN	12	11 —	23
MINNESOTA	0	6 —	6

Michigan attempts to move its "flying wedge" against Minnesota.

CHAPTER 5

GREAT CROWD STOPPED GAME WHEN MINNESOTA ELEVEN TIED

Special to The Detroit Free Press

MINNEAPOLIS, Oct. 31, 1903 - With two minutes left to play and the score tied, 6-6, the struggle between Minnesota and Michigan was brought to a premature close this afternoon when thousands of Gopher rooters swarmed onto the playing field making it impossible to continue play.

In those two minutes the game might have yielded a winner, though it is doubtful because of the stubborn manner in which the contest had been fought; and the slowness in which the touchdowns had been secured.

Those two minutes, however, were impossible to play, and one of the contests that was to aid in deciding a Western champion closed with the situation – as far as Minnesota and Michigan are concerned – the same as before the game.

Neither side was able to score in the first period. Michigan made her touchdown in the middle of the second half, after 75 yards of fierce, continuous line bucking. It looked like Michigan's game until Minnesota got the ball on a fumbled punt at Michigan's 45-yard line and pushed it over for the second touchdown of the game by the same sort of vicious straight football that had earned Michigan her score. As soon as Minnesota kicked the point-after the score was tied, 6-6, and the crowd swarmed out on the field in such numbers that it was absolutely impossible to clear the gridiron. With darkness rapidly spreading over the field and only two minutes left to play, the officials had no alternative but to call the game.

In the first half, Minnesota clearly outplayed Michigan. Minnesota took the ball in one stretch of line bucking from her own 45-yard line to Michi-

Willie Heston was Michigan's first 2-time all-America, earning this honor from Walter Camp in 1903 and again in 1904.

14

The third edition of Yost's "Point-a-Minute" teams went 11-0-1 in 1903 and outscored its opponents, 565-6. Minnesota was the only team to score against Michigan.

gan's 15. In the second half, Minnesota had the upper hand up to the time when Michigan started the spurt that resulted in her score. The performance of the Wolverines in snatching apparent victory from the jaws of apparent defeat was a remarkable exhibition of nerve and scientific football. Minnesota's feat in tying the score and gaining a draw was even more remarkable.

The surprise of the day was the way in which Minnesota ripped up Michigan's line. Even the much heralded John Maddock and John Curtis were buttoned up the whole game by George Webster and Fred Schacht. In the first half Webster ripped up the Michigan line and spoiled many plays before they were started.

The second half was a testimonial to the craft of Yost. The hurry-up coach evidently instructed his men between the halves to use trick plays and fake interference whenever possible. Nearly all of the gains

that earned Michigan's touchdown were made on these trick plays, and on the magnificent running of Willie Heston, who fully upheld his reputation as the best halfback in the West. The game was also a tribute to the skill of Keene Fitzpatrick. The veteran Michigan trainer brought his men on the field in splendid physical condition and 24 of the tiresome time-outs caused by injuries to players were due to the poor condition of the Minnesota men. Still, the game was the finest ever seen on a Minnesota field.

The first half of the game proved to be a grand exhibition of football. Through neither goal was in immediate danger during the half, Minnesota and Michigan fought an uphill, defensive game most of the time. Maddock, the sturdy Michigan right tackle, was forced to play his best game; for it was against this wing of the Michigan defense that Minnesota made most of her gains.

Although the half ended without either side scoring, Minnesota carried the ball 155 yards, against 60 yards by Michigan.

The second half opened with Minnesota's hopes bubbling over. The play of Michigan's halfback, Heston, was terrific, and easily 75 percent of Michigan's gains in its march from their 26-yard line to the Minnesota goal line were made by this plunging back. A first down brought the ball to the Minnesota 3. Tom Hammond was sent against the desperate Minnesota defensive formation to gain the coveted distance. He fell short only six inches from the Gophers' goal.

Then Heston was given the ball and the honor of carrying it over for the touchdown. After the point-kick was booted the score stood: Michigan 6, Minnesota 0.

In the play that led up to the making of this touchdown the Michigan team showed its mettle. The team raced and played with speed, while the Gophers were constantly taking time-out. The

Wolverines later got the ball again on their 35-yard and then gave the most brilliant exhibition of straight football in the game.

Later in the period Minnesota began the march which carried the Gopher eleven to Michigan's goal line and the quick ending of the game.

SCORE BY PERIODS

MICHIGAN 0   6 — 6
MINNESOTA 0   6 — 6

Left on the sidelines after their 6-6 tie with Minnesota, the Gophers later challenged Michigan to a rematch and an opportunity to reclaim their prized water jug. A rivalry was thus born.

CHAPTER 6

Michigan's 22-12 victory over Chicago earned the Yostmen their fourth straight national championship and extended their winning streak to 44 games.

MICHIGAN LINE TWICE CROSSED

BY JOE S. JACKSON
Special to The Detroit Free Press

ANN ARBOR, Nov. 12, 1904 - Never in all the four long years in which Michigan has been acknowledged champion of the West in football have the Maize and Blue been so badly frightened as during the first part of the second half of today's contest with the University of Chicago. The game closed with Michigan victorious, 22-12, but for a long time it hung in the balance at 16-12.

Never in those same four years had a Michigan eleven undergone the experience of this one of 1904.

In all the forty or more games played in this period no eleven had twice crossed Michigan's goal line in one day. No Chicago eleven had succeeded in doing it at any time, and in that agonizing second period there were those who wondered if Michigan coach Fielding Yost had not spoken more wisely than had been believed, when he said this team (Chicago) was one to be reckoned with.

Michigan pulled it out, however, and she did it by an exhibition of the sort of play that for three years made her the feared opponent of all other Western elevens, and that caused her supporters to believe her a worthy opponent for any of the big teams of the East. Michigan moved the ball the entire length of the field by a succession of fierce attacks that swept Chicago off its feet, and that finally landed the ball over the goal line. It was her great exhibition of an afternoon's play that was otherwise somewhat inconsistently brilliant at times, and at other times far from her standard. Michigan outplayed Chicago at all times except for the few minutes of the first half, in which the Maroons made their first touchdown, and a small portion in the second period.

Michigan's four touchdowns were all earned by hard-played football, marked by a few brilliant dashes and the onslaughts of Willie Heston, Tom Hammon, Frank Longman and Fred Norcross. Three of these touchdowns came in the first half, and one, by Heston, in the second.

Chicago got one in each half, the first earned by a great exhibition of line bucking, after an error of judgement in the backfield had put the Maroons within striking distance of the goal. The other was fluky in its nature, with Walter Eckersall snatching the ball out of the air after one of Michigan's numerous fumbles, and running unblocked for thirty-five yards for a touchdown.

A crowd of 12,500 packed Ferry Field, including 15 train loads of Chicago fans and three train loads of Michigan fans from Detroit. On occasion, when the afternoon got windy, smoke from the locomotives' stacks at times would make it difficult to see the game at the Western end of the field.

Germany Schultz, who was wearing a specially-built face mask, which had a most grotesque appearance, was the notable figure when the play began.

Only one of Michigan's regular eleven was forced to retire from the game; Tom Hammond giving way to just before the close of the second half. For the Maroons, only five who started were there at the finish.

At the start of the game it looked like another of those old-time Michigan slaughters of the Maroon. Until the Ann Arbor eleven had scored their first ten points, which they made long before the first half was half gone, Chicago not only never had the ball in Michigan territory, but never had possession of the ball except for the minute or two after John

Curtis kicked off to start the game. When Will DeTray, who caught the Michigan kickoff, had been stopped, he was at his own fifteen-yard line. Chicago, after a few short gains, was forced to punt. Michigan then began a march to the Chicago goal line, with Heston, Longman and Hammond hammering the line and making big gains through Chicago's right wing. Hammond was sent over for the touchdown but his point-after kick failed.

Heston made the long run of the day for the next score. Michigan got the kickoff near its 25-yard line and from that point Michigan never lost possession of the ball. Heston was in Michigan territory when he got the ball and broke lose around left end. He straight-armed Eckersall for 10 yards, and had but one man to pass when Eckersall got him from behind and brought him down inside Chicago's 15-yard line, after a run of nearly forty-five yards. From this point a touchdown was only a matter of a few minutes. Tom Hammond again got the call and scored. Fred Norcross stumbled on the extra point attempt. Michigan now led, 10-0.

Then Chicago broke the fast of four long years. Eckersall got the kickoff near his own 15-yard line, but Chicago was unable to budge the Michigan line. Norcross and Bill Clark dropped back for the expected punt. They underrated Eckersall's ability for he sent the ball high over Clark's head and it rolled over the goal line. It was brought out to the Michigan 25-yard line. Yost's squad then punted with Eckersall fielding it at Michigan's 45-yard mark. He returned it eight yards.

Chicago then surprised everyone by a steady and successful hammering of Michigan's line to drive for a touchdown. After the point-after was kicked, the Chicago band broke into "Hot Time" and the Maroon contingent went wild.

Michigan made it safe again with another touchdown before the half was done, holding Chicago after the latter had taken the ball on the kickoff. The Maroons tried a fake play, forming for a punt, and shifting to a quarterback sweep, but Michigan got through and downed Eckersall, taking the ball.

This was at Chicago's 20-yard line, and the march to the goal line was easy. Heston broke through for the touchdown after a number of short gains. Fol-

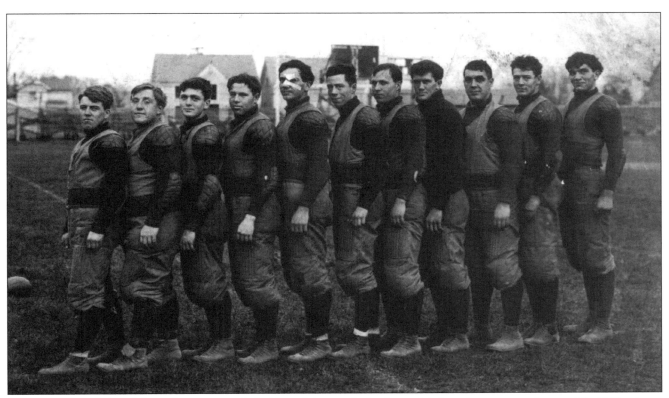

Willie Heston (4th from left) and Germany Schulz (far right) were the leaders in Michigan's 10-0 season in 1904. The Wolverines outscored the competition, 567-22.

lowing the extra-point kick, Michigan led, 16-6. At this point Chicago began to drop her cripples, and Michigan began to drop the ball, but no fumbles in this half were costly.

The Maroons took the breath away from Michigan rooters almost at the start of the second half. Michigan got the kickoff at her 20-yard line and Heston took the ball to the 35-yard line on the first play. On the next play there was a fumble, the ball bounced into the air and was grabbed by Eckersall. With no one in his path he ran untouched for a touchdown. Chicago added the extra point. This made the score 16-12. Another fumble as expensive as this one would put Chicago in the lead. And a chance for Eckersall to dropkick a field goal might mean a tie.

Finally, Michigan awoke and put on as fine an exhibition as Ferry Field followers have ever seen. After the kickoff, she held Chicago at its 25-yard line, only to lose the ball on another fumble, but recovered it at the Michigan 45-yard line. Heston went up the middle for fifteen yards and Chicago

then held Michigan with a similar brace, and took the ball on downs.

After another fumble and recovery Michigan was held for a second time and in turn forced Chicago to punt. Clark fielded the kick and was downed inside his own 15-yard line. Here was where the fighting began.

With the Chicago goal line nearly 90 yards away, Michigan carried the ball without losing it in a series of fast and vicious attacks. The backfield alternated in advancing it, until Longman finally went over for the touchdown. After Tom Hammond made the goal, Michigan was out of danger wih a 22-12 lead. Chicago, however, was weakening and the time was growing very short.

SCORE BY PERIODS

MICHIGAN 16   6 — 22
CHICAGO 6   6 — 12

Yost's 1905 "Point-a-Minute" team had amassed a 56-game unbeaten streak, but Chicago's 2-0 win brought this to a halt.

CHICAGO DEFEATS MICHIGAN IN FIERCE STRUGGLE

BY JOE S. JACKSON
Special to The Detroit Free Press

CHICAGO, Nov. 30, 1905 - By the smallest possible score in football, 2-0, and before the greatest crowd in the history of the game in the West – close to 27,000 persons – Michigan this afternoon lost the Western championship to Chicago. It was a bitter blow to both the team and to Fielding Yost, marking the first defeat the Ann Arbor school has sustained in five years, and the first championship that the Michigan coach has ever been beaten out of.

It was the irony of fate that Michigan should finish her season with more points to her credit and less against her than any team in this country, and yet, on the two points that were made, she should lose the sectional title. Both teams were unable to gain much yardage, but the contest was a remarkable one.

The two points that were made came midway in the second period; the game, up to that time, having been very evenly contested. Chicago had the ball and as had happened a dozen times earlier, Walter Eckersall, through failure of his teammates to advance it, was called upon to punt.

Chicago at the time was at Michigan's 43-yard line. Al Barlow and Bill Clark were playing back to field the kick, but it was a low punt and carried a good distance, and went between them. Clark went into the end zone after the ball with two Chicago players chasing him. With hardly a chance to get away, he could have played it safe and avoided a score by merely touching the ball down behind the line. Instead, Clark shook off the two tacklers and tried to run the ball back. A yard or so after crossing the goal line on the field, Mark Catlin threw him back, over his own goal line. The result was a safety, two points, and the game.

In a measure, Eckersall thus gratified his ambition to be the principal instrument in Michigan's defeat, his kick paving the way to safety. Otherwise he proved no great menace to Yost's men. Only once during the entire game did he have opportunity to try for a field goal. In the second period he tried to lift one from the 40-yard line, but his kick was low, and was blocked.

Looking back at the game, the slips that Michigan made stand out glaringly, though to the average rooter they bring not as much regret as the banishment of Joe Curtis which came early in the game. This greatly affected the Michigan attack.

Curtis has both Umpire Rheinhart and Eckersall to thank for his trip to the sidelines, a little skillful acting by the latter having its effect on the former. Eckersall was making a punt and Curtis broke through to block it. The momentum of his rush sent him against Eckersall, who claimed that he was kneed, went to the grass and there remained until the official decided that Curtis must leave the game.

This disqualification and fumbles at critical times told against Michigan. At the very start of the game Michigan had the ball on Chicago's twenty-five yard line but a fumble lost it to the Maroons. Later there were similar errors, all of them at most agonizing periods.

Michigan was represented almost as well in fan support as was the Midway institution.

There was not a vacant seat in the East stands. At either end were standing platforms similar to those at Ann Arbor, but much larger. These were jammed. Michigan and Chicago rooters jointly held the West stand. Before the game Chicago authorities figured the capacity of the field at better than 26,000.

If there was a man who stood out prominently in the contest, it was Johnnie Garrels, the Detroit schoolboy who plays left end for Michigan. When asked to oppose the best kicker in the West, Eck-

Adolph (Germany) Schulz won fame as a "roving center" on defense. Picked by Walter Camp as an all-America in 1907, he was later selected to the All-Time all-America team in 1951.

ersall, he held his own, and a little better most of the time. On offensive play he was one of the notable figures.

The only time Michigan threatened to score was in the second half when Garrels, on a trick play, taking the ball at midfield, got around Chicago's left end and had only Eckersall between himself and the goal line. Had there been a blocker near enough to brush off Eckersall, Michigan would have scored an easy touchdown and a victory. The longest run of the game, a dash of thirty-five yards around Chicago's right wing, was also made by Garrels. Though Eckersall robbed him of a touchdown, the Detroit lad had revenge in getting Eckersall behind his own line several times, throwing him for losses. The Chicago quarterback gave a great spectacular exhibition and was frequently successful in evading two and three Michigan tacklers when running back punts. Early in the game this netted him something. Later most of his runs, though long, were backward and across the field, and gained no yardage.

The entire game was marked by kicking and by open play. The first period bore a very strong resemblance to the second period of the Wisconsin game after Michigan had scored its touchdown. It looked as if Yost was trying to wear out the Chicago men without using his own line plungers to any great extent with the intention of coming back strong in the second half. This impression was furthered by the last two minutes of play in this first half when Michigan ripped up Chicago at will on the way to the goal line.

Chicago had just one promising chance to score in the first half. With only a few minutes left in the first period, the Maroons got the ball at the 35-yard mark and began to drive past midfield. A penalty of fifteen yards, however, spoiled their efforts and the ball went back to Michigan. This revived the hopes of her rooters for a grand finish. Garrels raced for fifteen yards on a fake punt and Fred Norcross made a quarterback sweep just before time was called.

The second half did not differ materially from the first one. There was almost as much kicking; Michigan punting nine times and losing the ball twice on fumbles while Chicago punted nine times, tried a drop kick once and was held once. Chicago resorted entirely to the kicking game after getting her two points, and Michigan used it to get the ball into Chicago territory apparently in the hope of securing it on downs, or through a fumble within a short march of the line. The Maroons, however, handled punts faultlessly, and took no chances on letting the ball go over on downs.

Eckersall's one try for a field goal came to him as a result of a Michigan fumble early in the period. Yost's boys had started out trying to rush the ball, but failed, the attacks seeming to lack speed and the team being unable to make consistent gains. Norcross fumbled a punt on Michigan's 38-yard line and Chicago got the ball. The Maroons advanced a little but not enough so, on third down, Eckersall dropped back for a drop-kick from the 40-yard line. The kick was too low and was half-blocked.

Michigan tried hard to score, but the powerful attack that drove the length of the field against Wisconsin was not there, or Chicago was a much better team. In the second half, Garrels made the only notable run, when he nearly got away for a touchdown on a trick play going around Chicago's left end as the blockers went the other way. Had he escaped Eckersall, there was no other man near him and it would have been a jaunt to the goal line.

Instead, it was a dying effort.

SCORE BY PERIODS

MICHIGAN	0	0 —	0
CHICAGO	0	2 —	2

Michigan utilized the forward pass for the first time late in the second half to break a scoreless duel with Minnesota.

BRILLIANT USE OF FORWARD PASS GIVES U–M VICTORY OVER GOPHERS

BY E. A. BATCHELOR
Special to The Detroit Free Press

ANN ARBOR, Nov. 10, 1910 - Two perfectly executed forward passes, each as swift and sure as a rapier's thrust; two plunges into the Minnesota line, and Michigan this afternoon had beaten the Gophers, won the undisputed championship of the West, established her claim to be considered the country's best and proved the superiority of skill and cunning over mere strength.

With less than five minutes to play in the final quarter of a desperate, punishing, but at the same time thrilling game, the Wolverines saw the opening for which they had been looking ever since the battle began. They were quick to seize it.

More than 55 minutes of the fiercest football ever seen on the new Ferry Field, football so grueling and intense that nearly every other play rendered some athlete a candidate for the trainers' attentions, had produced no score for either side, and had left the ball in Michigan's possession on her own 47-yard line. With the timekeeper's watch rapidly ticking off the few precious moments that remained before the close of hostilities, it was up to Michigan to adopt some plan of action that would produce quick results if she wished to escape the misfortune of a drawn battle.

The forward pass was decided upon as the maneuver most likely to result in a change in the tide and it proved to be exactly what was expected. First, the ball was shot to Stan Borleske, Michigan's left end, who caught it neatly and dashed to Minnesota's 30-yard line before they nailed him. Right here Michigan outguessed Minnesota's defense completely. The Gophers never anticipated that the pass play would be repeated. But it was, and with such success that Borleske lacked only three yards of the goal line when the desperate Maroon and Gold players dashed him to the turf.

First down and but three yards to go! Nothing short of a miraculous stiffening of the defense or the misfortune of a fumble could stop the advancing Wolverines now, and neither of these contingencies arose. Stanley Wells was called upon to make a path to the land of plenty behind the final chalk mark. On the first attempt he would get only a yard; with the Gophers, fighting with the courage of desperation and the fury of wild men, hurling themselves upon him before he well got underway. Again, Wells' signal was called and the line of blue locked with the line of red. For a moment the result of the plunge was in doubt to the eager thousands in the stands, but suspense was short-lived. When Referee Hackett separated the gladiators, Wells was found hugging the pigskin to his chest, safely over the goal line.

Then the crowd cut loose. There had been cheering all afternoon; some of it spontaneous, some inspired by the perspiring yellmasters. But what had gone before as a noise would have seemed a mere whisper beside the great Niagara of sound that broke from thousands of throats when Wells fought his way into the territory behind the Gophers' goal.

Venerable professors, giddy freshmen, staid and usually phlegmatic businessmen, small boys, pretty girls and even sweet-faced old ladies stood up and howled until their vocal cords refused to emit another sound.

Down on the field the Michigan team, substitutes, coaches, band and everyone else who managed to pass the barriers and gain admittance to the inclosure set aside for the elite, swarmed out on the battleground, mingling in one wild, joyous shouting, hugging, handshaking mob. The crisp November air was alive with blankets, hats, musical instruments and even money, some of the shouters being so excited that they threw away regular cash.

A crowd of more than 18,000 would jam Ferry Field to view Michigan's long-awaited season finale against undefeated arch-rival Minnesota.

Ferry Field served as the Wolverines' second home playing field until Michigan Stadium was opened in 1927.

It took some time for the officials, who had to preserve their dignity, however much they wanted to shout, to clear the field. When the last maniac had been herded to his placed on the sidelines, and the substitutes had gathered up the assorted trombones and bass drums, Michigan was given a chance to try for the point-after kick.

Neil (Shorty) McMillan, the little quarterback who handled the reins over that great Michigan team, booted the ball to Bill Edmunds, who heeled it. Then McMillan poised the oval for Fred Conklin and, when the latter got the angle just to his liking, he booted the ball squarely between the uprights. That made the score Michigan 6, Minnesota 0, which is the way it will endure through all the ages of football history.

Several minutes of playing time still remained. There have been times when the complexion of a game has been changed even as late in the day as

this, but such occasions occur mostly in books featuring the exploits of Frank Merriwell and other reliable heroes. Nothing of the sort was in the cards for Minnesota this time and the game for all intents and purposes had ended when Wells crawled over the goal line.

The Gophers didn't quit, though, badly as things looked for them after Michigan scored.

They received George Lawton's kickoff and were making fair progress working the ball down into Michigan's region of the field when the timekeeper blew his whistle. In these last few minutes the visitors really opened up some new football for the first time in the game and were getting away with it rather well.

Although all the scoring of the game occurred in the last part of the final quarter and came with a suddenness that was like a thunderbolt from a blue sky, there was action every minute of the whole four periods. Both teams had several chances to score points and there were thrills strewn liberally throughout the battle.

Minnesota started out like a winner, taking advantage of a Michigan fumble in the first period and getting the ball to the Wolverines' 8-yard line before the defense stiffened and compelled Johnny McGovern to try for a field goal. McGovern's famous toe wasn't working well on this occasion and he missed by a wide margin. This gave Michigan a breathing spell and enabled her to take the ball temporarily out of danger.

Before the end of this first period, however, there was another – and bigger – scare in store for the Michigan adherents. With the ball in Michigan's 25-yard line, big James Walker broke through like an elephant charging through a canebrake and blocked one of Lawton's punts just as it left his toe. Leonard Frank, a Minnesota end, was on the alert and he picked up the ball and carried it across the goal line without being touched. Gloom sat heavy on the Michigan thousands, while across the field in the Gophers' cheering section men were going mad with joy.

However, one of the officials had been touched by the ball while in play, so Michigan was permitted to try the play over again, based on the rule which says "that when the ball strikes an official, it becomes dead on the spot." Lawton then punted out of danger and Minnesota's last real chance to make trouble had fled.

Costly fumbling by Michigan's backfield kept the Yostmen on the defensive for almost the entire first period. Then the nervousness passed – and with it the penchant for putting the ball in the air – and the Wolverines came into their own. From the beginning of the second quarter on, the Wolverines outperformed the Gophers; the newer style of giving them the advantage.

Coach Henry Williams' team exhibited wonderful power at times and its famous shift play was productive on a lot of short gains.

Michigan played the most open game that she had shown all season, using the forward pass time and again.

Dr. Williams practically ignored their new brand of open football until after Michigan had scored. Then the Gophers tried it in desperation, realizing that they had everything to win and nothing to lose.

Michigan appeared to gain strength as the game progressed, playing much better football in the third and fourth periods than in the first and second. The final quarter was the one in which superiority was most in evidence, but the last few moments of the third stanza led up to some of the thrillers of the close. Just before third period ended, a forward pass, and some good line bucking and a dash by Vic Pattengill enabled the Yostmen to move the ball from midfield to Minnesota's nine-yard line.

It was maddening to the spectators to have action halted at this exciting juncture because the period had ended, but the rules make this sort of thing necessary and there was nothing for the nervous ones to do but sit and bite their nails for the three minutes during which the gladiators rested.

Play began in the last session with the ball in Michigan's possession, first down, on Minnesota's nine-yard stripe. Here the Gophers gave their grittiest defensive exhibition of the day, stopping two plays directed at the line. Lawton then fell back for the field-goal attempts but his kick missed the goalposts by a foot.

This turn of affairs gave the ball to Minnesota on a touchback and enabled them to get out of immediate peril.

Michigan later got possession of the ball at midfield and started the attack that was to turn Ann Arbor into a city of the insane and to hang crepe on the doors up in Minneapolis.

SCORE BY PERIODS

MICHIGAN..........0	0	0	6	— 6
MINNESOTA 0	0	0	0	— 0

Trailing, 21-0, Penn mounted one of the greatest comeback's in college football history to defeat the Wolverines, 27-21.

MARSHALL RALLIES PENN TO VICTORY OVER MICHIGAN IN FINAL MINUTE

BY E. A. BATCHELOR
Special to The Detroit Free Press

PHILADELPHIA, Nov. 9, 1912 - The Pennsylvania worm turned.

Three touchdowns by Michigan before the Quakers scored a point ought to have beaten the sons of Old Penn today, or at least ought to have discouraged them. Three touchdowns did nothing of the sort. On the contrary, the early advantage secured by the Wolverines only seemed to furnish the inspiration that the Red and Blue had previously lacked. With apparently certain defeat staring them in the face, the Pennsylvania men began to fight and they kept on fighting until the final whistle blew.

Four touchdowns, the last of which was scored in the final minute of play by quarterback Dick Marshall, who ran 50 yards through the entire Ann Arbor team, gave Penn a victory that will live forever in the memoirs of those who witnessed the contest as the finest exhibition of gameness ever witnessed on the gridiron.

Had the result and the manner of its achievement been reversed, Philadelphia would have been no place for a sane man tonight; as it is, they have turned out the fire department, the militia and the police reserves to keep the Penn students from making a bonfire of the city hall and that even more sacred edifice, the Broad Street station of the Pennsylvania Railroad.

Michigan was beaten after she apparently had the game won, but she lost to a team that, like the immortal John Paul Jones, doesn't know when it is licked. Expressed in cold numerals the final score was 27-21.

The score stood 21-0 in Michigan's favor, with the second quarter almost done. After making these three touchdowns the Maize and Blue appeared poised to run up the score higher.

As for the possibility of Penn's ever winning the game, that never occurred to anyone, but eleven Quakers who were out there struggling as no team ever had struggled before.

Then all at once Michigan lost her punch. The bottom dropped out of both the Wolverines' offense and defense at the same time. Beginning with the last five minutes of play in the second period, there was one good team on the field and one very bad one. The desperate Red and Blue managed to score one touchdown before the first half ended, but Michigan's 14 points looked like a big margin.

Right after the second half opened the Yost team got what looked like a touchdown.

Jimmy Craig ran half the length of the field and across the goal line only to be called back and Michigan penalized because somebody had been holding. That was the Maize and Blue's final chance. Before the period ended Penn had secured another seven points, which made Michigan's margin going into the last 15 minutes only seven.

And in this final quarter came the most desperate football of the day. Penn, outplaying her opponent always and gaining freely, was held scoreless until the final five minutes when a forward pass gave her a touchdown and a chance to tie.

Lon Jourdet caught the ball on this occasion and carried it over the goal line making the score Michigan 21, Pennsylvania 20. Chester Minds, the Quakers kicker, had a hard angle from which to make his try and he missed by inches, much to the joy of the Michigan contingent, which by this time was well content to win by any margin, however small.

With only about three minutes to play, it looked as though the Westerners would squeak though. It kept on looking so until there were just 23 seconds remaining. Then Michigan, having been held for three downs on her own 20-yard line, tried a kick on fourth down. George Thomson got away a beautiful long spiral that bored into the teeth of the wind for 35 yards.

Marshall, the Penn quarterback, caught the ball on his own 45-yard line and started goal-ward.

The Michigan tacklers, swarming like bees to the vicinity of the play, apparently had him down once, but Marshall stumbled, caught his balance again, and cutting across the field resumed his dash to the haven of victory. By this time there were four men blocking for Marshall and they brushed Michigan's defenders aside like flies.

Marshall is fast, faster in a football suit than any man on the Penn team – even the mighty Leroy Mercer – and he never ran better in his life. Once underway with that cordon of Red and Blue blockers protecting him, Michigan was helpless and Marshall didn't stop until he had carried the ball over the goal line.

The next five minutes of this interesting contest gave the Philadelphia police a chance to show their efficiency. The moment Marshall crossed the goal line somebody opened the door of the madhouse and several thousand of the most violent and dangerous inmates came swarming on the field. They hugged Marshall, shook him by the hand and even kissed him; the gridiron was literally paved with hats, canes, flags and everything that could be thrown. Apparently everybody thought time had expired, but it hadn't and according to the rules of the game, Michigan was entitled to a kickoff. Possibly Michigan could have made an equally inspiring dash and thus gained the victory that fortune had cheated her, the Wolverines hoped.

Players, officials, policeman and all others in authority united in trying to control the frenzied rooters. At first the task was about seven times too large, but finally the madmen were convinced they could break up their own hats and hug one another on the sidelines just as well as on the field. Minds then got an opportunity to kick the point-after, which Penn didn't need a bit.

Michigan received the kickoff and tried a couple of forward passes before the few remaining seconds ticked off. There was no Johnny Garrels present to add to the sensational happenings, however, and Head Linesman Crowell came out and honked his horn (to signal the end of the game) before anything important had happened.

Never since the introduction of football into the curriculum of American colleges had there been a more dramatic game, nor one which had such a climax. The matter in which Penn had outplayed Michigan in the last two quarters had filled the few

Wolverine rooters with fear that a tie might ensue, but when Minds missed the point-after kick following the third touchdown, it seemed as though the gods had decided to spare Michigan her victory after giving her a scare.

But the cards didn't lie that way and a play that originated in the fertile imagination of a writer of fiction dashed the Maize and Blue to the ground.

SCORE BY PERIODS

MICHIGAN	14	7	0	0 —	21
PENN	0	7	7	13 —	27

Yost's 1912 Wolverine squad went 5-2, losing to Syracuse and Penn.

CHAPTER 10

All-America John Maulbetsch runs for tough yardage against Harvard.

HARVARD'S LONE TOUCHDOWN BEATS MICHIGAN ELEVEN

BY E. A. BATCHELOR
Special to The Detroit Free Press

CAMBRIDGE, Mass., Oct. 31, 1914 - One battering, bruising march down the field in the second period gave Harvard a victory over Michigan today.

Before and after this Crimson assault, which resulted in a touchdown and a point-after kick, the Wolverines outplayed their opponents but they never could cross the Harvard goal line and the count stood 7-0 against them when a magnificently fought game ended in the gathering dusk. The score might well have been 14-7 or even 14-0 in Michigan's favor,

for the Maize and Blue once carried the ball to Harvard's 4-yard line and another time to the 5-yard stripe, only to lose it on downs.

It looked as though nothing in the world would stop the fighting Westerners on the two occasions, but Harvard did it, rallying on the threshold of her goal and hurling back the assaults with a determination and fury that defied defeat. Michigan lacked the punch in the "pinches" and that was why she was beaten.

Harvard is welcome to the victory for Michigan has honor enough in the possession of Johnny Maulbetsch, who outshone any other man on the field as an arch light outshines a tallow candle. He did the work of three men, yes, of half a dozen, but he could not be a whole eleven in himself. Had there been any other Wolverine to match him Harvard would tonight be explaining her defeat instead of celebrating her victory.

Michigan's attack was Maulbetsch. The other backs were useful only in blocking for him or resting him. Sometimes one of them gained a few yards but it was the Teuton who really convinced Harvard that Michigan was a foe to be reckoned with. They stopped Maulbetsch once on the Harvard 5-yard line when he had only a yard to make for a first down; but the play was badly chosen and he got neither a hole to dart through nor any blocking.

Once the Wolverine star carried the ball six times in seven rushes that netted Michigan a total of 41 yards. John Lyons was called on once in the march and grabbed two yards while the other 39 were placed to the credit of Yost's human battering ram. It was one of the greatest feats of individual strength and durability that ever has been seen on the Crimson field and even Harvard cheered for "Mauly" after the home team had taken the ball on downs and punted out of danger.

It was after his wonderful fighting advance that Maulbetsch could not negotiate the first down that would have meant a touchdown. On the play before the final effort he had been knocked cold. On another drive Maulbetsch carried the ball 10 times in 11 Michigan assaults.

The game was divided in a rather peculiar way so far as the advantage was concerned.

Michigan made a regular show of the Crimson in the first and third periods while Harvard outplayed the Wolverines in the second and fourth periods. The Wolverines gained 98 yards to seven for Harvard in the first period and 68 to Harvard's 13 in the third. Altogether the Westerners negotiated 11 first downs, while Harvard had nine. Five of these went to Michigan's credit in the first period.

Right off the bat, Michigan's fans had cause for joy. Following an exchange of punts, Michigan recovered a Harvard fumble, made on the first rushing play the Crimson tried. This advantage was soon lost and Michigan had to punt. Harvard punted back

and the exchange was about even. Then the Wolverines started a march that brought them 47 yards in eight plays and took the ball to the Harvard four-yard line.

Michigan's rooters were fairly frantic as they saw Maulbetsch with occasional assistance from the others rip the Harvard line to shreds. A double-pass brought the longest gain of this advance and the most spectacular Michigan run of the day. It measured 17 yards.

"Touchdown, touchdown," yelled the Maize and Blue cheering section. Cheerleader Haff did his best to get some unified shouting from his command, but no mortal man could be expected to wait for a signal to yell at such a time. It was every one for himself until his throat cracked or his lungs burst.

Over across the field, Harvard was imploring her men to "hold em." Walter Trumbull, the Crimson team captain, raged up and down the line like a wild man encouraging, plotting, threatening his men.

And Harvard did hold. She held so well that on a fourth down with three yards to go, Michigan had to give up her line-smashing and try something else. There was a conference among the Wolverines and a forward pass finally was agreed upon. Unfortunately, Lawrence Splawn gummed up the signals and, instead of passing to either of two men who were uncovered over the goal line, he tried to run with the ball and was thrown for a loss. Harvard had saved the day.

Immediately the Crimson punted out of danger and for the remainder of the quarter there was no great advantage on either side. In the second period came the "break" that gave Harvard her victory. It arrived through the medium of a long punt by the Crimson and a short return by Michigan. The Cambridge team secured the ball on its own 46-yard line and began a pounding attack that would not be denied. Using only one forward pass which was good for a 12-yard gain, the Percy Haughton-coached machine slowly fought its way down the field until Tad Hardwick finally plowed through for the touchdown that decided the issue. Hardwick also kicked the point-after.

Michigan came back for the second half determined to do or die. A lecture in the field house had

The Wolverines got a big send-off from the Michigan student body at the Ann Arbor train station before departing to play Harvard.

impressed upon every man that victory lay within Michigan's grasp if she would only play at the top of her form, and as soon as the whistle blew the Maize and Blue team went to work with new confidence and dash. The Westerners got their chance following a punt over the Harvard goal line by Splawn. Harvard was unable to move the ball at her 20-yard line and Hugo Francke got away a kick that was below his standard. The ball was downed by Michigan on the Crimson's 47-yard stripe.

Then came Mulbetsch's splendid exhibition. Using a variety of plays but always the same raging, tearing German dynamo to carry the ball, Michigan

fought her way by straight line plunges to the Crimson six-yard mark. Only a yard was needed for a first down and a first down meant a touchdown. Again Maulbetsch was asked to tote the pigskin. But the whole right side of the Harvard line was on him this time, and when the officials sorted out the struggling mass of players the ball had not been advanced the necessary distance. Again Harvard had met the test with the courage of desperation and Michigan's star had set.

The Crimson, of course, punted out of danger and took good care not to get into any more. In the fourth quarter Harvard seemed to be fresher than

Lawrence Splawn punts against a heavy Harvard rush.

her guests and at the very end of the game she was engaged in a campaign that seemed likely to result in another touchdown.

Taking one of Splawn's punts at the Harvard 27-yard line, the Crimson battled to Michigan's 36-yard stripe when the whistle blew. A well-executed forward pass was the last play. Hardwick's toss was gathered in by J. Collidge for a gain of 15 yards.

Harvard's superiority in this last few minutes was very marked. Michigan apparently had shot her bolt in her desperate effort to score in the third period.

Michigan men have much reason to be proud of their team. Harvard will probably be champion of the East this fall and the Western boys refused to grant Harvard an inch that was not earned. In the last quarter the Wolverines seemed to be tired. But they were just as game as ever and they might have stopped the Crimson avalanche before it reached the goal line even if the whistle hadn't terminated hostilities when it did.

Defeated but a long way from disgraced is a fair way to sum it up this contest. A bunch of green men who gave the best it had were forced to bow before an adversary that had just that finesse that comes with football experience. It was a good fight all the way through and there is honor enough for both victor and vanquished.

SCORE BY PERIODS

MICHIGAN 0	0	0	0	—	0
HARVARD 0	7	0	0	—	7

Michigan's 19-0 victory spoiled the dedication of the Buckeyes' new football cathedral, Ohio Stadium.

MICHIGAN DOWNS OHIO STATE AS BUCKEYES OPEN STADIUM

BY HARRY BULLION
Special to The Detroit Free Press

COLUMBUS, Oct. 21, 1922 - There is a great splotch on the brand new 80,000-plus Ohio Stadium that Ohio State University, amid much pomp and ceremony, dedicated this afternoon.

And tonight the old town is raining with the cheers of the maddening throngs from Michigan, whose football warriors lowered the proud Scarlet and Gray of the Buckeye school before a crowd never before equaled at a game on a gridiron of the West. If ever a triumph was sweet to the Wolverines, this victory, 19-0, this afternoon was. For three years Fielding Yost and his loyal followers have been

burning for the revenge they achieved on this, the red letter day in all the history of the Western Conference.

Ohio State was whipped to a standstill, damaged as no team coached by John Wilce ever had been before, and there is a deep thick pall hanging over every supporter of the Scarlet and Gray. In one blow, the Wolverines whipped out the fruits of Ohio State's triumphant years; pushed back again the chesty Buckeyes, and while about it, jumped again on a position that will command the esteem of the West.

Before the third period was concluded it was a foregone conclusion that the Ohioans were over their heads against the dashing attack and defense of the Wolverines, and many in the vast throng began to make their way to the exits.

Those who stayed were struck with awe by the Yostmen's precision in executing plays. For once, the spirit of Ohio State was killed and her supporters were almost speechless with the horror of the catastrophe.

Walter Camp was in the press box. He came to see the greatest football field in the country, and the caliber of pigskin toters in the wild and woolly West.

He saw Kipke, a blizzard in action, Goebel, Kirk, Roby, Cappon, Muirhead and Uteritz outwit, outplay and with the help rendered by their mates virtually crush the Ohio State battle front that its legion followers boasted would win over Michigan through superior intellect, better coaching and psychology they believed was created by the three past defeats of the Wolverines.

Michigan gave them thrust for thrust and never was worried in a single exchange. Ohio tried every phase of football she knew, but seemed dumfounded when the men of Yost solved every trick and actually led the Buckeyes to their doom.

Michigan scored two touchdowns and a pair of field goals this afternoon. Paul Goebel put the Wolverines in the lead in the first quarter with a field goal from the Ohio State's 11-yard mark. In the final period, Harry Kipke booted a dropkick from the 38-yard line. The touchdowns came in between, in the second and third quarters.

Both touchdowns were scored by Kipke, the first one on a double pass that sucked the whole Buckeye team over to the left while Kipke, taking the ball from Doug Roby, sped around right end for 25 yards and the first Michigan touchdown scored against Ohio State in four years.

Ohio State had not fully recovered from that blow when in the third quarter the little blond marvel of the Yostmen speared a pass out of the air and, evading a broken field, ran 35 yards and desecrated the Buckeye goal line again.

Like a unit, the Michigan line constantly attacked the enemy. Her ends nailed the Ohio State backs almost in their tracks and the tackles, particularly Stanley Muirhead, were as venerable as the Rock of Gibraltar. And realizing early that Ohio State could do nothing to stop Michigan's charging defensive

All-America Harry Kipke proved to be a one-man wrecking crew against the Buckeyes. Kipke scored 2 touchdowns and kicked one field goal in a spectacular performance.

Kipke was college football's premier kicker of the 1920's.

linemen from quarterback Vince Workman – who it is said, can hit a dime with a forward pass at 50 yards – the Buckeyes began to blacken the air with heaves.

Only once was Ohio State dangerous, but the alertness of the Wolverines' backfield thwarted her designs. This happened in the third period, the roughest spot in the whole game for Michigan and one where the Yostmen were confronted by two serious ordeals.

Ohio State had the ball on the Michigan 10-yard line, with fourth down and 2 yards to gain.

Workman elected to try a pass that fell safely in Wilmer Isabel's hands, but Herb Steger tackled him so hard that the ball, slipping from his hands, fell into Frank Honaker's. Just Frank Cappon stood between the Buckeye end and the Michigan goal and it looked as though the Michigan fullback would not be able to get past the Buckeye blockers. But he dodged two burly linemen, swung around in front of Honaker and brought him to earth. Kipke immediately kicked out of danger. Later in the quarter Workman, favored by a slight wind, kicked the ball dead inside Michigan's 5-yard line. The Wolverines tried one play around end to get away from the uprights and Kipke booted the ball out of danger again.

The Michigan contingent was on hand early – nearly 18,000 strong. Special trains from Ann Arbor and Detroit were loaded to the vestibules and the roads were black with automobiles, each draped in the colors of the Wolverine school. One party made the "grade" from the university seat of the Wolverine state in an ancient car of standard make and tethered the machine to a hitching post just outside The Deshler Hotel by employing a halter. The car, from front light to rear bumper, was smeared with yellow and blue paint – and with the same lack of care that a novice applies calcimine in a bungalow kitchen.

Victory for Michigan will mean "hell" in this place tonight.

SCORE BY PERIODS

MICHIGAN.........3	7	6	3	—	19
OHIO STATE......0	0	0	0	—	0

Red Grange turns the corner against the Michigan defense. Grange would finish the afternoon with 5 touchdowns – 4 by rushing, and a 95-yard kickoff return. He also tossed a touchdown pass.

GRANGE SCORES FIVE TD'S AS ILLINOIS DEFEATS MICHIGAN

BY L. H. NORTHARD
Special to The Detroit Free Press

CHAMPAIGN, Ill., Oct. 18, 1924 - Illinois and Harold (Red) Grange dedicated the $2 million stadium of the Indians this afternoon with the Orange and Blue all-America back leading his teammates to a 39-14 victory over Michigan, virtually assuring Illinois the Big Ten championship.

Flashing across the newly sodded field of the Illi-ni, Grange appeared more like a specter than a mortal. He was as elusive as a ghost to the Michigan tacklers. Four times in the first period and once in the third he evaded outstretched Wolverine arms and ran across the goal line.

Fighting back against odds they knew were too great to overcome after the end of the first quarter, Michigan staged a valiant losing battle, scoring in the second and final periods.

It was dedication day here, but in the years to

come 70,000 persons who witnessed this game will remember it as Red Grange Day. If Grange earned all-America rating by his play last year he proved his right to retain the place among the elite by his showing today. No back ever raced through a Michigan defense as did this flame-thatched youth from Wheaton, Ill.

Grange was the Illinois offense. He was the Indians' one means of gaining ground. All of the other backs alternated with him in order that Red might have a breathing spell, but their efforts either resulted in a small gain or no advance.

When histories are written on the feats of red-haired warriors, Grange must be given his place with those old heroes, Richard the Lion Hearted, Eric the Red and Frederick Barbarossa.

Somewhere in the spirit world today these fighters of old must have smiled to see this young man with his red shock covered by an orange helmet racing through the desperate Wolverines as they once went forth to victory.

Michigan's hopes of continuing as an unbeaten team were dashed to the ground on the first play. Herb Steger kicked off to Grange, who lined up behind as perfect interference as any conference team

has ever given a back. It would be the first of Grange's five dashes across the Maize and Blue goal.

In this one period he scored four touchdowns on four long runs. Never in Michigan's leanest years had any one man ever equaled the feat of Grange. Four times he was given the ball and on those four attempts he scored four touchdowns, his total yardage being 263 yards.

Never was he stopped and seldom was he forced to slacken his pace. Last year, Grange had Jim McMillian, the all-America guard, to lead his interference. Today, Illini coach Bob Zuppke produced another McMillan in L.T. Slimmer of Millville, N.J. Dropping out of his position at guard, Slimmer charged around the ends to take out the first of the Michigan tacklers.

Slimmer wasn't Grange's only assistance. Wally McIlwain and Harry Hall were equally as effective in getting the next Wolverines in the path of the flashing redhead. Earl Britton, the one man that Michigan expected to see head the interference, did figure in at times but he was overshadowed by the others.

There was something uncanny about the way Grange gathered blockers as he continued his dash-

This photo shows how good Grange really was. No one got close to him on this October afternoon.

Benny Friedman runs for big yardage as a rare opening in the Illinois defense opens up.

es down the field. Illinois linemen, supposed to be stopped by Michigan linemen, seemed to drop from nowhere to get in front of their star and bowl over Wolverines.

In the first quarter, Grange displayed some remarkable twisting, side stepping, change of pace and ability to reverse his field. Three times he crossed the field on a diagonal line from one sideline to the other, leaving a line of fallen Wolverines in his path.

Today's dedication was all Grange's. He was taken out before the first period ended and Illinois stopped gaining. There wasn't any punch left in the attack of the Indians. They seemed to lose efficiency, and Michigan, welcoming the sight of the troublesome young man going to the sidelines, took heart.

Then when Britton punted poorly the Maize and Blue attacked with renewed vigor. This drive carried them to the Illinois 15-yard line, where Steger broke off tackle for a touchdown.

Grange came back in the third period and Michigan's attack was stopped. Illinois was fighting again with Grange as the weapon of offense. His dashes around the ends and off the tackles took the ball to within 12 yards of the goal and then, unaided by any interference, he swept around right end and outraced three Wolverines to the goal.

Not wishing to take any unnecessary chances, Grange was ordered to throw more passes and do less carrying of the ball. His aim was almost as

unusual as his running. He passed to the ends or one of the backs, often for good gains and one of his tosses to Marion Leonard resulted in the final Illinois touchdown.

Good fortune smiled on Michigan in the fourth period. Steger kicked a field goal but one of the officials discovered Jim Miller clipping after the ball was declared dead and the Wolverines were given the ball on the Indians' 13-yard line. Steger hit the line twice and Bill Heath once for a first down. F.A. Rockwell then quarterback-sneaked it over the goal line for the touchdown.

Coached since the beginning of the season to stop Grange, the Maize and Blue defense against his sensational dashes today was almost powerless. Michigan's ends had to bear the brunt of the burden and they weren't equal to this almost super-human task. Phil Marion and Charles Grube fought hard but failed. Equally powerless was the secondary.

Regarded as only a line plunger and work horse, Miller was the one back who seemed able to pull down the elusive Grange. In the fourth period, Miller was taken out, exhausted from the fight he had made against the Illinois ghost.

Michigan went down to defeat but it went down fighting as hard as any Michigan team has ever fought. The Maize and Blue was beaten but not disgraced. Thousands of Wolverine followers came to Champaign to witness this game; most of them expecting to see Michigan win.

They left the stadium saddened by defeat but singing the praises of a fighting team. But Wolverine fans know how to be strong in defeat as well as in victory.

After the final whistle, the Michigan band formed in front of the Michigan section and played "The Yellow and Blue." With bowed heads, most of them silently weeping, the Michigan players stood in a little groups, the stronger-hearted trying to cheer their sorrowing comrades. It was a touching scene, one that spoke volumes for the spirit that moved these young men in face of failure.

Three words graphically tell the tale of today's victory for Illinois.

They are "too much Grange." It was his day and he made the most of it. Grange will continue to be a star at Illinois, but it is doubtful if he ever will rise to the heights he reached this afternoon.

Fighting against great odds, Michigan fell before "too much Grange."

SCORE BY PERIODS

ILLINOIS............27	0	6	6 —	39
MICHIGAN..........0	7	0	7 —	14

All-American halfback Benny Friedman eludes an Ohio State defender on a romp through the Buckeye secondary.

WOLVERINES SURVIVE BUCKEYES' LATE RALLY

BY M. F. DRUNKENBROD
Special to The Detroit Free Press

COLUMBUS, Nov. 13, 1926 - Far below, at the bottom of this human canyon, Michigan and Ohio State waged a fierce battle today for Western Conference supremacy, the Wolverines finally winning by the narrowest possible margin, one point. The score was 17-16, and the Buckeyes lost because Myers Clark failed on a dropkick for the extra point after Ohio State's touchdown late in the game.

For Michigan it was a hard-earned, highly prized victory. For Ohio State it was another defeat at the hands of a foe it has been striving to conquer for

five years without success. The Buckeyes came close to gaining a tie this time, but obtained little solace out of that. For weeks they had been dreaming of a triumph today.

To win Michigan had to show resourcefulness and fight like the greatest Wolverine teams of the past. The Yostmen were placed in a hole when their rivals seized a 10-point lead through a dropkick and a touchdown in the first quarter.

At that stage Ohio State seemed an unbeatable combination while Michigan was just an ordinary one struggling along to prevent the Ohioans from crowding too far ahead. The invaders braced in the second quarter, and matching Ohio State's scoring by a great spurt which thrilled a crowd officially announced as 90,411, came to the halfway stage with the count at 10-10.

A passing attack, typical of Michigan, produced the second-quarter touchdown and its captain, Benny Friedman, personally attended to the making of the three precious points, which squared the total, by a thrilling placekick of 43 yards.

A touchdown on the fourth play in the final quarter, and the extra point were supposed to have won for Michigan. They did, but not until a new Ohio State team, charged with a new spirit and led by a demon named Byron Eby, had given the Wolverines a scare they won't forget for a long time. A swift march saw the scarlet-jerseyed athletes, driven by desperation, go catapulting down the field to a touchdown, which matched Michigan's earlier score. But then came the calamity which undermined the Buckeyes' brilliant stand – Clark's failure in his bid for the extra point.

Those were stirring scenes compared to the first half, where first one side and then the other was on the rampage. But it was in the last two quarters that most of the game's action was crowded, and it was to leave broken-hearted tonight one of Ohio State's greatest fighters, Elmer Marek, the rugged young Iowan, and to make a hero of Syd Dewey, a Michigan lineman.

Forced back almost under his own goal to receive a wind-driven, swirling ball from Louis Gilbert's foot, Marek elected to catch it on one of its crazy bounces rather than permit it to roll dead. He failed to hold it, however, and when it fell to the ground Dewey – a power in Michigan's play throughout the game – pounced on it seven yards from the Ohio goal line.

At the beginning of the fourth quarter, Benny Friedman passed over the goal line into Leo Hoffman's arms for a touchdown. The Michigan captain then kicked the extra point, which was to determine the outcome of the game.

A few minutes before Marek's muff, Eby was seen prancing up and down in front of the Buckeye bench. It was apparent that he was preparing to relieve the injured Marek, as he did at the end of the quarter. But Dr. John Wilce, the Ohio State coach, waited one play too long.

Once in, Eby made a desperate effort to repair the damage done by the youth he relieved. Eby accomplished this by sprinting eight yards around his left end for the touchdown, which was followed by Clark's failure to produce the point needed to tie the game.

There can be no denying that it was a bad break for Ohio State when Marek fumbled Gilbert's punt. This was one game though, when the breaks nearly evened themselves. Marek's fumble matched one made by Gilbert earlier in the first quarter, when Michigan's great punter dropped the ball on an end run after several Buckeyes hit him. The Buckeyes recovered on Michigan's 11-yard line. That put the home team in a position for the first score of the game. A few plays later, Clark's dropkick from the 15-yard line added three points.

Michigan had been placed in a hole a few plays before Gilbert's fumble when Friedman, after signaling for a fair catch on one of Clark's long punts saw the ball wafted out of his reach by the wind. Instead of Friedman making the catch near his 23-yard line, an Ohioan downed in it on Michigan's 10-yard line. It was on the next play that the Buckeyes recovered the Wolverine fumble.

With less than five minutes of the first quarter remaining, the ball went over to Ohio State on its 40-yard line after Michigan missed a first down by less than a yard. A sprint of 18 yards by Fred Grim started the Scarlet and Gray on a march down the field which was climaxed by Fred Karow's short buck for a touchdown, a score made possible by Fred Bell's forward pass to Clark for a gain of 42 yards.

Three passes almost in succession for nice gains made possible Michigan's touchdown in its second quarter rally. On the third play, with the ball eight yards from the Buckeyes' goal line, Friedman tossed it into Bennie Oosterbaan's arms for the score.

Gilbert, Oosterbaan and almost every man in the Wolverine lineup, shared with Friedman in that touchdown but the three points which came just before the close of the half was solely a Friedman achievement, coming on his placekick of 43 yards from an angle.

Statistics reveal that Michigan's greater success

A packed house of 90,411 at Ohio Stadium watches as Michigan dominates the Buckeye defense.

with the forward pass was a factor in its victory. The Wolverines outgained Ohio State, 132 to 98 yards, and got two touchdowns through the airlanes. Michigan's rushing strength matched the Buckeyes, with the Wolverines picking up 93 yards on the ground and Ohio State 95.

Colorful to the extreme was the setting for today's classic of the Western Conference, which attracted a throng that filled every seat in the huge stadium and every nook and corner about the field. It was a typical football mob with the colors of both teams equally rampant in the stands.

Ohio State wanted to win this game more than any other and the words "Beat Michigan" predominated. This war chant first appeared in big letters on bicycles that eight Buckeye cheerleaders rode when they entered the field. The same words appeared on a huge sign stretched the length of the playing field, and then later when the Ohio State band formed a special formation at midfield proclaiming "Beat Michigan."

SCORE BY PERIODS

MICHIGAN	0	10	0	7	— 17
OHIO STATE	10	0	0	6	— 16

Bennie Oosterbaan, Michigan's first three-time all-America, stretches to receive a high pass against the Gophers' double coverage.

OOSTERBAAN RACES 60 YARDS TO TOUCHDOWN AND MICHIGAN VICTORY

BY HARRY BULLION
Special to The Detroit Free Press

MINNEAPOLIS, Nov. 20, 1926 - Michigan remains supreme on the gridirons of the West.

The Maize and Blue won by the smallest margin in which a football game can be determined this afternoon before 60,000 on a snow-covered field, 7-6. It was a case of Minnesota's bad luck and Michigan's good fortune.

One fumble, a careless piece of work of which a sturdy Gopher back was guilty, cost Minnesota a victory that ordinarily she would have achieved.

Minnesota pulverized Michigan's line on a march of 70 yards to a touchdown in the second quarter and Michigan appeared helpless in its efforts to get through, around or over the Gophers' forward wall.

But Michigan won because one of her alert young men seized a fumble on the Minnesota 40-yard line and ran 60 yards to a touchdown. Melvin Nydahl failed to kick the extra point after Minnesota's touchdown, but Benny Friedman booted the ball squarely over the crossbar for Michigan.

Outplayed in every department of the game by a powerful and in a measure, a resourceful eleven, Michigan won because she was lucky. Yet the

Wolverines might have made the score even more decisive had Louis Gilbert kept his feet after intercepting a forward pass just before the timekeeper's first-half gun.

Minnesota had just started a forward pass before the pistol was heard, and leaping high for the ball, Gilbert caught it with a clear hole ahead of him. The fleet Michigan halfback then headed for the goal and had covered all but five yards of the distance when he stumbled and a Gopher fell on him.

It was a tough way for Minnesota to lose, but for the same reason Michigan's victory was all the sweeter to the Wolverines. Twice on successive Saturdays, Michigan won because from the Wolverine caste a kicker came forth who booted the extra point when it was needed.

But Friedman's accurate toe would not have aided the Wolverines had it not been for Oosterbaan, who alertly picked up the loose ball and ran 60 yards to paydirt. Oosterbaan was all alone when Nydahl fumbled the pigskin. The Michigan end wasted little time in picking up the loose ball and carried it over the goal line.

Quick to rally to Oosterbaan's aid, the Michigan linemen started taking out tacklers until only Robert Peplaw was left unattended. But the fleet Gopher halfback never was nearer than five yards to Oosterbaan as they raced over the chalk marks. Running with free arms, Peplaw picked up enough ground on the Wolverine to make a dive for him, only to miss when Oosterbaan side-stepped him and crossed the goal line straight up.

That Michigan was clearly outplayed is attested to by the fact that she made only two first downs against 19 by Minnesota. Yet the Wolverines were so fortunate that they almost made two touchdowns on two first downs. In rushing the ball from scrimmage the Gophers made 328 yards, and Michigan in its two first downs advanced the ball 48 yards.

It was the eighth straight time that Michigan beat Minnesota and the Gophers are beginning to wonder what they must do to end the oppression by the Wolverines.

In this game today, Minnesota beat Michigan in everything but points scored. Only a game eleven that is Michigan's could recover from the mauling it

Oosterbaan was voted to college football's All-Time team in 1951.

absorbed in the second period and come back to survive to win one of the greatest football games ever played in the West.

Men with hearts less courageous than those of the young men who were fighting in this crucial battle of the season to keep Michigan's record unsullied in the West, were resigned to what seemed to be disastrous fate, as the Gophers ran their plays from deceptive formations, scattering the Wolverines all over the turf.

Nothing could stop the Gophers in that never-to-be-forgotten march of 79 yards down the field, with Peplaw, Nydahl, Harry Almquist, Harold Barnhart and Herb Joesting taking turns in ripping huge holes in the staggering defense of the Wolverines. But it wasn't Minnesota's day to win, no matter what that smashing backfield was capable. The recovered fumble by Oosterbaan and his run of 60 yards proved it beyond question.

Mute witness to the changing tides of battle was The Brown Jug, the most famous of college football trophies, on the sidelines. It will go back to Ann Arbor tonight to stay another year at least.

To each of the elevens the jug was a mascot, the Gophers scoring while it rested on a table on their side of the field and the Wolverines matching the touchdown when the trophy rested on the other side.

From the shift formation, Joesting, Almquist, Barnhart and Peplaw bent and broke the Michigan line repeatedly in the first quarter, but when danger threatened, the blue-jerseyed young men stiffened and, altering the Gophers' plan of attack, forced a kick and took possession.

Throughout the first quarter Minnesota had the advantage as long as the Gophers adhered religiously to their running and plunging attack. Resorting to the passing game, Minnesota invariably lost the ball and a resounding kick by Gilbert sent the pigskin back deep into the maroon and gold's territory.

But the power of the Northmen could not be so easily thwarted. Shortly after the second quarter opened, Barnhart caught a punt on the Minnesota 30-yard line, where he was nailed in his tracks by two Michigan tacklers. It was the last time Minnesota was stopped en route to the Wolverines' goal, which Joesting crossed on a short plunge after a steady march of 70 yards downfield. There was deception as well as drive in Minnesota's smashing line plays.

Frequently the hard running, vicious backs went catapulting past the secondary and Michigan only prevented their escape to the goal line by pulling the runners down from behind.

Not since Michigan used to be piled up on a gridiron in the lean days of Fielding Yost's regime has another eleven torn its line asunder as it was distributed over the chalk marks on that drive of 70 yards in the second quarter. Never did the Gophers fail to gain. On a drive into the sorely oppressed Maize and Blue line the bullet backs always made a yard or more. Once it was necessary for the head linesman to take the measurement to determine the first down, but it was over the required distance and the march continued.

John Molenda was bruised and battered from coming up to the scrimmage line in a brave but fruitless effort to stop the advance. Leo Hoffman relieved him as the Gophers slowly but steadily got nearer to the goal line. In all that time Michigan's only glimpse of the ball was when it appeared under the pro-

Benny Friedman, an all-America in 1925 and 1926, connected with Bennie Oosterbaan on many memorable passes.

Benny Friedman pauses in mid-air to intercept a Minnesota pass.

tecting arm of a charging Gopher.

Between halves the Wolverines got the opportunity to rest they needed and the coaching staff devoted the necessary time to correcting the faults of the line, or the parts of the game plan that could be pieced together. Temporarily, Yost's halftime oratory had the desired effect, since in the early stages of the third quarter, it stopped the Gophers' line plunging and forced them to kick. Oosterbaan cut in and blocked the ball, which Ray Baer recovered on the Minnesota 20-yard line. But the Minnesota forward wall that opened the holes in Michigan's line to let the backs through hurled back the Michigan attack, and on fourth down Friedman's pass to Oosterbaan behind the line was incomplete.

Taking the ball out to the 20-yard line, Minnesota smashed through for two first downs and created the impression that another offensive parade was in order. But Michigan stiffened again, forcing Minnesota to kick. It was apparent that the Gophers were cherishing their 6-point advantage and were prepared to protect it. This was evident in that the Gophers, if they had three yards to go on third down, chose to kick – three yards on a plunge meant nothing to them in their sensational march of 70 yards in the second period.

Michigan never stopped trying nor slackened its

hopes, however. Michigan knew that its break would come if it was patient. Frequently the pigskin was permitted to slip out of the grasp of a Gopher, only to have one of them recover. But the fatal fumble was to happen. Minnesota let the ball loose once too often and an alert Wolverine turned it into a touchdown.

Nydahl went crashing into the line, as he had done frequently before. But in the collision the ball was knocked out of his arms and was exposed to the agile hands of Oosterbaan.

Scooping up the leader on his 40-yard line, Oosterbaan turned and sprinted 60 yards across the sacred Minnesota goal line.

SCORE BY PERIODS

MICHIGAN	0	0	0	7	— 7
MINNESOTA	0	6	0	0	— 6

CHAPTER 15

Yost showed U-M the way

By Joe Lapointe
Special to The Detroit Free Press

Ann Arbor, Nov. 6, 1986 - Eighty-five years ago, when Fielding Yost started coaching football at the University of Michigan, the sport was a rough version played by men without helmets. The ball was much larger and rounder. Linemen would play with loops attached to their belts so they could tow ball carriers through enemy lines. Touchdowns and field goals counted for five points each.

One of Yost's most famous plays, "Old 83," required a fake in which the halfback would take the center snap, fall down after faking a pitch to a runner, then get up and pitch to a different back who would run around the other end. This play would be illegal today, as the play is over once a ball carrier is down.

"Football in those days was a man-to-man fight on the field," Yost told sportswriter Grantland Rice in 1922. "Almost anything went. Today the rules have changed most of this. There are penalties for clipping, for piling on, for roughing the kicker, for striking with the palm of the hand – for anything that looks like intentional roughness."

This week, Michigan coach Glenn E. (Bo) Schembechler was asked about Fielding H. (Hurry-up) Yost at a press luncheon in Ann Arbor. Though they coached decades apart, Yost and Schembechler have something in common. Both rank among college football's most prominent coaches of all time, and Saturday at Purdue, Schembechler can equal Yost's U-M record of 165 victories.

Schembechler (164-38-4 at U-M) recalled that, when he took the Michigan job in 1969, his wife, Millie, became a friend of Eunice Yost, Fielding Yost's widow.

"I went up to his house," Schembechler said. "He lived not far behind where I live. I went up there several times. Walked around to see all the artifacts on Fielding Yost, Stagg and Pop Warner – those were

Legendary college football pioneer Walter Camp of Yale (left) visits with Yost prior to the 1903 Michigan-Chicago game.

the real pioneers. 'Hurry-up' Yost. Must have been a heck of a guy."

You could say that. The spirit of Yost is not only an Ann Arbor ghost. Yost was something of a football Johnny Appleseed at the turn of the century, helping to spread through the Midwest and West Coast the popularity of a sport that was as undefined as it was rugged.

Born in West Virginia in 1871, the son of a Confederate Civil War soldier, Yost never saw a football game until he was a young adult, but he soon found he had a knack for playing and coaching the game.

Although he had a law degree, Yost quickly took to coaching football. At first he was a wanderer, playing line at West Virginia in 1895 and 1896, then coaching at Ohio Wesleyan (7-1-1 record in 1897), Nebraska (7-3 in 1898), Kansas (10-0 in 1899) and Stanford (7-2-1 in 1900).

He later explained he wanted "to see as much of the country as I possibly could" and that football was a good way to see it.

He found a football home at the University of Michigan in 1901, living there part-time (during football seasons) for two decades and full-time from 1921 until his death in 1946.

Yost was U-M's athletic director from 1921 to 1941. He quit coaching in 1926 with a 165-29-10 record.

In addition, he was a lawyer and businessman involved in a cement company, a furniture firm and a bank in Tennessee.

He was a military history buff, often visiting the site of Custer's Last Stand and interviewing Indians who had fought the battle. He looked beneath land, too, in speculative enterprises for various minerals.

"In fact," he once wrote in a letter to a friend, "I actually had a fling at oil, gas, coal, gold, flurospar, silver, bauxite, graphite, asbestos and copper."

Aside from coaching and private business, Yost's greatest success came as an athletic director. On the campus at Ann Arbor, he built a golf course, the huge Michigan Stadium and Yost Field House, now known as Yost Ice Arena, home of the hockey team. To compare him to modern Michigan men, he was something of a combination of Schembechler and athletic director Don Canham.

"He was a tremendous genius from the stand-

point of management of an athletic department," Canham says. "He made Michigan (sports program) what it is. Looking at the minutes of the meetings (of his era) he was pretty autocratic. He had to be."

When Yost supervised construction of what is now a 101,000-seat, single-deck football stadium, he included footings that would support a second deck, Canham said.

When Yost coached, it was at smaller stadiums called Regents Field and Ferry Field. His most famous teams, from 1901-05, were called the "Point-a-minute" teams because they outscored their foes 2,841 to 42 in 57 games. Only one of those games was a defeat (2-0 to Chicago, in the last game of 1905). He won the first Rose Bowl, in 1902, with a 49-0 victory over Stanford.

This was in an era right before a crackdown on the sport that came from the White House and President Theodore Roosevelt. Educators of the time said the sport had become excessively brutal. They wanted to curb the practice of tramp athletes moving from campus to campus, transferring their services almost as professionals.

"Sure, Yost recruited," Schembechler said with a chuckle the other day, recalling that some of Yost's early stars played for him at different schools.

At the time, not everyone regarded these tactics as violations. One such incident, which came to light in 1935, took place in 1899 when Yost coached at Kansas. A player named George Krebs showed up there, tried out for football, became a starting lineman and led the team to a victory over Nebraska. Krebs had graduated that spring from West Virginia, where he had starred with Yost on the football team.

"(Yost) wrote me, asking me to play on his (Kansas) team," Krebs said in 1935. "That was all right in those days, you know."

Yost himself had left the West Virginia team for one game and played for Lafayette against Pennsylvania. And when Yost was coaching at Wesleyan in Ohio in 1897, he brought his team north to play the Michigan Wolverines.

When he arrived, Yost – a 6-foot, 195-pound college graduate with a law degree – explained that he had been able to find only 10 players. Would it be all right, Yost asked, if he filled in on the line?

Yost (at far right) gathers with fellow 1920's sports celebrities (left to right) Glenn (Pop) Warner, Knute Rockne, Babe Ruth, Christy Walsh and Tad Jones before attending the 1925 Coachmen's Dinner in New York City.

Permission was granted. Yost helped the team to a scoreless tie.

"This was in the so-called barbarian days of football," journalist Westbrook Pegler once wrote of Yost, "long before Mr. Yost distinguished himself for his ethical piety at the University of Michigan."

Yost, born April 30, 1871, was the son of Permenus Esley Yost and Elzena Jane Ammons Yost. He was a farm boy who later taught rural school and worked as a deputy sheriff in a mining county. He was large in build for his era and wore a handlebar mustache as a young man (in the era called "The Gay 90's.") He attended Ohio Normal, a Methodist university in Ada, Ohio, and played first base on the baseball team, before he studied law and played football at West Virginia.

Later, Yost was frequently seen with an unlighted cigar in his mouth. Cartoonists frequently drew his shock of unruly white hair falling across the top of his forehead.

Writers of his time sometimes quoted him in dialect. Yost would go in to an alumni meeting and tell the grads: "Doncha know I believe you men are

behind me, but too far behind me."

Yost didn't drink alcohol and opposed the repeal of prohibition in 1933. "Some people can drink alcohol and it does them no harm," he frequently said, "but alcohol never helped anyone." It seems he knew how to talk to people.

"He was a politician," says Will Perry, Michigan's associate athletic director, who has written a book about Michigan football. "He had a great sense of public relations. He would go up to The Michigan Daily (the student newspaper) and help them write headlines."

His brother, Ellis Yost, wrote in 1948 that Yost was "a lover of the outdoors. Fielding was fond of hunting both big and little game. He bagged big game in the West Virginia mountains, California and Canada."

One animal that particularly interested him was the wolverine. Yost was envious that supporters of the University of Wisconsin brought a live badger to their games. So he searched for a year and finally got 10 live wolverines from Alaska. They grew so vicious that Yost had to give them up, keeping one at a campus zoo.

When Yost was courting his future wife in Nashville, Tenn., she introduced him to her father and, after Yost had left, asked what he thought of Yost.

"There," pronounced the father, "is a man."

Most of all, however, the man was known as a football coach.

"He believed in defense," Schembechler said earlier this week. "They didn't score very often on him."

Yost's first Michigan team didn't allow a point scored against them; his first five teams shut out 50 of their 57 opponents.

Yost poses with two of his greatest players, Bennie Oosterbaan (left) and Benny Friedman (right).

Yost believed in punting as a weapon, not only as a surrender of the ball when the offense failed to move it. He advocated surprise quick kicks on third down, saying that field position was sometimes more important than ball possession.

In a 1948 article, Detroit lawyer Charles F. Delbridge recalled Yost's football philosophy.

"How often have we heard him say: 'Pass, punt and pray,' " Delbridge wrote. "What's the easiest way to gain ground? Pass or punt her way down the field. Then hold 'em and pray for a break. If they fumble, fall on it. If they pass, grab it. Hold 'em. Take the ball away from them deep in their territory. If ya can't take it away from 'em, you can't win anyway. Then you're in 'po-zee-shun.' In po-zee-shun to use a scoring play. Only yardage that really counts is that one yard across the goal line, y'know. 'Why risk losing the ball on a short or lateral pass, the distance ain't worth it, y'know?' "

Bennie Oosterbaan, who played end on Yost's last two teams in 1925 and 1926, recalled Yost as a "very likable, loveable person who knew his stuff.

"A very good teacher who could get it across with a smile on his face," Oosterbaan, a pallbearer at Yost's

funeral, said in an interview this week. "Bo is a different personality. Yost never raised his voice. Most coaches do."

He wrote the book "Foot Ball for Player and Spectator," published in 1905. He had one losing season at Michigan, in 1919, with a 3-4 record. He won 10 conference championships.

He left coaching for one season, 1924, then returned for two seasons before leaving the job for good. Yost then concentrated on supervising the building of athletic facilities on the campus and supervising the program until he retired on July 1, 1941, at the age of 70. He died five years later.

One of Yost's chief rivals was Amos Alonzo Stagg of the University of Chicago. Yost was not especially fond of Knute Rockne, the Notre Dame coach. When the University of California at Berkeley asked Yost's opinion of Rockne for a possible job, Yost wrote a letter that said in part: "Knute Rockne is a graduate of Notre Dame University but is a Protestant. My information is that he is interested only in competitive athletics. In my opinion, he would 'fret' under the administration and restrictions as exist in our Western Intercollegiate Conference Universities."

And now, in the list of football's legendary names, Stagg, Rockne, Yost and Warner, there is another, a modern one: Schembechler. How does he really feel about being in such company? Isn't he a little bit excited about tying Yost's Michigan victory mark?

"Very much so," said Schembechler's wife, Millie. "With all the humility in the world.

"Both of us are very, very excited about this bit of history to be made. We never thought we'd be here this long. It is an awesome, awesome, position. It's wonderful."

Yost instructs a young Wolverine prospect on the art of kicking a football.

CHAPTER 16

All-America halfback Tom Harmon (98) sweeps left end against Iowa. Harmon scored all of Michigan's points in the 27-7 win.

HARMON LEADS WOLVERINES IN WIN OVER IOWA

BY TED ROCKWELL
Special to The Detroit Free Press

ANN ARBOR, Oct. 14, 1939 - Michigan today ranked with the foremost football teams of the nation as Tom Harmon, with one of the most brilliant all-around performances presented by a modern Wolverine halfback, paced his team's offensive powerhouse to a crushing 27-7 triumph over Iowa's Hawkeyes. It was Michigan's Big Ten debut and it was impressive.

More than 27,000 watched Harmon rally his mates, after Iowa had taken a seven-point lead in the first five minutes of the game, to score all of Michigan's

points with four touchdowns and three point-after kicks.

And in addition, Harmon was a blocking ace in Wolverine rushes. He never appeared better stepping forward and knocking down rival runners at the line of scrimmage. His pass defense was brilliant. He was Michigan's leader.

Before the Michigan team appeared to appreciate fully that the Western Conference schedule had begun, they were trailing by seven points. It was a nicely-timed 40-yard heave from Nile Kinnick, the Iowa triple threat, to Floyd Dean, the senior halfback, which caught Michigan napping.

Dean took the pass on Michigan's 30-yard line and

trotted alone over the goal line for a startling 70-yard touchdown. Then Harmon set out to even the count in the first quarter and chalk up two more scores in the second period.

Harmon climaxed his great performance for Michigan by intercepting a Kinnick pass on the Michigan 10 and running 90 yards for Michigan's final score in the third quarter.

After Iowa's startling 70-yard touchdown pass the Michigan line asserted itself and continued to seal off the acclaimed Kinnick to reduce his threat. The line pressure exerted against him did not relax thereafter. And the game pressure that slowed down the Hawkeye passes also reduced the efficiency of the Iowa running game.

Two of Michigan's substitutes gained much recognition today. They were Fred Trosko, who handled kicks faultlessly and punted well in the left halfback position of Paul Kromer, and Joe Rogers, a bright and big sophomore who successfully alternated for veteran end John Nicholson. Nicholson was used sparingly today.

Opening the game, Michigan's Forest Evashevski, the Wolverine quarterback, leisurely was testing Iowa's might at the supposed weak spot at the center of the line with Bob Westfall smashes. But the Iowa guards were stout and they stopped the Michigan fullback.

There was an exchange of punts with Bill Smith, the Michigan tackle and kicker, actually gaining (in yardage) over Kinnick against the wind, and Iowa got the ball on its 20. The Hawkeyes smashed twice at the Michigan line, moving the ball to the 30.

Then on third down – the right down to pass – Kinnick faded back. Dean rushed down the west sideline, getting behind young Westfall.

Kinnick flicked his arm and the ball arched from him in a beautiful spiral 50 yards in the air to the outstretched fingers of the flying Dean. He caught the ball on the Michigan 30 at full speed and, with no one between him and the goalposts, raced alone and unhampered and unhurried to the Michigan goal. Kinnick dropkicked the extra point.

Then Michigan woke up, pouncing on three breaks of the game, a pair of fumbles and a blocked punt, to move out in front.

Kinnick fumbled on the Iowa 39-yard line and big Roland Savilla, the Wolverine tackle, recovered the ball.

Taking the ball on the Hawkeye 39, Harmon passed to Ed Frutig, who was stopped on the Iowa 2. Evashevski sent Westfall through the Hawkeye middle for a yard. On second down, Harmon cut back over the Hawkeye right guard for a yard and the score. Harmon added the extra point, which tied the score at 7-7.

Early in the second period Dean fumbled on the Iowa 36, and the alert Savilla made his second brilliant recovery. A Michigan passing attack was halted, when Bill Green intercepted a Harmon toss on the Iowa 2-yard line, where he was hauled down by Frutig.

Then the Michigan line pressure was turned on fully. Kinnick's hurried punt from the Iowa end zone was returned eight yards to Iowa's 27 by Trosko. Harmon added 12 yards by smashing through Iowa's right tackle. Next Harmon flipped a flat pass to Evashevski to the Hawkeye four. Westfall spun for two yards up the middle. Finally, on second down Harmon, on a cross buck, hit over to the Iowa left tackle for his second touchdown. Harmon's point-after kick failed.

Iowa received following Michigan's second touchdown. Savilla was pacing Michigan's line pressure. He blasted his way into Kinnick's kicking alley and blocked a punt. There was a question about the recovery, but it was ruled Michigan's ball on the Iowa 29.

Harmon then circled Iowa's right end and bowled over Hawkeye defensive backs as he drove to the Iowa nine. Afterward, Harmon circled the opposite end with a great burst of speed and plowed over the goal line to give Michigan a 20-7 lead at halftime. Harmon's extra point kick was good this time.

Two 15-yard holding penalties in the same series of downs early in the second half slowed Michigan considerably. Forced back to the Michigan 3 by the penalties, Smith sliced a punt off his left foot, and the ball rolled around crazily. It was downed on Michigan's 16.

Kinnick hit at the center of the Michigan line, but was stopped. Then he tossed a flat pass to his left. Harmon quickly diagnosed the ball's flight, and inter-

Harmon leaps high to intercept Heisman Trophy winner Nile Kinnick's pass at the Michigan goal line.

Harmon returns a pass interception as Iowa's Bill Kelley (43) chases in pursuit.

cepted it on the Michigan 10.

Harmon then cut in and out, avoiding two Iowa tacklers, and then streaked straightaway for the Iowa goal line. At every stride the great Harmon widened the distance between himself and his nearest pursuer. He was 40 yards in front of both Hawkeyes and Wolverines when he scored the touchdown. Afterward, Harmon added the third point-after conversion kick.

The early part of the fourth period largely was a punting duel in the middle of the field.

Halfway in the period, Michigan coach Fritz Crisler sent in his substitutes. Desperately, Kinnick tried a dozen passes. Michigan's line pressure thrust him back. The duel that was expected between him and Harmon never seriously developed. By all standards Harmon was the outstanding back on the football field today.

But it was the Michigan line superiority that contributed most to Harmon's brilliance.

Savilla, in particular, set up the stage for three of Harmon's touchdowns. Iowa's best offensive drive against Michigan personally was stopped by Harmon in the first period with the score deadlocked at 7-all.

Iowa took the ball at its 30 and Dean smashed to the Hawkeye 44 around Michigan's right end. Kin-

nick then tossed a delayed pass to his fullback, Bill Green, who drove 34 yards to the Michigan 29. Dean gained 14 yards through the Michigan guards in two downs and Michigan fans became uneasy as Iowa lined up on the Wolverine 16.

Green smashed off tackle to the Wolverine 12. On the next play, Harmon batted down a Kinnick pass. Harmon then stopped the Iowa threat on the next play when he intercepted Kinnick's next toss in the Michigan end zone for a touchback.

Although Harmon had a lot of help, it was his day.

SCORE BY PERIODS

MICHIGAN	7	13	7	0	— 27
IOWA	7	0	0	0	— 7

Tom Harmon had one of his most memorable games as a Wolverine against Penn. He finished the afternoon with 202 yards rushing, scored 2 touchdowns and tossed the game-winning pass to Ed Czak.

HARMON OUTDUELS REAGAN IN MICHIGAN VICTORY

BY THE ASSOCIATED PRESS
The Detroit Free Press

PHILADEPHIA, Nov. 18, 1939 - Michigan nipped Pennsylvania, 19-17, today but the football game, although a thriller right down to the finish, was just a backdrop to the brilliant duel staged by two of the year's finest backs in any league, Tom Harmon and Frank Reagan.

This pair of aces, Harmon, the Michigan flyer, and Reagan, the Quaker quarterback, played out their string to just about a tie in a gaudy battle of triple-threaters as 57,000 cheered them on in perfect Indian summer weather at Franklin Field.

However, the game had an unscheduled finale when Penn tried an onsides kickoff on the last play and the final gun sounded while Michigan was disputing with the officials about it. After that the crowd ran on the field and some overzealous spectators took a few punches at Referee H.O. Dayhoff and Umpire William G. Crowell for not taking a time-out.

In the Harmon-Reagan rivalry, it was Harmon who received just a mite more support from his teammates to turn the tide to the Wolverines in this eighteenth renewal of an historic gridiron series dating to 1899. The break came in Harmon's favor when he converted an apparent 15-yard loss into a sprinting, swerving, 65-yard gallop for a touchdown. This occurred before the folks had even settled down in their seats at the start of the second half.

Michigan had taken the kickoff on its own 35 and Harmon started a sweep to the left. It was here that Reagan's support failed. Three times his mates had sure tackling shots at Harmon and three times they missed. Harmon's path was blocked to the left, so he calmly turned around and, as Penn defenders chased him, he dashed all the way back to his own 20-yard line before heading in the right direction again.

Hastily formed interference saw him through his pursuers and, suddenly, he was in the clear, running for what spelled the difference between victory and defeat.

Even with that beautiful piece of running, however, Harmon didn't have a thing on Reagan, who was as fine a back today as the Quakers have had in years. Although Harmon scored two touchdowns, passed for a third and kicked an extra point, Reagan tallied one six-pointer and was the spearhead of marches of 92 and 73 yards before bowing out in the closing minutes, injured but still wanting to fight.

Harmon gained 202 yards in 29 rushes for an average of 6.1 yards per crack for the afternoon. Overall, the Gary Ghost turned in 294 yards for rushing, passing and punting and kicks returned.

Reagan wrapped up the contest with 356 yards in total yards, including 14 pass completions in 26 attempts for 188 yards. He gave a performance at quarterback – particularly in the Quakers' 92-yard touchdown drive in the third period – in which

there wasn't a flaw. The Quakers used 13 plays in that drive and Reagan was in on 10 of them, picking up 35 yards on the ground and passing for 41 more before he sliced inside right end for the touchdown.

Pre-game reports noted that Harmon would likely have a big game today because his injured blocking sidekick in the Michigan backfield, Forest Evashevski, was back in action. But Harmon's ball carrying today would have been A-1 in any game. It was his day to howl. And he did. So Reagan made it a duet.

Statistically, there wasn't much to choose between the two teams, although the Quakers had gone into the game as 2 to 1 underdogs in the betting. At the windup, Pennsylvania had 17 first downs to Michigan's 13, but the Wolverines were way on top in marching through the line with a net gain of 291 yards to 142 for Penn. However, the Quakers did a lot of sailing through the air with the greatest of ease, and their 15 pass completions gave them 195 yards to a total of 45 for Michigan.

Throughout the first quarter the party didn't shape up as much of a ball game. Penn couldn't get anywhere at all and Michigan was unable to keep a consistent offensive going, although the Wolverines once reached the Quaker 30 and later the 24.

Shortly after the second quarter opened, Reagan, starting from his own 45 after the Quakers had received a punt, launched a drive which gave the hometown boys first blood. The Quaker ace passed to Jim Chandler for a short gain, then alternately tried each end and the middle of the line for a total of 23 yards. A.A. Chizmadia, a substitute back, picked up 17 yards through the line and, when the attack stalled, Gene Davis brought his educated toe into the line-up to kick a field goal from the 14-yard line.

This gave Penn a temporary advantage but, more important, it woke the Wolverines out of their nap. Back they came after the kickoff and didn't stop until they scored. Harmon ran the kickoff back 39 yards to his own 48. In the following furious drive, he picked up 20 yards and Bob Westfall, Michigan's second best back today, ripped off 25 before Harmon dived over from the one-foot line. Harmon added the extra point kick, the only one he converted in three tries.

That marked the end of the first half scoring, but

Michigan coach Fritz Crisler at practice with his venerable Wolverine backfield: (left to right) Forest Evashevski, Bob Westfall, Tom Harmon and Fred Trosko.

Penn made a desperate bid in the waning minutes, and had marched 45 yards to the Michigan 20 in three plays – two of them passes by Reagan – when the field judge's gun called the intermission.

Michigan took a two-touchdown edge in the first minute of the second half on Harmon's hurricane sprint, and from then on the Wolverines protected their lead.

Midway of the period, Penn staged its 92-yard drive. After receiving a punt on its own eight, Reagan turned right end to the 24, passed to Hi Gustafson on the 37 and to Chandler on the 47. Then he swept left end for 15 yards, passed to Gustafson on the Michigan 31 and to Chandler on the 22. Jim Connell picked up 13 yards. Reagan pitched to Ed Allen for

seven more yards and then Reagan knifed over standing up and added the extra point kick.

By this time there was mild hysteria going on in the stands, and it kept right on growing as Michigan took its turn "at bat." Westfall intercepted a Penn pass on the Wolverine 37, and there the Midwesterners were on the prowl again. Harmon picked up 23 yards in four tries, Westfall hit the middle for 16, and then Harmon tossed his high pass one to Ed Czak in "amen corner." It was no trick at all for Czak to stumble across.

Penn took up the chorus again as Reagan ran the kickoff back 47 yards to midfield and passed twice – to Gustafson and Chizmadia – to move the Quakers to the Wolverine eight. But John Nicholson intercepted another pass to end the threat.

A good punt by Harmon sent the Quakers back to their 22, so they started all over again.

Two Reagan passes – to Bob Stephens and Gustafson – gained 57 yards to the Michigan 16.

Chizmadia carried it to the five, where Reagan was injured and left the game. His replacement, Bill Koepsell, passed to Stephens for the touchdown and Davis added the point-after kick, with less than half a minute to go.

Penn tried an onsides kickoff in order to get possession of the ball and, although the officials ruled in Penn's favor on the play, giving the Quakers possession on the Michigan 43, the Michigan protest which ensued took up the game's remaining few seconds.

Coach George Munger, of Penn, ran across the field to protest to Referee Dayhoff and Umpire Crowell over the fact that time had not been taken out while the conference with the Michigan players was going on.

His protest, however, was overruled and he stalked off, but by this time several hundred spectators had surrounded the officials. One or two were seen to toss a punch or two at the officials before the group pushed its way through the gates and broke up the gathering.

SCORE BY PERIODS

MICHIGAN..........0	7	6	6 —	19
PENN 0	3	7	7 —	17

Fritz Crisler with 1939 team captain Archie Kodros.

Chapter 18

SMITH'S 80-YARD RUN LIFTS GOPHERS TO 7-6 WIN

By John N. Sabo
Special to The Detroit Free Press

Minneapolis, Nov. 9, 1940 - Michigan's luckless Wolverines pushed a giant Minnesota team all over the rain-soaked turf of Memorial Stadium this cheerless afternoon, only to be subjected to one of the most bitter and truly undeserved defeats in Michigan's football history.

By an unjust 7-6 score this gigantic Minnesota team dropped Michigan from the ranks of the unbeaten. By that precious one point the Gophers took over the Big Ten leadership. By that hairline edge Minnesota registered its sixth straight victory of the year and its seventh in as many years over Michigan. Yet, except for that final one-point difference, Michigan outplayed Minnesota by a distinctive margin.

Minnesota won today before 63,894 rain-soaked fans because the Gophers executed one perfect play and produced a substitute, Joe Mernik, who is nothing short of a placekicking magician.

The play came with four minutes to go in the first half and in it halfback Bruce Smith streaked 80 yards through a momentarily bewildered Michigan team for the Minnesota touchdown. The score was tied, 6-6, after that touchdown and in came Mernik. It was the same Mernik whose placekick beat Northwestern, 13-12, last week. With George Franck holding the ball, he split the goalposts to give the Gophers a 7-6 lead.

So Minnesota won this game, won it in a way it had never hoped or wanted to win.

Minnesota came in the winner after having been outplayed by a Michigan team that advanced inside the 5-yard line on three different occasions only to lose its scoring punch.

Once, Michigan marched 86 yards to the Minnesota 1-yard line and failed to score. Next, Michigan found itself on the Gopher 3-yard line after a blocked punt. Then Michigan marched 75 yards to the Minnesota 4-yard line. Each time the luckless Wolverines were stopped by a Minnesota line that outweighed Michigan's line 16 pounds to a man.

At the finish Michigan had scored only once, on a 2-yard touchdown pass, Tom Harmon to Forest Evashevski, in the second period. Harmon missed the point-after kick by less than three feet. When Smith and Mernik collaborated for the seven Minnesota points later in the same period, Michigan was a sad one-point loser.

In losing, Michigan made 15 first downs to five for Minnesota. The Wolverines didn't permit Minnesota to get inside the Michigan 30-yard line at any time except for Smith's 80-yard run. Michigan kept Minnesota on the defensive throughout the last half.

Minnesota did a good job of stopping Harmon today as the Michigan all-American simply could not untrack himself in the slippery going. It rained throughout this game and Harmon, although he played the entire 60 minutes, gained only 59 yards in 29 attempts. He also lost 31 yards, leaving his net for the day a sad 28 yards. Thus one of the greatest backs Michigan has ever had could not score on Minnesota in his collegiate career.

Fullback Bob Westfall paced Michigan's 86-yard march in the first half, which roared to the 1-yard line and died. On this march Michigan was on the 2-yard line on second down and still couldn't score with Harmon carrying the ball three consecutive times. Harmon should have scored because on fourth down he had a hole at right tackle. But Harmon

Crisler instructs 1940 Wolverine captain Forest Evashevski during a pause in the action at practice.

slipped on the soggy turf and Minnesota took the ball on the 2-yard line.

Then Michigan finally came through by pouncing on a Minnesota fumble. Fullback Bill Daley, of Minnesota, fumbled on the Gopher 5-yard line and Westfall recovered. On third down Harmon tossed the touchdown pass to Evashevski. Harmon, however, missed his placekick for the extra point.

That gave Michigan a 6-0 lead and a few minutes later Michigan kicked away another golden opportunity. This time end Ed Frutig blocked George Franck's punt from the end zone and Rube Kelto recovered for Michigan on the Gopher 3-yard line.

Again, Michigan couldn't connect. On third down Harmon passed and the toss was intercepted by Bob Paffrath, the Gopher quarterback, in the end zone. This gave Minnesota the ball on its 20.

It was here that gridiron lightning hit Michigan. Smith took the ball on first down and cut over his own left tackle. Eighty yards he streaked over that slippery turf and he went the last 50 yards without a Michigan man within 40 feet of him. That made it 6-6 and Mernik was rushed in to the game by Gopher coach Bernie Bierman. He replaced the breathless Smith and Mernik did what he was supposed to do. He kicked the point that won the game.

Trailing, 7-6, at the half, Michigan came back with an offensive that had Minnesota's 214-pound line groggy. But Minnesota's line wasn't groggy when Michigan was within touchdown distance. Michigan, with Westfall's plunging and some good passing by Harmon to Davey Nelson and Frutig, marched 75 yards down the field and reached the Gopher 4-yard line.

With first down on the 4, Harmon fumbled but recovered on the 7-yard line. On the next play Evashevski fumbled. Urban Odson, the 247-pound Minnesota tackle, jumped on the ball at the 9-yard line and that was all for Michigan. Only five minutes remained to be played and Michigan was finished, although the Wolverines did get to the 26-yard line once more before the game ended.

What kept Minnesota in the ball game until Smith's great run was some extra fancy punting by Franck. Once in the first quarter he got away a 64-yard punt with the slippery ball, which went out of bounds just 18 inches from the Michigan goal line. Another time he punted 39 yards out of bounds on the Michigan 5.

Franck, the speedster of the Minnesota backfield, netted only 17 yards on the wet turf.

But he didn't have to run. He punted like a demon and Smith's running was more than enough to offset Franck's dashing.

It marked the fourth time in 32 games between the Gophers and the Wolverines that a game has ended 7-6. Each team has won twice by that margin. However, Minnesota's two 7-6 victories are of very recent vintage. Two years ago Minnesota beat Michigan by the same score in Minneapolis.

Minnesota now must beat only Purdue and Wisconsin to clinch the Big Ten championship and a claim to the mythical national title. The Gophers should win those two games. It's a certainty that Minnesota will not find Purdue and Wisconsin as tough as Michigan was today in the rain.

The crestfallen Wolverines left tonight. It was still raining. And as they left, no one spoke. Misery that comes only after a one-point defeat by Minnesota in Minneapolis is a misery that even a great Michigan team couldn't shake off.

SCORE BY PERIODS

MICHIGAN	0	6	0	0 —	6
MINNESOTA	0	7	0	0 —	7

Tom Harmon cuts back against the grain against the Buckeyes. His Heisman performance (3 rushing and 2 passing touchdowns) led the Wolverines' 40-0 rout of Ohio State.

HARMON TOPS GRANGE'S RECORD IN WIN OVER OHIO ST.

By John N. Sabo
Special to The Detroit Free Press

COLUMBUS, Nov. 23, 1940 - In a glorious climax to the greatest football career of modern times, Tom Harmon and his Wolverines annihilated the Ohio State Buckeyes, 40-0, this wet November day as 73,648 rain-soaked spectators looked on in absolute amazement.

When Harmon & Co. had finished this football funeral in Ohio Stadium, Ohio State had suffered its worst defeat in 35 years. Not since 1905, when Michigan beat the Buckeyes by an identical 40-0 score had an Ohio State team been beaten so completely and unquestionably.

Harmon finished his collegiate career by surpassing every Big Ten football player of modern times, including Red Grange. Harmon scored 22 points over

a slippery turf. He made three touchdowns, passed for two others and kicked four extra points.

Today's 22 points brought Harmon's three-year total to 237. His three touchdowns made his total 33, compared to the 31 Grange scored while galloping for the Illini.

Harmon, a one-man club today if one ever existed, finished his career on the same turf that Grange did in 1925. But he was greater than Grange. In his final college game in 1925 Grange did not score a touchdown but gained 277 yards rushing and passing. Harmon made that record look pale.

The Michigan all-America netted 149 yards rushing. He completed 11 passes for 148 yards. That's a total of 297 yards. He had a hand in five touchdowns. But that's not all.

Harmon did all the Michigan punting with a wet ball and averaged 50 yards.

He did all of the passing, plenty of blocking and furnished some smart tackling. He simply dissected the Ohio State team which only a year ago had been the Scarlet Scourge that swept to the Big Ten championship.

When Harmon left the field after his third touchdown dash of the day, with only 38 seconds remaining to be played, the whole crowd, friend and foe alike, stood up and cheered.

As Harmon left, the Michigan section of the stands emptied. Ten thousand Michigan rooters mobbed Harmon and formed a guard of honor to escort him to the locker room.

As evidence of the one-sidedness of this game, consider these facts: Harmon's three touchdowns came on runs of seven, 18 and seven yards. He passed 17 yards to Forest Evashevski for one touchdown and 16 yards to end Ed Frutig for another. He also kicked four extra points.

Harmon also did some fine blocking in the first period when another senior, Paul Kromer, exploded with the longest touchdown run of the day. Kromer took a punt by Don Scott and went 81 yards for the second Michigan touchdown. That was the

Harmon attempts a field goal against the Buckeyes.

With this interception, the Michigan defense shuts down the Buckeyes once more. It would be a familiar sight all afternoon.

only touchdown on which Harmon didn't handle the ball, but he knocked down two Ohio State players with fine blocks on this dash.

Ohio State, beaten in three other games, had dreams of redeeming itself when this game started in a cold drizzle. The largest Buckeye crowd in five years was on hand in hopes of seeing Ohio State salvage some glory from this sorry season. When the battle was over, the Buckeye fans had forgotten about their football team and were cheering Harmon.

Francis Schmidt, the Buckeye coach, sat on that cold, wet Ohio State bench. He sat, winced and wondered where he would be coaching next year. Harmon & Co. not only took all the punch out of the Buckeyes but punctured an Ohio State line which averaged 213 pounds so full of holes that it looked like a touch-football line.

Statistically Michigan's supremacy over the dazed Buckeyes was just as one-sided as the final score indicates. Michigan made 22 first downs to 6 for

Ohio State, 299 yards rushing to 82 and 148 yards passing to 33.

All Ohio State had to show for 50 minutes was the biggest Buckeye headache in 35 years.

Not once was the woefully weak Ohio State team inside the 20-yard line.

Whatever trepidation was in the minds of Michigan supporters at kickoff was extinguished pronto. Michigan scored in every period, led 20-0 at the half, and simply toyed with the Buckeyes at the finish.

Harmon & Co. started puncturing the Ohio State line quickly. In the first quarter Harmon and his mates bent, ripped and then crushed the 212-pound Buckeye line on an 80-yard touchdown drive.

This drive took 11 plays and Harmon finished it with a seven-yard dash through left guard.

At least five Ohio State players in white jerseys had their hands on Harmon as he went for the touchdown 11 minutes after the start of the game. Harmon missed his the point-after try.

Exactly 69 seconds later Michigan resumed its scoring. This time Kromer took a high punt by Scott on Michigan's 19-yard line. Scott punted to Kromer all afternoon, not wanting Harmon to get his hands on the ball any more than necessary.

But Kromer was just as big poison on this occasion. He took the punt near the sidelines, cut completely across the field and headed for the goal line. Behind beautiful blocking, he went 81 yards. On the 6-yard line, Jim Langhurst, the Ohio State captain, made a do-or-die tackle and got only a mouthful of mud for his efforts. Kromer scored sanding up and Harmon kicked the extra point.

Just to show the bewildered Buckeyes that Michigan had more than a running attack, Harmon started passing in the second period. He rifled one pass to Evashevski which netted 17 yards and the third Michigan touchdown. This ended a 77-yard advance and Harmon booted the extra point.

Leading, 20-0, at the half, the Michigan boys continued their festival. In the third period Michigan took the kickoff and advanced 77 yards to another touchdown. This time Ed Frutig, playing his last college game, snagged a 16-yard touchdown pass from Harmon for the finishing touch. Harmon's place kick was wide.

By this time nobody was thinking about the eventual outcome. Everybody was thinking about Harmon. So Harmon gave the boys and girls what they wanted. He scored two more touchdowns. He got one on an 18-yard end run which finished a 52-yard march in the third period. He added the next one on a seven-yard dash with only 38 seconds to play.

It was the last time Harmon carried the ball in his collegiate career and he carried it as Michigan expected him to – right over three men to a touchdown. Harmon added the extra point and then Davey Nelson replaced him.

This was Harmon's show, but there was a fine supporting cast. Fullback Bob Westfall did his share. He gained 130 yards net rushing, 48 more than the entire Ohio State team gained. He slammed through that line with a consistency which certainly shocked the Buckeyes.

When Harmon was kicking up the mud, Westfall was bouncing through the line. It was like a one-two punch. Westfall softened 'em up and Harmon finished 'em.

The defeated Buckeyes have a lot of sad memories. It was their fourth setback of the year, the most defeats they have suffered since Schmidt became coach in 1934. When Harmon scored the first touchdown, that added to another miserable mark. It was the first time since 1890 that every Ohio State opponent had scored in one season. Seven previous 1940 foes had scored on the Buckeyes.

Michigan finished the year with seven victories in eight games and thereby clinched second place in the Western Conference. Only the 7-6 defeat at the hands of Minnesota kept the Wolverines from the title.

SCORE BY PERIODS

MICHIGAN	13	7	13	7	40
OHIO STATE	0	0	0	0	0

A rare photo of Tom Harmon wearing a number 6 jersey, the number he was first assigned after entering Michigan.

Harmon awarded Heisman Trophy

BY ROBERT F. KELLEY
Special to The New York Times

NEW YORK, Dec. 10, 1940 - A tall, dark-haired young man who has moved a football forward one way or another 3,533 yards in the last three years came to the city yesterday, registered with his coach at The Warwick Hotel and last night stood before hundreds of cheering diners at The Downtown Athletic Club to receive The Heisman Memorial Trophy for being chosen the player of the year. Quiet and unassuming, Tom Harmon of Michigan became the sixth player to receive this trophy, following in the footsteps of another Middle Westerner, Nile Kinnick of Iowa.

Harmon and H.O. (Fritz) Crisler, Michigan's coach, arrived in time to visit with a few friends and tour the city. Both spoke at the dinner, the feature of which was the presentation ceremonies, held in the D.A.C. gymnasium. Harmon received the big trophy from Walter P. Holcombe, the president of the club.

Among those present were Fielding H. Yost, director of athletics at Michigan; Harmon's parents, Mr. and Mrs. Louis A. Harmon of Gary, Ind.; Mayor Ernst Schaible of Gary and twelve other leading citizens of that city.

Other leading college coaches on hand were Tad Wieman, Princeton; Herb Kopf, Manhattan; George Munger, Pennsylvania; Major Swede Larson, Navy; and Dr. Marvin A. (Mal) Stevens, N.Y.U. J. Walter Bennett, the captain of Michigan's famous 1898 team and President of the "M" Club, also was present.

Mr. Holcombe outlined the history of The Heisman Trophy and also paid tribute to Willard B. Prince, the originator of the idea, who was one of those in charge of the dinner.

In making the presentation Mr. Holcombe told Harmon: "You have won a great distinction, but I remind you that in so doing you have acquired a great responsibility as well, that of setting to our American boys as fine an example in after life as you thus far have shown them as a student, an athlete, a sportsman and a gentleman."

Harmon thanked every one, starting with his mother and father and including his coaches, and teammates. The Gary Ghost said: "They have provided me with the equipment for whatever success I obtained and this evening marks the happiest in my career." He concluded by thanking every one again and said, "I am very thankful that I am an American."

In a brief interview prior to the start of the dinner Harmon reiterated his determination not to play professional football.

The Heisman award is given on the basis of a nationwide vote of sportswriters and officials. The star, who finished his Michigan career with a superb showing as his team gave Ohio State the worst defeat in its football history, 40-0, received a total of 1,303 votes, 462 more than John Kimbrough of the Texas Aggies, in second place.

Last year Harmon was runner-up to Kinnick in

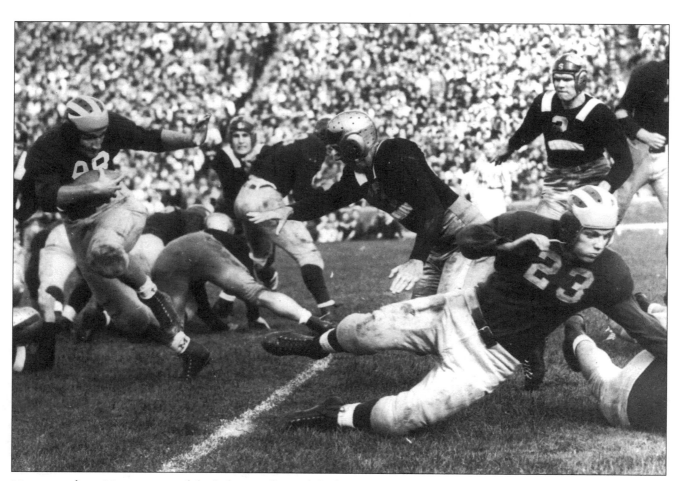

Harmon strikes a Heisman pose while eluding an Illinois defender.

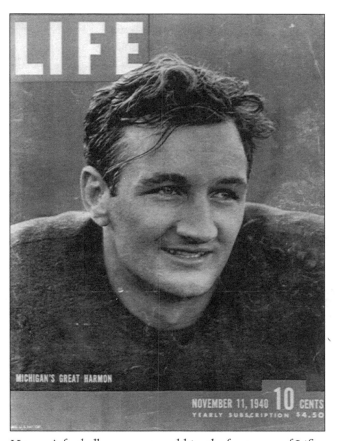

Harmon's football prowess earned him the front cover of Life *in November 1940.*

the voting. His name now goes into the records alongside those of Jay Berwanger of Chicago, Larry Kelley and Clint Frank of Yale, Davey O'Brien of Texas Christian and Kinnick.

When Harmon, in that closing game with Ohio State, scored three touchdowns, passed for two more and kicked 4 points after touchdown, he put the seal on a remarkable record. That brought his touchdown total to 33, two more than Red Grange scored for Illinois.

During the three years he played, Harmon made 2,134 yards overland in 398 rushes and threw 101 passes for 1,399 yards.

Michigan this year was one of the great teams of the country, losing only to Minnesota by a single point. In addition to the Ohio State game, Harmon's most widely watched performance was that against Penn in 1939. When both teams were undefeated, country-wide attention was focused on the meeting with the Quakers' fine back, Francis Reagan. Harmon led Michigan to a clean-cut victory that day and moved on to a brilliant season.

Harmon, weighing about 195 pounds in action, not only ran and passed, but blocked fairly well and did much of his team's punting, doing that job very well. He had the added value of being a durable player, being in for most of the time and playing two sixty-minute games as a sophomore, three as a junior and three as a senior.

CHAPTER 21

Michigan's fake field goal against Notre Dame led to holder Don Robinson's (46) dart around left end for a touchdown and an eventual 32-20 victory.

MICHIGAN'S FIVE TOUCHDOWNS BEAT IRISH, 32-20

BY JOHN N. SABO
Special to The Detroit Free Press

NOTRE DAME, Ind., Nov. 14, 1942 - Michigan's wild Wolverines, playing 50 minutes of football at its furious best, commemorated Notre Dame's centennial anniversary today and what a commemoration it was!

In an offensive barrage productive of eight touchdowns, Michigan pounded through Notre Dame's 202-pound line for five touchdowns and a 32-20 victory which will go down in football history as one of the greatest scoring exhibitions of all time.

This was no defensive scrap. It was a wild-run-ning, wide-open game which saw Notre Dame take the lead twice, only to have an offensively-superior Michigan team bounce back hard and often. It was a game which saw Tom Kuzma roar through for two touchdowns and Don Robinson, George Ceithami and Paul White rip across for one each.

Notre Dame tried desperately to stem this Michigan avalanche. The Irish punctured the Michigan defenses for touchdowns once by end Bob Dove and twice by Creighton Miller. But the Irish had nothing to offset a great Michigan surge in the third period which saw the Wolverines turn a 14-13 Notre Dame halftime lead into a 32-14 Michigan margin within 15 minutes.

Wolverine triple-threat halfback Tom Kuzma scored two touchdowns in Michigan's comeback win over the Irish.

To get a true perspective of what Michigan did today, one needs only look at the records.

Not in 36 years – since Army's 38-10 victory over Notre Dame in 1916 – has any team scored as many points against Notre Dame as Michigan did today.

When this furious battle before 57,200 fans had subsided, there remained little doubt as to which was the superior team. Today it was Michigan by everything the final score would indicate.

The Michigan line, outweighed 10 pounds to a man and with five of the Wolverine forwards playing the full 60 minutes, put the heat on in attacking the Irish in the third and fourth periods, when this game was decided.

The Michigan backs, with Kuzma, Robinson, White and Bob Wiese taking turns at lacerating the Irish forward wall, outrushed the Notre Dame backs, gaining 319 yards to 170.

Michigan also had the edge in first downs, 19 to 11, and gained most of them with an attack which refused to acknowledge the Irish's edge in weight.

So Michigan goes into its last two Big Ten games against Ohio State and Iowa with every chance to win or tie for the conference championship. The Wolverine team of today certainly looked like a squad which had the offensive weapons necessary to became a championship club.

In this spectacular victory Michigan had no picnic. The Wolverines needed every bit of their offensive astuteness and power to batter down a Notre Dame team which was primed to make this its best effort. Any team which has to come from behind twice to score a victory is pulling no punches.

To show how wild this game this was, Notre Dame not only led twice but it scored six minutes after the opening kickoff. The Irish produced another touchdown the second time they had their hands on the ball in a way indicative of their desire to repeat that 11-3 victory of 1909 in the last encounter between these schools.

Notre Dame's first touchdown came after a 44-yard drive and required only eight plays.

The score came on third down and the ball on the Michigan's 7-yard line. Angelo Bertelli calmly flipped a pass to Dove, who had skimped past White in the end zone. Bertelli added the point-after kick

and Notre Dame was off to a 7-0 lead.

That was just the beginning. No sooner had the Irish's John Creevey kicked off than Michigan was off to the races. The Wolverines charged 68 yards in 10 plays and a touchdown.

Wiese and Kuzma took turns at churning up the turf before Ceithami plunged over from the 1 on a first-down quarterback sneak. Jim Brieske kicked the extra point and the score was tied, 7-7.

Thereafter it was give and take until the third period. Michigan rushed in front, 13-7, on a 37-yard touchdown drive in the first three minutes of the second quarter.

That drive was started when defensive end Elmer Madar recovered an Irish lateral, Bertelli to Bob Livingstone, which Livingstone fumbled on the Irish 37. In 10 plays, Michigan scored and the touchdown came on one of those moth-eaten Wolverine plays, a fake place kick.

With the ball on the Irish 4-yard line on fourth down, Michigan coach Fritz Crisler rushed Brieske in as though to try for the field goal. Robinson held the ball on the 11 but Brieske didn't kick. Instead, Robinson tore around left end and into the end zone. This time Brieske's point-after kick was blocked by Dove.

Notre Dame didn't let this lapse upset its plans. Midway in the period Bertelli punted and Kuzma fumbled. George Murphy, the Irish team captain, managed to touch the loose pigskin before it bounced out on the Michigan 12 and again Notre Dame was pounding at the touchdown gates. This opportunity turned into a 14-13 halftime lead when Miller plunged over right guard from the 3-yard line and Bertelli kicked the extra point.

It was anybody's game at this stage, but Michigan didn't let it remain so.

The Wolverines let loose all of their touchdown thunder in a one-sided third period which saw Michigan score three times. What's more, Michigan had the ball so much in his quarter that Notre Dame had only five running plays.

The Wolverines started running almost immediately. When Creevey's kickoff went out of bounds on the Wolverine 42, Michigan opened up with a 58-yard drive which required only 10 plays. White's two-yard plunge on a reverse inside left tackle was the scoring play. Brieske's kick made it 20-14 and Notre Dame wasn't in front for the rest of the afternoon.

On the next kickoff Creighton Miller was tackled hard by guard Julius Franks and the ball bounced out of the Notre Dame back's hands. Bob Kolesar, another Wolverine guard, recovered for Michigan on the Irish 25. Again the Wolverines were off. Seven plays and Kuzma had a touchdown after powering three yards over right tackle for the score. Brieske's kick was wide by inches.

The fifth and last Michigan touchdown came when the Irish started taking desperate chances. With the ball on their own 1-yard line, Bertelli dropped back to pass on second down.

He heaved a long one, but White intercepted it and Michigan started touchdown operations from the Irish 24.

The Wolverines actually scored this touchdown twice. The first time Robinson went six yards through left tackle into the end zone but the play was called back for holding and Michigan was penalized to the 16. On the next play, Kuzma passed 15 yards to end Phil Sharpe, who went to the one. Then Kuzma rammed over right tackle. When Brieske missed the extra point, Michigan had a 32-14 lead, which proved more than enough.

Still game, the courageous Irish came back with an aerial attack which was good for a 65-yard touchdown drive. The touchdown came on the old Statue of Liberty play when Creighton Miller took the ball from Bertelli and went 14 yards around left end. Bertelli missed the extra point kick and so ended the scoring.

In victory the Michigan line played a great game. Tackle Al Wistert was so outstanding that his teammates lifted him to their shoulders and carried him off the field. It was Wistert's great charging, blocking and tackling which punctured the right side of the Notre Dame line repeatedly. It was through that right side that Michigan made most of its 319 yards.

There were plenty of other outstanding men in the Michigan line. Julius Franks never tackled more sharply, center Merv Pregulman and ends Madar and Sharpe played the full game in this give-no-quar-

ter-and-ask-none tussle.

The Michigan backs gained the touchdown glory but it was that outweighed Michigan line playing with only two substitutions which battled Notre Dame into defeat today.

SCORE BY PERIODS

MICHIGAN 7   6   19   0 — 32
NOTRE DAME 7   7   0   6 — 20

CHAPTER 22

U-M GOES DOWN FIGHTING AGAINST ARMY

By Wilfrid Smith
The Detroit Free Press-Chicago Tribune Wire Service

New York, Oct. 13, 1945 - Michigan sent its football boys on a men's errand Saturday afternoon in Yankee Stadium but before Army's national champions proved their experience and skill with a 28-7 victory, 70,000 fans thrilled to the Wolverines' battle against the Cadets' power and speed.

In winning their twelfth consecutive game and third of the season, Army had to go all out all the way.

Army's stars were its 1944 all-America players, Glenn Davis and Felix (Doc) Blanchard.

Blanchard ran off Michigan's left tackle 69 yards for Army's second touchdown in the second quarter and Davis sprinted 70 yards around Michigan's left flank for the final score in the last period. Without either one of these superb backs, Michigan might well have contained the Cadet attack and turned the football trick of the year. It was no parade for Army, and the score belies the ferocity of the competition.

Michigan, trailing, 14-0, at the start of the second half, took the kickoff and drove 75 yards to the Cadet

goal. In possession again, the Wolverines were checked on a march for the tying touchdown by a fumble.

From this point, there was no doubt of the final result, but Michigan's youngsters fought to the end.

They made six first downs in the last 15 minutes to one for Army.

Army's veterans were forced to the limit. Blanchard and Davis carried the ball 40 times from scrimmage. The crashing tumble of Blanchard, who hit from tackle to tackle and never was completely stopped, were complementary to Davis' sweeping sprints.

Blanchard carried the ball 21 times for 179 yards. Davis carried 19 times and covered 191 yards. In addition, Davis completed three of five passes for 47 yards.

Blanchard's power through the line forced Michigan to bunch its defense and thus become vulnerable to wide plays. The weakness was apparent, but the Wolverines had no choice.

Army's initial attack used no deception and Davis and Tom McWilliams alternated in wide runs after taking a deep lateral from Arnold Tucker, the Cadet quarterback of the T formation.

Michigan, on the other hand, while continually alternating several platoons of teams throughout the contest, made the most of deception against the Army defense, which rarely substituted. And the Yankee Stadium onlookers perhaps saw the slickest backfield maneuvers – spin plays, double laterals, and reverses – possible to plan.

Michigan's stalwarts were Joe Ponsetto, a team captain, and center Harold Watts, 60-minute men who bulwarked the line and stabled the attack.

At the kickoff Michigan had Jack Weisenburger at fullback in place of Dan Dworsky, a surprise which gave the Wolverines aid from their best punter. Dworsky played his part as did Pete Elliott and Henry Fonde.

These speedsters and Walt Teninga, who opened at left half, were exceptional against a defense which always was a step faster than Michigan's blockers.

Although each team only received one 15-yard penalty, the assessments were barriers to touchdowns. In the first quarter Davis caught a long pass from Tucker for a 61-yard gain and a touchdown which was called back when Army held. The penalty put the ball on Army's 24-yard line.

In the second period of a scoreless game Fonde carried Elliott's lateral 16 yards for a first down on the Cadet 10, but the Wolverines held and were set back to Army's 36. On fourth down, two plays later, Weisenburger was stopped on Army's 33.

The Cadets marched 67 yards in 13 plays for the first touchdown of the afternoon.

McWilliams then swung wide around Michigan's right end to score. Dick Walterhouse made the first of his four conversions and Army led, 7-0.

After Michigan received the kickoff and Teninga kicked out on Army's 31-yard line, Blanchard struck outside Michigan's left tackle and ran 69 yards to the Wolverines' goal. After the conversion, Army led, 14-0, and that was the score at the intermission.

Bob Nussbaumer took Blanchard's second-half kickoff in the end zone and returned to his 25-yard line. Ten plays later Art Renner caught Teninga's pass in the Cadet end zone to score.

Ponsetto kicked the point-after and Michigan trailed, 14-7. Here was Michigan's high tide of performance.

Army's counterattack was stopped when Bob Derieth recovered Tucker's fumble on Michigan's 26. Eventually Blanchard recovered a fumble on the Wolverine 31. Davis swung around Michigan's left end for 15 yards and McWilliams turned right end for 15 more. On the last play of the third quarter Blanchard drove through the line to score and put Army ahead, 21-7.

In the last period Michigan, although definitely beaten, rallied to mark up two first downs and advanced 35 yards to Army's 30. Elliott's low pass to Len Ford on fourth down ended the assault.

Then came Davis and there went Davis. On the first play the Cadet ace outran all opponents straight across the gridiron and turned down the sideline to cover 70 yards for the final touchdown.

Thereafter Michigan marked up three first downs, but the futile assault was only the enthusiasm of youngsters who would not accept defeat.

SCORE BY PERIODS

MICHIGAN	0	0	7	0 —	7
ARMY	0	14	7	7 —	28

Heisman Trophy winner Doc Blanchard (35) stiff-arms a Michigan defender in an attempt to escape to open field.

DAVIS ROMPS AND ARMY MARCHES ON

BY LYALL SMITH
Special to The Detroit Free Press

ANN ARBOR, Oct. 12, 1946 - Army was the winner, 20-13.

But the football glory of the University of Michigan was as great in defeat as it could have been in victory over a mighty team that ran its perfect record to 22 straight victories over a span of two and one-half seasons.

There were 86,000 fans jammed into Michigan Stadium to see what the Wolverines could do against an Army juggernaut that had steamrollered all opponents by the liberal usage of fullback Doc Blanchard (Mr. Inside) and halfback Glenn Davis (Mr. Outside).

Those fans were out of their seats more than they were in them as Michigan rose to the heights to give Army its most severe test over its long domination of football foes.

Mr. Inside, all 210 pounds of him, was stopped time and again by an alert Michigan line.

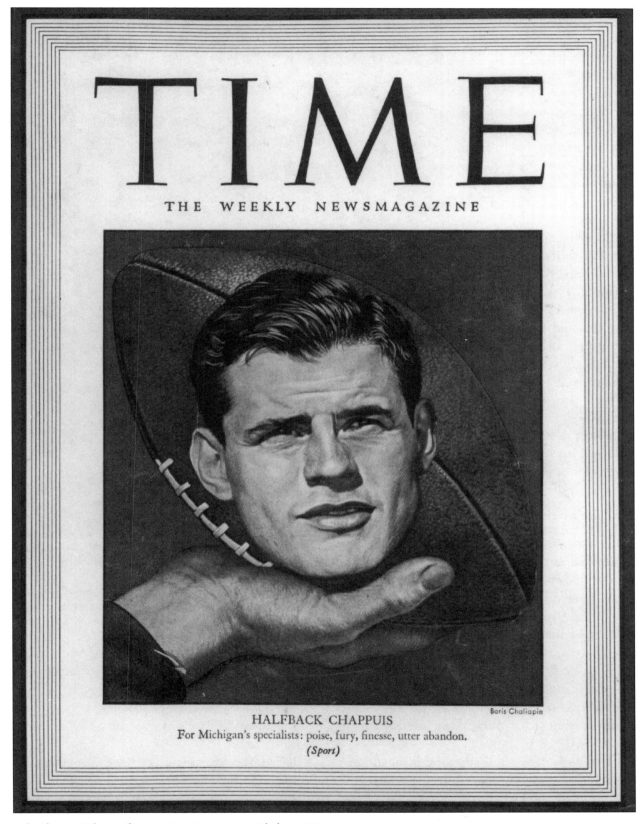

TIME

THE WEEKLY NEWSMAGAZINE

Boris Chaliapin

HALFBACK CHAPPUIS

For Michigan's specialists: poise, fury, finesse, utter abandon.

(Sport)

Bob Chappuis' heroic feats against Army in 1946 led to a Time cover story in 1947.

Mr. Outside, a fleet-footed sensation, broke loose once on a 57-yard touchdown junket but he, too, was stopped time after time.

So much so, in fact, by the four-man line defense concocted by Michigan coach Fritz Crisler, that Army took to the air. And that decision was the one that spelled the narrow margin between Army's victory and Michigan's defeat.

The Wolverines scored first with halfback Bob Chappuis flipping a 12-yard pass to Howard Yerges after nine minutes in the first period to climax a 41-yard drive.

But Davis, sticking to running maneuvers, evened the count with only 50 seconds left in the same quarter when he shot through a hole on his own 43-yard line, ducked over to the western sidelines and feinted his way all the way to the Wolverine goal.

Jim Brieske had converted after Michigan's score and Jack Ray did likewise after Army's initial one and then the Cadets took to the airways.

As the first half neared its close, Army had the ball on its

Gene Derricotte (41) turns the corner against the Cadets.

own 33. Davis, who tried seven passes and completed all seven of them, fired a 44-yard pass to Blanchard. Then, with only 29 seconds left before the intermission gun, Davis again rifled a long pass to end Bob Folsom for a touchdown, putting Michigan behind, 13-7.

But the Wolverines, still smarting from the 28-7 defeat handed them by this same team last year, drove back after the kickoff that opened the second half to roll 83 yards to tie the score.

Paul White climaxed it with a six-yard sprint that gave Michigan a tie score, which stood until Davis again turned into an aerial wizard to pull the game out of the fire.

The Cadets marched 76 yards by land and by air to finally send Blanchard over the goal line from the 8-yard marker.

It had been the custom of the Cadets to use both Davis and Blanchard sparingly. But with Michigan playing out its collective heart, both players were in the battle all but a few minutes.

Blanchard carried the ball 14 times but gained only

44 yards. Davis scampered away on 17 attempts and wound up with a net gain of only 64.

Stopping these stars and opening up with a tricky assortment of its own offensive maneuvers, Michigan made 12 first downs to 12 for Army. The Wolverines gained 141 yards on the ground to 152 for the team that never has been outgained and usually totals more than 300-plus yards per game.

But the story was in the air. Davis threw the ball seven times and hit his seven receivers for an overall gain of 159 yards. Most of the passes were long ones.

So intense was Michigan's will to win that in the closing minutes, the Wolverines were down on the Army 10-yard line. John White, the center on Crisler's line, recovered a fumble by Davis on Michigan's 33 and Chappuis, a brilliant star even in defeat, hit Yerges with one of the six passes he completed in 11 attempts, for a 16-yard gain.

Arnold Tucker, the Army quarterback, intercepted a Wolverine pass on his own 25 to momentarily stall the march. But after Michigan had thrown Davis for an eight-yard loss and Blanchard for three more, the Wolverines took a punt on the Army 43 and started to roll with only 55 seconds left in the game.

Bump Elliott followed up by hitting Don Robinson with a pass on the 25. Then Robinson rifled one to Elmer Madar, a sensation in all departments of play, who carried to the 10. Two fifteen-yard penalties, however, then halted the march to the tying touchdown and the game ended when Tucker intercepted a pass by Chappuis on the Cadets' 35.

A punt off the side of Jim Rawer's toe gave Michigan the ball on Army's 41 to start its first touchdown drive. White, Chappuis and Bob Wiese lugged the ball down to the Cadet 25 before Chappuis passed to Madar on the 18. Chappuis and White hit to the seven. A penalty moved Michigan back to the 12 before Yerges gathered in a pass from Chappuis and walked the tight rope down the sideline to score.

The brilliant 57-yard run by Davis knotted the score at the end of the first period and Army came back to score again in the second period only to have it called back by a penalty after Davis went over from the 10 on a lateral from Tucker.

But after a Michigan punt, Davis wound up on his 7 with the ball in his hands and a horde of Wolverines after him. Seemingly in desperation, he threw a long pass that was gobbled up by Folsom to give the Cadets their first-half margin.

After the second-half kickoff, Yerges lateraled to Chappuis, who reeled off 11 yards to the Michigan 30. On an end-around play, Leonard Ford rambled for 18 additional yards and Yerges sneaked through center for 10 yards to the Army 42. Madar made a great catch of a pass by Chappuis on the 23. Chappuis banged to the 16 and then passed again to Yerges on the eight.

White ran to the four before Chappuis lost two yards. Then on a nifty cutback play which sent him from the right side of the Wolverine backfield far to his left, White drilled over for the tying score.

Brieske's kick was no good for the first time in seven tries this season.

SCORE BY PERIODS

MICHIGAN	7	0	6	0 —	13
ARMY	7	6	0	7 —	20

Michigan's 1947 Dream Backfield: (left to right) Bump Elliott, Jack Weisenburger, Howard Yerges and Bob Chappuis.

MICHIGAN ROUTS U.S.C. IN ROSE BOWL

BY BALDWIN HILL
Special to The New York Times

PASADENA, Calif., Jan. 1, 1948 - The University of Michigan's dazzling football machine capped an all-victorious season today by slashing almost at will up and down the Rose Bowl greensward to defeat the University of Southern California, 49-0.

93,000 spectators, headed by General Omar Bradley, the grand marshal of the Tournament of Roses, saw Fritz Crisler's gridiron supermen run up

a score unparalleled since Fielding Yost's point-a-minute Michigan team massacred Stanford by the same margin in the first Rose Bowl game in 1902.

With this triumph setting a modern Rose Bowl scoring record the Wolverines challenged Notre Dame's claim to mythical national gridiron supremacy.

With its twin offensive and defensive machines working so much like well-oiled parts that their intermittent replacements of each other on the field even were almost imperceptible, Michigan struck for a touchdown before the first period was ten minutes old.

During a Hollywood visit prior to the 1948 Rose Bowl actress Marlene Dietrich poses with Wolverine stars (left to right) Bump Elliott, Bob Chappuis and Bruce Hilkene.

While Southern California struggled vainly to get possession of the ball for a decisive hitch, Crisler's wolfmen crossed the Trojan goal line – once in the first period and twice in the second period. They coasted along on a single tally in the third, but closed with a crescendo of three scores in the fourth period.

Each touchdown was neatly converted by the adroit toe of Jim Brieske, with Gene Derricotte holding. Their last two successful efforts set a new Rose Bowl extra point record.

Other records also were shattered. It was U.S.C.'s worst defeat in sixty gridiron years.

Michigan's total yardage – 491 – topped the mark of nearly twenty years standing set by the Trojans

against Pittsburgh in 1930 – 427.

This was the twenty-fifth actual bowl game and the thirty-fourth staged in connection with the annual Tournament of Roses. The weather was bright and balmy, with just enough briskness.

The Trojans fought valiantly, with nary a hint of despair or dispirit, but were manifestly outclassed. The Wolverines' passes, chiefly from the talented fingers of Bob Chappuis, darted like precise bolts of lightning, and their plunges along the ground were like piledrivers. Trojan coach Jeff Cravath's previously spectacular outfit, by contrast, seemed to move in slow motion.

U.S.C. never could generate the power to get a consistent touchdown drive started.

Efforts to fight her way out aerially were unavailing, too.

Three Wolverine jackpots were rung up by fullback Jack Weisenburger and two resulted from passes by all-America halfback Chappuis to halfback

Chalmers (Bump) Elliott and quarterback Howard Yerges, respectively. One touchdown was on a pass from halfback Hank Fonde to Gene Derricotte, who replaced Chappuis in the final quarter, and the finale on a pass from Yerges to Dick Rifenburg.

Tactics starred rather than strategy. Crisler used his regular single-wing variations throughout the game, while Cravath's men stuck to the old and previously reliable T.

Michigan won the toss, received, and yielded possession of the ball momentarily before embarking on a 63-yard, eleven-play drive. Sparked by Chappuis' flings, the Wolverines made the first score on a 1-yard plunge by Weisenburger.

As the first quarter neared its close, Weisenburger punted from his 47 out of bounds on Troy's half-yard line. That put U.S.C. in a corner where it had to kick out for safety and set up another Wolverine touchdown drive.

Going into the second stanza, Chappuis sent a 15-

Fritz Crisler and his Wolverine team at practice prior to the 1948 Rose Bowl.

yard heave to Bob Mann, the fleet left end, for a first down on Troy's 26. One play later Chappuis spiraled one 22 yards to Yerges on the four, from where he battled his way to the 1. Weisenburger barreled over left guard for the Western Conference champions' second tally.

Goaded into redoubled efforts, the Trojans drove from their 12 clear to Michigan's 10 on more than two dozen bitterly-fought plays, only to lose the ball when quarterback George Murphy's pass was intercepted by Michigan's Dick Kempthorn.

Then the Wolverines went eighty-three yards in eight plays. Elliott made the third touchdown on an eleven-yard Chappuis pass.

Early in the third quarter Weisenburger and Chappuis spearheaded another apparent touchdown drive that was

The Michigan team gathers to board the train for their journey to Pasadena.

thwarted by a fumble by Yerges on the 9, which was recovered by Walker McCormick, the Trojan center. However, U.S.C. again floundered, and Dean Dill punted at midfield to Derricotte, who returned 12 yards.

Failing to gain a first down, Weisenburger punted into the end zone, and Troy started its third scoring try of the third quarter. On the second play, fading back to pass, Dill was smothered by the Michigan forward wall and fumbled.

Don Dworsky, the Michigan center, recovered on the 18. One play later Chappuis tossed to Yerges on the 13, and he went all the way.

In the final quarter Michigan, in possession of the ball thrice, capitalized each time. Going fifty-four yards in five plays, the Weisenburger-Chappuis combination scored with the fullback bucking the final yard. A Trojan fumble on the U.S.C. 45 was recovered by Joe Sobeleski, the Michigan guard, and diminutive Hank Fonde passed to Derricotte, who raced 21 yards for No. 6.

The final score resulted from two passes. Derricotte threw to Ford on the 40, and he drove to the 28. Then Yerges rifled one to Rifenburg, who made a sensational snare on the 7 and tallied.

SCORE BY PERIODS

MICHIGAN	7	14	7	21 —	49
U.S.C.	0	0	0	0 —	0

Bump Elliott (left) and his brother, Pete, were both standouts for Fritz Crisler's powerhouse Wolverines.

Crisler says best team 'Played greatest game' against Trojans

BY THE ASSOCIATED PRESS
The New York Times

With their greatest display of cheers, back-slapping, hugging and yelling of the year, the mighty men of Michigan expressed their joy today after their superb exhibition of football. It was an exhibition which wrote a new page in Rose Bowl history and left Southern California bewildered.

The walls of the dressing room reverberated with the emotional blow-off as the Maize and Blue boys surged in from the field after posting the identical score that Michigan had run up in 1902 in the Wolverines' only other Rose Bowl engagement.

The boisterous forty-four men of the squad turned their enthusiasm to their handsome coach, Fritz Crisler, when he arrived at the dressing room about ten minutes later. After the frenzy had died down a bit, the doors were opened to reporters, who poured uncounted questions at the smiling Crisler.

"This is a great team," he said, "and this was their greatest game. Yes, I think it's the best team I ever coached, though the teams I had at Princeton in 1933 and 1935 were great teams.

"No, I don't feel there were any individual Michigan standouts. It was a matter of squad play – that's been characteristic of this group all season."

Of course, the inevitable comparison with Notre Dame, which whipped the Trojans, 38-7, was invited. With a smile, the Wolverine coach answered, "Yes, I think this was a wonderful game."

Queried about the Trojan team whose only other record blot during the regular season was a 7-7 tie with Rice, Crisler termed it a "good" team and one that would compare favorably with "the best teams we've played in the Western Conference.

"But the breaks were swell for us," he added. "Everything worked swell for us.

"Don't think U.S.C. hasn't got some good men. Paul Cleary (the all-America end) and Walt McCormick, the center, are top-notch ballplayers in any league."

Through the gloom of the Trojan dressing room, U.S.C. coach Jeff Cravath was still able to speak.

"We knew we were outclassed," said Cravath, "but we didn't think we would be outclassed that much. We expected to do a better job."

He didn't see how Michigan "could have been much sharper."

Was Michigan better than Notre Dame? (Michigan had a 49-point margin over Troy, the Irish 31.)

"Michigan wouldn't beat Notre Dame's first team, but the Michigan reserve strength is far superior," Cravath said. He pointed out that Johnny Lujack, the Irish ace, hadn't thrown any passes in the second half against U.S.C., and opined the Irish score could have been higher.

Who would Cravath take – Lujack or Bob Chappuis?

"Both," said Honest Jeff.

CHAPTER 25

Prior to his last game as Michigan's coach, Crisler addresses his squad at practice for the 1948 Rose Bowl.

The man who modernized football

By TIM COHANE
NRTA Journal

NEW YORK, November 1979 - In 1945, a weak University of Michigan football team went up against Army's best squad ever, a powerhouse led by backs Doc Blanchard and Glenn Davis – Mr. Inside and Mr. Outside.

The place: Yankee Stadium.

On that wartime Michigan roster were many spindly, rosey-cheeked youngsters, 12 of them freshmen. But their coach was the great Fritz Crisler.

What a game! Not only did the spectators see Blanchard and Davis in action, they saw some very strange maneuvering by Crisler.

When Michigan had the ball, Crisler pulled out eight players – the linemen and linebackers – and put in substitutes. His idea was to rest the eight.

Amazingly, it worked for most of two quarters. Crisler's kids were holding the mighty Cadets to a scoreless tie. However, late in the second period Army broke it open with Blanchard galloping for one touchdown and Davis two.

But history was made: Crisler gave birth to two-platoon football.

"It was not ingenuity on my part, but desperation. When the other fellow has a thousand dollars and you have a dime, it's time to gamble. Our below-

Crisler retired at the peak of his career after his Michigan squad won the 1948 Rose Bowl and was named national champions.

Crisler observes from the sidelines at the 1948 Rose Bowl.

par wartime squad couldn't possibly have stood up against that powerhouse for 60 minutes. Therefore, we gambled."

It worked so well that Crisler platooned for the rest of the season, substituting all 11 players when the ball changed hands. It created, for the first time, offensive and defensive teams.

"Many coaches wrote and phoned to know what we were doing," Crisler adds. "By the following season many of the colleges and secondary schools had begun to adopt platooning."

As a leader on National Collegiate Athletic Association rules and administrative committees, Crisler

was responsible also for the two-point conversion, which adds drama to the game, and for widening the goalposts from 20 to 24 feet. But it is for two platoons that he is best remembered.

Even if he had never influenced a single change, Crisler would have been ushered into the Hall of Fame, as he was in 1954, for his coaching.

In his 18 years (1930-1947) as head coach, his record of 116-32-9 was 14th best in the all-time totals at the game's centennial in 1969. His record includes two seasons at Minnesota, 10-7-1; six at Princeton, 35-9-5; and 10 at Michigan, 71-16-3. He had three perfect seasons: 9-0 at Princeton in 1933 and 1935, 10-0 at

Michigan in 1947.

The Wolverines, who thrashed Southern California, 49-0, in the 1948 Rose Bowl game, surely were among the top offensive teams ever put together. With their spinning and buck-lateral sequences from the single wing, they were among the most spectacular, as well.

In 1930, the year before Crisler went to Princeton, Tiger practices for the Yale game saw 50 or more former players in uniform trying to help out with the coaching. There was scarcely room on the field for the undergraduate players. The chaos contributed to a 51-14 trouncing by Yale.

When Crisler took over in 1931, the first non-alumnus to coach Princeton, he was regarded warily by some. However, he mailed all interested alumni passes to practice with two stipulations: that what

they saw would remain secret, and that they would stay off the field.

The reaction at first was negative, but when his 1932 Tigers tied Yale, 7-7, and his 1933 team capped an unbeaten, untied season by beating Yale, 27-2, the grumbling faded.

This was a typically smooth Crisler operation. Of all the football coaches who might have done well in other careers, Crisler was tops.

As a diplomat, he would have been at home in any embassy.

When someone once remarked to him that his freshman squad of 1932 included 30 former high school and prep captains, he replied with a grand blandness that it was an interesting coincidence.

Thereafter, the football Class of 1936 was known as "The Princeton Coincidentals."

Fritz Crisler, in his first job as head coach at Minnesota, visits with Stanford's Glenn (Pop) Warner.

Asked to compare his strong Princeton teams with the Tommy Harmon-led Michigan teams of 1938, 1939 and 1940, Crisler wrote, "I would not risk picking a winner. A break (in the game) would probably decide it. Both had an abundance of ability and competitive desire."

Harmon, of course, was Crisler's greatest player. He ranks with Red Grange of Illinois, Chic Harley of Ohio State, Bronko Nagurski of Minnesota, and Nile Kinnick of Iowa in a special pre-World War II pantheon of the Big Ten Conference. Harmon was also one of the greatest ball-carriers of all time.

Harmon's principal blocker was quarterback Forest Evashevski, later an outstanding coach at Washington State and Iowa. Even the coach could not quell Evy's free spirit and sense of humor. He often referred to Crisler as "Chris Fisler" and when the coach in one of his rousing speeches said he wanted "11 tigers on defense and 11 lions on offense," Evashevski raised his hand and said he wouldn't play unless he could be a leopard.

"Offense is poise, defense is frenzy," was Crisler's number-1 motto. Since opponents were invariably pointing for Michigan, he was in the habit of assuring his squads, "Our plan is simple; theirs is one of desperation."

No matter the halftime score, Crisler would ask his players, "What's the score?" and they would chorus, "Nothing to nothing." Inevitably a sophomore spoke out one day: "You fellows are all wrong. The score is 21-0 and we're ahead." There was no more halftime seriousness that day.

In Crisler's 10 years at Michigan, the Wolverines were the team to beat in the Big Ten.

They won the title in 1947, tied with Purdue in 1943, and finished second six times. In Harmon's three seasons the record was 19-4-1, with three of the losses, two of them 7-6, administered by Bernie Bierman's Minnesota machines.

There was irony in this. Crisler, upon leaving Minnesota where he had recruited well, signed Bierman as his successor. "Little did I suspect," he sighs, "that act would haunt me in later years."

Away from the gridiron or council table, Crisler was a sociable soul who liked to stay up late with old friends. Unlike his old coach and mentor at the University of Chicago, Amos Alonzo Stagg, Crisler favored a stronger beverage than milk.

Born January 12, 1899, on a farm near Earlville Ill., Herbert Orin Crisler was brought up in a devout Methodist family. At first he leaned toward the ministry, later toward medicine. But sport got its hooks into him.

He was a star end at Chicago under Stagg, and excelled in basketball and as a baseball pitcher. He was a superior scholar, winning the Big Ten's senior medal for proficiency in academics and sports.

After graduation he became an assistant to Stagg, who gave him the nickname Fritz when he was a young player with much to learn.

"Crisler," said Stagg, "there's a celebrated violinist in this country. The name sounds like yours but it is spelled differently: K-r-e-i-s-l-e-r. He's world-renowned because he has certain attributes and knows how to use them. He had genius, skill, coordination. From now on, Crisler, I'm going to call you Fritz, too, to remind myself that you are absolutely his opposite."

The nickname stuck. Years later, when the violinist was giving a concert in Ann Arbor, University of Michigan students arranged for the two Fritzes to meet. They chatted briefly, found they were not related – the coach's ancestry was Dutch; the violinist's Austrian. The artist asked the coach if there was something he could play for him. The request was "Danny Boy."

Once, Stagg summed up Crisler with this accolade: "Balance, judgement, dependability and loyalty are his predominant characteristics. In my talks to young people I have often used him as an illustration of these qualities well supported by eloquent mental gifts."

Those mental gifts gave football much, but nothing more far-reaching than two platoons.

CHAPTER 26

Chuck Ortmann (49) scampers through the Minnesota secondary en route to a Michigan touchdown.

MICHIGAN RIPS MINNESOTA MYTH, 14-7

BY LYALL SMITH
Special to The Detroit Free Press

ANN ARBOR, Oct. 22, 1949 - A tow-headed blond from Milwaukee made a piker out of Frank Merriwell as he put the might back in mighty Michigan.

It was this 20-year-old junior halfback, Charley Ortmann, who staged a heroic one-man show to lead the twice-beaten Wolverines to an upset 14-7 victory over a vaunted Minnesota eleven before 97,239

amazed fans.

Amazed, perhaps, is not the word. But the fact remains that Michigan went into this 40th battle with the gigantic Golden Gophers as a two-touchdown underdog. The Wolverines came out of it with a triumph which will go into the books as one of the greatest upsets of this or any football campaign.

The Gophers had been hailed as an unbeatable team. Their pride was their invulnerable forward wall, called the greatest in the land. The Gophers had won four straight games, including an easy victory over a Northwestern eleven which had humbled Michigan one week ago for the Wolverines' second straight defeat.

Michigan was without halfback Leo Koceski, Ortmann's sidekick and running mate. But with him or without him, the Wolverines never before rose to such heights against what looked to be insurmountable odds.

The only thing which doesn't tell the true story is the final score. The game wasn't that close.

It was Michigan all the way, with the brilliant Ortmann accounting for 207 of the 228 yards, as the Wolverines poured through an out-charged, out-fought Gopher forward wall.

The Milwaukee Kid was the dagger whose thrusts punctured the Gopher bubble of invincibility, but the Michigan line, vulnerable in its last two starts, was just as great this sunny October day.

Faced with its biggest obstacle, it threw back the mastodonic men from the North and swarmed over their ball carriers like a plague of locusts. Minnesota could run for only 67 yards.

It could pass for only 77 more.

The first two quarters were the ball game. In those minutes the Wolverines proved this was their day of glory. They arose out of their unaccustomed class of mediocrity and proved they still were in a battle to retain their twice-won crown of Western Conference king.

It was in that first half they scored all their 14 points. It was in that same half they gave the Gophers the ball nine times and then took it away from them every time.

The Wolverines thwarted all assaults and held Minnesota to only four yards on the ground and 45 more in the airways.

Starring with Ortmann was little 167-pound Charles Lentz. It was he who intercepted a Gopher aerial midway in the first period to set up a 39-yard march to Michigan's first touchdown.

It was this same halfback who twice more raced up to intercept Minnesota passes in the final quarter.

The Gophers took the first kickoff. When they punted they had lost one yard. They recovered a

fumble by Don Dufek two plays later on their own 45. When Billy Bye punted again, the ball was on his 39, a loss of six more yards.

Third time Minnesota got the football, Dick Gregory, realizing the Gopher backs couldn't budge the Michigan line, flipped a pass from his own 34. Lentz grabbed it at midfield and lugged it back 11 yards to the Minnesota 39.

Ortmann, who was to throw 17 passes and complete nine, threw one in the first play to end Harry Allis, who lugged it to the 20. A five-yard penalty advanced the ball to the 15, and Dufek swept wide to the 11.

Then it was Ortmann again. He took the ball and rammed over his own right tackle into the Gopher secondary.

He got back toward midfield and then propelled himself into the end zone in a half-dive, half-fall, which brought the fans up out of their seats in one great roar of glory and pride.

When Allis kicked the point-after, it was Michigan on top, 7-0, with less than eight minutes gone in the period. The score stood that way as the Wolverines continued to throw back the Gopher line and break up every drive.

With 90 seconds left in the half, Bye tried to pass from his 42. This time Lentz wasn't there, but Dufek was. He grabbed it off the fly and returned it across midfield to Minnesota's 45.

Ortmann was thrown for an eight-yard loss on the first play. Then he grabbed the ball and started on as if to sweep around his own right end. He pulled up short, arched his arm and again fired a pass to Allis, his favorite target.

Allis was tripped up finally on the Gopher 28. Now there was only 75 seconds left before the half and the Wolverines raced the clock. They beat it with 30 seconds to spare as they ran and tossed the baffled Gophers off their feet.

Halfback Don Peterson was handed the ball by Ortmann on a fake pass play and sped 11 yards to a first down on the 13. Now there were 28 seconds to go and the crowd was on its feet.

Don's brother, fullback Tom Peterson, rammed behind center to the 12 (18 seconds now).

Bill Putich – One-Play Bill – flipped a seven-yard

pass to Irv Wisniewaski, who scrapped his way to the 5-yard line (14 seconds to go).

Putich (Call him Two-Play Bill, now) grabbed the ball again and flipped a lateral to Wally Teninga, who swept wide to his right and was denied an immediate touchdown by six inches when he was thrown out of bounds.

Then, with 10 seconds to go, Teninga smashed straight into what was supposed to be Gopher power – the middle of the line – where Clayton Tonnemaker and Leo Nomellini had held sway until Michigan burst Minnesota's bubble this day. Teninga broke into the end zone, and when Allis again converted, it was 14-0.

Michigan trotted happily off the field for a respite and then came back to run into short-lived adversity. Dufek fumbled the first time the Wolverines got the ball and end Bud Grant recovered for the Gophers on the Minnesota 45.

With Bye passing to Gordon Soltau and Grant for gains of eight and 24 yards, plus some block-busting by fullback Frank Kuzma, the Gophers made their first serious bid. The pass to Grant reached the Michigan 13 for a first down and the goal in sight.

Bye made one yard, and then one more. Kuzma smashed for four yards but Michigan's line wouldn't give, and when he lunged ahead on fourth down, he was stopped on the five.

Michigan then took over.

Three plays made nine yards and Ortmann went back to punt. The pass from center was a bad one. Ortmann fumbled the ball, dropped it and finally tried to kick it while it was bouncing crazily on the turf. It rebounded off the charging Gopher line and careened into the end zone.

Ortmann dove for it, but end Art Edling, of the Gophers, finally cradled it. And that's how Minnesota scored.

Soltau converted and it was 14-7 after eight minutes and four seconds of the period.

This was a Gopher break and if there was to be a time that would rally Minnesota, this was it. But it wasn't.

Next time the Gophers got the ball Ozzie Clark smeared Bye for a six-yard loss. On the very next play Bob Hollway cracked through to smear Bye

again for nine more.

Not until the first play of the final period did Minnesota pick up its initial first down by rushing. Bye, whose net gain in 22 rushes was only three yards, picked up eight and Minnesota had achieved something it had not attained before.

Two plays later Bye took a lateral and swept 15 yards. Then it was time for a pass, and Lentz intercepted at midfield.

Now it was time for Ortmann to put on another one-man show. He cracked center twice and passed to Allis for a new series on the Gopher 33. Ortmann got to the 40 before two fumbles put the ball back on the 49.

On the next play Ortmann regained 12 yards. Then Teninga's punt was partly blocked and the Gophers recovered on their 48. Bye made one yard before Kuzma tried a jump pass.

Once again Lentz was on the spot to intercept. Then it was Ortmann for 12 yards. Bob Van Summers made one. Ortmann passed to Johnny Ghindia for eight more.

Now it was fourth down, one yard to go for a new series and nine minutes left, in the battle. Ortmann gambled for the one yard and crashed through for six to the 33.

The drive fizzled there, and Teninga punted out of bounds on the six. The Gophers took over, but couldn't gain and punted out to Michigan's 38.

Two plays lost one yard before Ortmann faked a pass to his right halfback, who was sweeping around to the left. He kept the ball and darted around the other flank.

Ortmann was on his own, but when he finally was pulled down, he had legged 44 yards to the 13-yard line. It was a perfect climax to his greatest day and Michigan's greatest triumph in its venerable series with the Gophers.

SCORE BY PERIODS

MICHIGAN..........7	7	0	0	—	14
MINNESOTA 0	0	7	0	—	7

Only 50,000 fans braved the 30 m.p.h. winds, 0° temperature and heavy snow in 85,000-seat Ohio Stadium to watch Michigan's 9-3 win.

WOLVERINES ROLL SNOWBALL INTO BIG TEN TITLE

BY LYALL SMITH
Special to The Detroit Free Press

COLUMBUS, Nov. 25, 1950 - "Punt and pray"– that's what Michigan did.

And on that fabled combine made famous by Fielding Yost, the Wolverines conquered Ohio State, 9-3, in a terrific blizzard which blew them straight into an undisputed Big Ten title and a return trip to the Rose Bowl on New Year's Day.

"Punt and pray" that Michigan did. It didn't make one single first down all day. It didn't complete one single pass on a wintry afternoon which forced the game to be played under arctic conditions.

The Wolverines just punted and prayed while 50,503 frozen fans shivered and shook. The snow swirled in from the north in 10-degree temperatures, completely wiped out yard markers and sometimes obliterated the players from the sight of the huddled fans in the stadium.

The blizzard forced a 20-minute delay of the battle as workmen struggled to clear the field of the heavy blanket of snow which paralyzed this section of the Midwest. There were doubts that the game would be played at all, so horrible were the conditions. But the show went on as the wind whistled in to numb the players and send the fans beneath blankets which soon were weighted down by the snow and ice.

Michigan punted and it prayed. Every point in the blizzardly battle was scored as the slippery and frozen football came off somebody's toe.

At first, the Wolverine prayer appeared to be working in reverse as one of halfback Chuck Ortmann's 24 – that's right – 24 punts was blocked early in the opening period.

The Buckeyes took over on the Michigan eight-yard line – or where that mark would have been if you could have seen beneath the blanket of snow and ice.

Three plays later Ohio was back on the 21, from where Vic Janowicz booted a field goal straight into the gale and over the crossbars to give the Bucks an early 3-0 lead.

But the success formula still was ahead for the Wolverines, who retrieved two points later in the same period when team captain Al Wahl blocked one of the 21 kicks by Janowicz. The ball spun back out of the end zone and it was 3-2 on an automatic safety.

With only 20 seconds left in the first half, Ohio State again was pushed back to its own goal line by Ortmann's punting toe. On third down Janowicz tried to kick out.

Before he kicked, Michigan called time-out to set up some way to block that punt.

When play was resumed, the Wolverines sent Tony Momsen crashing in from the left side.

The ball smashed into his chest and bounced crazily through the snow back over the Buckeye goal.

Momsen kept right on going. He dove for the ball and it slipped away from him. He dove for it a second time. This time he nestled it beneath him as if to warm it as the Buckeyes piled in on top of him. It was a touchdown, and when Harry Allis kicked

the point, the game actually had been ended, 9-3.

It was punt and pray the rest of the way, with the brilliant Ortmann getting the ball away time after time to keep the Buckeyes away from the door.

To say that the prayers were unanswered is no sacrilege.

For when Northwestern upset Illinois, 14 to 7, Michigan had become Big Ten champions for the fourth straight year and the third straight time since Bennie Oosterbaan replaced Fritz Crisler as head coach.

The Wolverines had to share the title with this game Ohio State team last year. They shared it with no one this time. Their record of four victories, one loss and one tie is better than Wisconsin and Ohio State's 5-2 marks. Illinois wound up in fourth place with a 4-2 record in conference competition.

This was a battle with the chips down and the Wolverines reached out with icy fingers to rake them in – fingers which were frozen this day but will be warmed on Jan. 1 when they play a repeat performance in California.

They punted and they prayed, but they hit and tackled, too.

This was a battle when you had but one idea. That was to make the other team handle the ball and then pray that you could make them fumble, or else crash in to block their own punts to get the slippery football back.

On the first play of the game Ortmann punted out to the Ohio State 31. On the third play Janowicz punted back to the Michigan 6. On the next play Ortmann tried to kick out again.

Tackle Joe Campanella broke through to knock down the ball. Leo Koceski recovered it on the 8. But since the ball had crossed the line of scrimmage, it was just a punt and the ball belonged to the Buckeyes.

On the first play Janowicz went back to pass, he was hopelessly trapped and chased back to the 29, from where he threw the ball away to draw a penalty for intentionally grounding the ball. That five-yard deficit pushed it back to the 34. Then Janowicz passed to Tom Watson, who reached the 21.

That was one of the three passes the Bucks completed in 18 tries all day. On the next down Janow-

Because of the difficult conditions, the Michigan-Ohio State game turned into a punting duel and a struggle for short stretches of yardage.

icz had Carroll Widdoes hold the ball on the 27-yard line for a field-goal try.

It was good, although Michigan protested that the wind had blown it astray before it sailed over the bar. So Ohio State led, 3-0.

Late in the same period Michigan slashed into that lead after Ortmann had punted out of bounds from midfield to the Ohio State 4-yard marker.

On first down Janowicz dropped deep in to his end zone to punt after scraping the snow away so he would have solid footing. Wahl sliced in to block it, and Allan Jackson chased it and fell on it.

The officials ruled that it had gone out of the end zone when Jackson grabbed it. Instead of a touchdown, the Wolverines had a safety and instead of six points they had two. But they took those two points and remembered the way they had scored them. Then they punted and kept praying.

The ball changed hands eight times in the second period, before Michigan took over on the Ohio State 28 after a weak kick from his 18 by Janowicz.

Ortmann hit to the 22. Don Dufek was stopped. Bill Putich fired a pass which barely eluded Lowell Perry's grasp at the goal. Then Harry Allis tried a field goal from the 30, but the ball soared far to the left of the posts.

Janowicz later punted from the 20 and Ortmann punted back to the Buckeye 10 with just 47 seconds remaining in the half.

Janowicz and Walt Klevay then tried to run out the clock. They couldn't gain, so Janowicz dropped back to punt again – his 12th attempt of the opening half.

Michigan called time-out, set up it's charging strategy and maybe the Wolverines really did say a prayer. I don't know. But Momsen crashed in to block the kick and then fell on it to provide the points which will enable Michigan to leave snow and ice far behind in another month.

The Wolverines held, 9-3, the lead at the intermission.

Ohio State had only the consolation of making the first of its three first downs in the game in the same half. That came when Janowicz made nine yards from his own 17 after Chuck Gandee had picked up an earlier three feet.

The second half was more punt and prayer. Ortmann punted 12 times, making Ohio State handle the ball which Michigan did not want to toy with. He kept the ball in Buckeye territory as the storm grew so terrible that at times the players could not even be seen from the press box.

Neither team crossed midfield in the third period, but Ohio State took life as it fought to ward off its third defeat of the year.

That was when Ralph Straffon, whose 14 yards in 15 tries made him Michigan's leading ground-gainer, fumbled at the outset of the final quarter. Tom Anderson recovered for Ohio State on the Michigan 31, but on third down Ozzie Clark slid up to intercept a Janowicz pass and return it to the Michigan 40.

On first down Ortmann quick-kicked to the Ohio 21. From then until the gun finally ended this icy battle, it was punt and pray, punt and pray. It ended with the ball somewhere close to the 50-yard line you couldn't tell how close as Ohio tried four desperation passes which failed.

And so it came about that the punt-and-pray formula of the late Fielding Yost won a game and a championship for one of his prize pupils, Bennie Oosterbaan.

SCORE BY PERIODS

MICHIGAN	2	7	0	0 —	9
OHIO STATE	3	0	0	0 —	3

Michigan coach Bennie Oosterbaan watches from the sideline during the 1951 Rose Bowl.

WOLVERINES RALLY TO WHIP CAL, 14-6

BY TOMMY DEVINE
Special to The Detroit Free Press

PASADENA, Calif., Jan. 1, 1951 - The University of Michigan inscribed two more names among its all-time gridiron immortals as it made an amazing comeback to whip California, 14-6, in the 37th Rose Bowl game.

Into the record books alongside the names of Wolverine brilliants like Willie Heston, Johnny Maulbetsch, Harry Kipke, Benny Friedman, Harry Newman, Tom Harmon and Bob Chappuis will go Chuck Ortmann and Don Dufek.

It was the needle-threading passing of Ortmann and the ram-rodding, up-the-middle rushes of Dufek which sparked a sensational second-half comeback.

Ortmann and Dufek literally picked Michigan off the emerald green turf in the Rose Bowl and catapulted this Wolverine team into a triumph that must be ranked among the greatest ever by a Michigan team.

Sure, there were other stars in the Wolverine constellation as Michigan gave the Big Ten a monopolistic sweep of the five-year series with the Pacific Coast conference.

There were youngsters like quarterback Bill Putich and lanky Fred Pickard, an end, who came into the game late in the second half and put new life and zest into Michigan's aerial game.

There were tough, rugged defensive performers like the ever alert Tony Momsen, sophomore Roger Zatkoff and the durable Tom Johnson.

But the glory of this Rose Bowl victory rests primarily with Ortmann and Dufek. They were the gridders who stole completely the spotlight from California's vaunted trio of Jim Monachino, Pete Scharbarum and Johnny Olszewski.

Ortmann and Dufek, a pair of seniors playing their final game for Michigan made it, by far, the greatest of their respective careers.

How good were they? They were simply the difference between victory and certain defeat.

It was Dufek, a real work horse, who made Michigan's ground attack click under as heavy pressure as a fullback ever faced.

The burly blond from Chicago carried the ball more than all the other Michigan backs combined. He made 23 rushes out of the total of 39 for the Wolverines. Dufek picked up a net of 113 yards for an average of 4.9 yards per carry.

The efficiency of this hard-hitting youngster is attested by the fact that only once all afternoon was the big and powerful California line able to throw him for a loss. That deficit amounted to only one yard.

Michigan made a net of only 145 yards on the ground, so you can see how clearly Dufek dominated the play. Fittingly enough, Dufek scored both Wolverine touchdowns.

As for Ortmann, he was a passing wizard at the very peak of his career.

The kid from Milwaukee took to the air 19 times. He completed 15 of them. That's right, 15 completions, just one short of the all-time Rose Bowl record.

When the California defense closed in, in a vain attempt to throttle Dufek, Ortmann took to the airways and sent the Bears reeling with his passes.

It was a combination California couldn't stop or match.

This was a football game which was divided into two parts. The first was all California. The second was equally one-sided in favor of Michigan.

The Wolverines went into the fourth quarter trailing, 6-0.

They had scoring chances and fizzled them. That they weren't farther behind was something of a football miracle. But there on the scoreboard were just six points for California and nothing for Michigan.

On the third play of the final quarter, a pass by Putich was intercepted in midfield by California. The Bears couldn't roll, however, and Don Robinson punted over the goal line.

Michigan took the ball on its own 20. And that's when and where the Wolverines finally began to jell.

The situation was desperate and so Michigan gambled. On first down from that spot deep in his own territory, Ortmann passed to Pickard, who had just entered the game. The aerial was good for 15 yards.

Another toss to Pickard. On this one he made a great shoestring catch for nine yards.

Dufek hammered for the first down.

Then Ortmann passed to Putich for three yards and tossed a screen pass to Dufek for 14 more to California's 37.

An offsides penalty against California and another slam at center by Dufek made it first down on the Bears' 27.

Here Putich called for a switch in patterns. Ortmann went back into the old double wing – an obvious passing maneuver, but still California couldn't stop it.

From the double wing, Ortmann hit Lowell Perry for 12 yards. Dufek was tossed for a one-yard loss. Then off the double wing again, Ortmann passed to Harry Allis for 12 yards and a first down on the Bears' 4.

Here came the real dramatic, heart-throbbing moment of the contest for the 98,939 spectators.

Dufek hammered for two yards. Dufek slammed for one. Third and a yard to go. Again it was Dufek who hurtled over the line. He was stopped just one foot short of the goal line.

This wasn't a time for finesse. It was a time for straight-ahead power. That meant Dufek again, and this time he got the touchdown by bare inches at the expense of a valiant Bear line.

Then Allis calmly stepped back and converted to put Michigan ahead, 7-6.

When the touchdown came there were only five minutes and 37 seconds to play.

On the first play after the ensuing kickoff, Robinson fumbled and Allis recovered for the Wolverines on California's 38.

Here was a chance to sew the game up quick. And momentarily it looked as if Michigan would do it.

Dufek – always Dufek – drove 21 yards in two smashes at the tiring Bear forward wall. Then on the next play Dufek fumbled, and Ed Bartlett, the Cal end, recovered on his own 15.

One play failed and then California was penalized back to the six for roughing. Then the Bears could pick up only six more yards in two tries.

It was fourth and 13 on California's own 12. There were four minutes to play.

The Bears gave it the "all-or-nothing" try. They weren't going to play it cozy for a one-point defeat. They wanted victory without regard for the possible margin of the loss.

So on the fourth down Jim Marinos passed. The toss was incomplete and Michigan took the ball on downs.

Michigan didn't boot this opportunity. It was Dufek for two. It was Dufek for three more. And, once again, it was Dufek for the remaining seven yards and the touchdown.

On the scoring play, Dufek swept wide around right end and outran all the Bear defenders.

Again Allis converted to make the score 14-6.

California ran five plays after the kickoff and the game was over.

The second half was dramatic and punch-filled for Michigan. By contrast the opening two periods were a gridiron nightmare.

And oddly enough, it was Michigan's two heroes – Dufek and Ortmann – who were the "goats" of

California's only touchdown.

Early in the second quarter, California couldn't gain and Robinson punted to the Wolverines' 37.

On the first play, Ortmann's pass was intercepted by Ray Solari, the Cal linebacker, on the 45 and he ran it back to the Michigan 39.

Then the Bears struck fast. Marinos faded back and, with fine protection, hit Bob Cummings on the five-yard line and he raced across for the score.

On the play, Cummings out-maneuvered Dufek, got behind the Wolverine star and took the toss untouched.

Les Richter, the Bears' all-America guard, missed his try for the extra point. It didn't seem important the way California was pushing Michigan around with ridiculous ease.

SCORE BY PERIODS

MICHIGAN	0	0	0	14 —	14
CALIFORNIA	0	6	0	0 —	6

CHAPTER 29

Lou Baldacci (27) attracts a crowd as he battles the Michigan State defense.

U-M FRUSTRATES
INSPIRED SPARTANS

BY HAL MIDDLESWORTH
Special to The Detroit Free Press

ANN ARBOR, Oct. 1, 1955 - They said Michigan would fill the air with passes.

They said Michigan State would have to put a gang defense on Ron Kramer, the Wolverines' all-America end.

They said the Spartans would do well to hold the No. 2 team of the nation to a two-touchdown margin.

So what happened?

Michigan attempted exactly two passes all afternoon and one of them was a mistake.

Kramer barely got his hands on the ball.

And the Wolverines counted themselves fortunate to drag out a 14-7 decision from a hustling young M.S.U. team which turned out to be much better than a lot of people suspected.

Before 97,239 fans, the eighth straight sellout in this intense intrastate rivalry, the Wolverines scored once after an intercepted pass and another time after

a blocked punt.

The Spartans got their tally after a weak punt by Kramer. They missed three other good chances when Michigan's defense stood firm in the shadow of the goal.

It was the Wolverines' 35th victory in the long series. Like many of the others, this one saw Michigan collect on its poise and stubborn defense.

By most measuring sticks, it was the Spartans' day. They ran and passed for 215 yards to 151 for the Wolverines. They had twice as many first downs, 14 to 7.

But when it came to crossing the goal line, it was methodical Michigan which kept the upper hand to open its Big Ten campaign with a narrow victory after last week's 42-7 romp over Missouri.

The loss left M.S.U. 1-1 in the conference after a

20-13 opener against Indiana.

Kramer, who was the whole show against Missouri, took a back seat this time. The 6-foot-3 giant, who already is on everyone's all-America team, added only two yards to Michigan's yardage total, carrying the ball once on an end-around. He punted six times for a 30-yard average, had one partly blocked and got off another for 24 yards, which set up Michigan's lone score.

In his stead, the Wolverines turned loose some hungry runners to capitalize on their breaks. Tony Branoff, who was supposed to be slowed by leg injuries, galloped 38 yards with a pass interception and almost alone covered the remaining 20 yards necessary for Michigan's first touchdown. Then, after State had tied the score, Branoff and quarterback Jim Maddock teamed up for the deciding score after a

Ron Kramer and Tom Maentz (in 3-point stance) were a formidable pair of receivers for any defense to stop.

blocked punt late in the third quarter.

Branoff scored the first counter from a yard out and it was the same distance on Maddock's game-wining tally after Branoff had sprinted 13 yards to set it up.

Kramer kicked both extra points, giving him seven straight for the young season.

Although they didn't figure in the scoring, a couple of Michigan's substitute fullbacks, Dave Hill and Ed Shannon, totaled 66 yards between them after taking over for Lou Baldacci when he was hurt early in the second quarter.

But the best runner on the field was Jerry Planutis.

State's waspish fullback dived one yard for the Spartan's only touchdown halfway through the third period. He also kicked the extra point which tied the score at that point.

Planutis, a peewee at 175 pounds, lugged the ball 17 times for 69 yards as he and Clarence Peaks, a 198-pound halfback, cracked into the Michigan line repeatedly. Peaks wound up with 63 yards on an equal number of rushes.

The pattern for the game was established early.

On Earl Morrall's first Spartan passing attempt, Branoff snagged the ball and ran it back 38 yards to State's 20-yard line.

In six plays the Wolverines had their touchdown. Balducci carried the ball three times and Branoff twice before Branoff stepped through left guard for the touchdown which gave Michigan a 7-0 lead after Kramer's conversion.

A quick kick by Peaks set the Wolverines back on their heels and they were in real trouble when Terry Barr's fumble was recovered by Embry Robinson on Michigan's 23.

But the Spartans were turned back when Kramer pulled down Peaks for a five-yard loss and Morrall's fourth-down sweep wound up three yards short of the goal line.

The Spartans probed into Michigan territory at the start of the second quarter before sophomore Jimmy Van Pelt made a daring interception of Morrall's long pass on the Wolverines' 11-yard line.

But a second Michigan fumble, this one by Shannon, started the Spartans on still another futile march near the end of the period.

After Norman Masters recovered on the Spartan 40, the long drive reached the four but went to waste when, with 20 seconds to play, Morrall couldn't find a receiver and had to gamble on a run. Once more he wound up on the three-yard line and the half ended with Michigan leading, 7-0.

That situation lasted only halfway through the next quarter, however, as Kramer's punt wobbled crazily out of bounds on the Michigan 39 and the Spartans moved in to score in 11 plays.

Planutis made three straight first downs, the last one on the 5.

Morrall sneaked twice to come within inches of the goal line and Planutis took a handoff to get the touchdown. Then he jubilantly tossed the ball high in the air before calming down to kick the extra point which tied it. At that point, it appeared State might move in for the kill, but an important blocked punt turned the tide in Michigan's direction for keeps.

Kicking from his 42, Morrall saw big John Morrow barge in to block the boot. The ball bounced wildly back to State's 21, where Michigan's captain, Edgar Meads, downed it.

In five running plays Michigan went across to score. When Kramer converted, it was 14-7. The rest of the way neither team got inside the 20.

Michigan's lone pass completion came during the fourth-period sparring when Maddock hit Shannon with a 15-yard running toss for a first down on State's 25.

The only other aerial the Wolverines even attempted was in the third quarter when Maddock hurled one in desperation and saw guard Dick Hill, an ineligible receiver, reach up and touch the ball as it went past. For that, the Wolverines were fined 15 yards.

SCORE BY PERIODS

MICHIGAN	7	0	7	0 —	14
M.S.U.	0	0	7	0 —	7

Michigan end Ron Kramer was honored on the Ed Sullivan Show after being selected to the 1956 all-America squad.

MICHIGAN RALLY UPSETS MIGHTY IOWA, 17-14

BY TOMMY DEVINE
Special to The Detroit Free-Press

IOWA CITY, Nov. 3, 1956 - The rosebuds that had miraculously sprouted on every corn stalk in Iowa suddenly wilted Saturday under the University of Michigan's red-hot second-half rally, 17-14.

Not since the great drought or the corn borer plague has a catastrophe occurred to match the one which struck the University of Iowa in the final minutes of play.

A record homecoming crowd of 58,137 saw the Wolverines drop Iowa from the ranks of the undefeated. The loss snapped a five-game winning streak, which had been the longest compiled by a Hawkeye team since 1928.

It also shattered long-held hopes that Iowa might win its first Big Ten championship since 1922 and earn the conference's berth in the Rose Bowl game at Pasadena on New Year's Day.

All those cherished dreams appeared about to be realized this mild, overcast November afternoon. But then an old jinx – a voodoo sign Michigan has waved frequently over the Hawkeyes – took hold.

Only twice in 18 games of this series have the Hawkeyes been able to win. Their last triumph in the series came in 1924 and since then it has been wait, wait, wait for a victory that still is to come.

This was still another bitter pill in the dosage Forest Evashevski, the former Michigan quarterbacking great who now is Iowa's head coach, has taken at the hands of his alma mater.

In each of the last four seasons, Evashevski has had his teams geared to high pitch against Michigan, and each time they've blown golden opportunities

In 1953 and 1954, the Hawkeyes dropped one-point decisions to Michigan, 14-13.

Last year they held a 14-0 lead at halftime and then blew it, 33-21.

After Michigan took a 3-0 lead in the first quarter on a 12-yard field goal by Ron Kramer, Iowa bounced back to score twice and hold a 14-3 edge at the intermission.

Iowa appeared to have the manpower and the tools this time to get the job done. It appeared, too, that it had the psychological edge, for it had the Rose Bowl incentive and the old search for a victory over Michigan going for it.

But in the stretch the Hawkeye defense couldn't hold the inspired Wolverines who just wouldn't be denied.

There was an abundance of thrills in an 80-yard march Michigan made to gain its game-deciding touchdown with only one minute and six seconds of play remaining.

The Wolverines bounced back after last week's loss to Minnesota.

For much of this game, the Wolverines were listless and plodding. But when they finally put their heads and their hearts to the task, they went about it in a workmanlike and polished manner.

They drove 69 yards for their first touchdown and then ground out yardage the hard way in the waning minutes of the contest to move 80 yards for the clincher.

Two performers stood out in the Wolverines' victory. Sophomore fullback John Herrnstein and a seldom used junior halfback, Mike Shatusky.

Herrnstein became the true "bread-and-butter" man of the Michigan attack. Shatusky, who got his chance after spending much of the season as a third stringer, scored both Wolverine touchdowns.

Michigan had the ball for 52 running plays. Herrnstein and Shatusky ran with it on 31 of these occasions. The burly sophomore fullback from Chillicothe, Ohio, picked up 66 yards in his 18 smashes at the Iowa line and Shatusky was credited with 41 yards in 16 attempts.

They combined to pick up 107 of the 154 yards Michigan netted on the ground.

From the opening game of the season, when Herrnstein broke in as a regular, the burly Ohioan has been destined for stardom. Recognition for Shatusky has been slow and painful in coming, however.

Shatusky got his big chance against Iowa primarily because of an ankle injury to first stringer Terry Barr. Even then, the starting berth went to Ed Shannon with Shatusky as his replacement.

Strangely, the field goal that in the final analysis provided Michigan's winning margin, appeared to be an extremely poor maneuver when the Wolverines made it in the first quarter.

Michigan had moved 58 yards in 15 plays to reach the Iowa 5-yard line.

It was fourth down and three yards to go. This early in the game it certainly seemed logical to try for the yardage and a touchdown. But Wolverine coach Bennie Oosterbaan decided instead to make the conservative move.

His second unit, which had been responsible for the drive, was withdrawn and the starting team returned to the field. Kramer promptly dropped back to the 12 and placekicked the field goal.

Michigan had three points, but before long they looked useless.

Midway through the second period, Iowa got a tremendous break.

Back on a pass attempt, Jim Van Pelt was hit by Hawkeye end Frank Gilliam and the ball was knocked from his hand. Tackle Alex Karras fell on it on the Wolverine 24-yard line.

Six running plays carried the ball to the Michigan 13. After two more running plays failed, second-string quarterback Randy Duncan threw a perfect pass to Delmar Kloewer in the end zone. Bob Prescott converted and the Hawkeyes were in front, 7-3. The touchdown came after eight minutes and five seconds of play.

Four minutes later, Iowa had another touchdown and seemingly was on its way to victory in the process of taking a giant step toward Pasadena.

The second Hawkeye score came on a beautiful 34-yard sprint by quarterback Ken Ploen.

Ploen, who was brilliant most of the contest as he engineered the Hawkeyes' winged T attack and ran the option from it, rolled out to his right on a run-pass option.

Wolverine end Kramer smashed in and missed Ploen. Then two blockers cut down Herrnstein who was moving in from the corner-linebacker spot. That gave Ploen plenty of daylight and he burst into the clear with only Jim Pace making a futile dive at him on the 10.

Again Prescott converted and Iowa led, 14-3.

The Hawkeyes had the clear-cut advantage in statistics and actual play on the field during the opening half.

But they still had 30 minutes to go. They survived 28 of those still holding an edge, but then the executioner's axe fell on their title chances as the scoreboard clock ticked off the final and fatal seconds.

Immediately after taking the kickoff to open the third period Michigan hammered from its own 31 to the Iowa 2-yard line. From there, Shatusky plunged over.

The 69 yards of the drive had required 12 plays – 11 on the ground with one key pass plus two costly Iowa penalties. Kramer converted after Shatusky's plunge and the score was 14-10.

After an exchange of punts, Iowa took the ball on its own 17 and promptly began to move. Then a veteran Iowa back lost his poise and made a foolish play.

With possession and time both now key factors, halfback Don Dobrino recklessly tried to get rid of the ball after he was trapped behind the line.

The Hawkeyes were called for intentionally grounding a pass. That set Iowa back to its own seven and it had to punt.

A Michigan touchdown didn't develop immediately, but the incident seemed to unnerve the entire Iowa team and to rob it of its poise at the time it needed it most.

Michigan's winning drive started immediately after another exchange of punts that put the ball on the Wolverines' own 20.

Then Herrnstein and Shatusky went to work, carrying the ball on 11 of the 19 plays Michigan required to move 80 yards for the winning marker. The longest run of the march was only six yards, but Herrnstein and Shatusky were relentless in grinding out the yardage.

Twice in the march Michigan came up fourth down and needing short yardage to keep the drive and its victory chances alive. Each time the powerful Herrnstein put his head down and rammed the middle of the weary Iowa line for the necessary ground.

When Michigan reached the Iowa two, the clock showed one minute and 20 seconds to play. Now quarterback Jim Maddock called Shatusky's signal again.

Shatusky responded by hammering across for the touchdown that broke the homecomers' hearts and caused the rosebuds to drop from the corn stalks.

Kramer's conversion was just an unneeded point.

SCORE BY PERIODS

MICHIGAN	3	0	7	7	— 17
IOWA	0	14	0	0	— 14

John Henderson (81) grabs a pass from halfback Rick Sygar to score the Wolverines' winning touchdown against rival M.S.U.

MICHIGAN SNAPS M.S.U. JINX WITH 17-10 VICTORY

BY TOM ROWLAND
Special to The Michigan Daily

EAST LANSING, Oct. 10, 1964 - Michigan's offensive machine sputtered, coughed and waited until late in the fourth quarter to roar alive with two touchdowns that whipped Michigan State here yesterday afternoon, 17-10, ending a nine-year winless

string against the Spartans.

It is also the first time since 1955 that the Wolverines have won their first three games of the season.

A stadium-record crowd of 78,234 watched sub halfback Rick Sygar haul in a five-yard pass from quarterback Bob Timberlake for one tally and then throw one himself to end John Henderson from 31 yards out for another as the Wolverines erased a 10-3

After a heralded career playing for Fritz Crisler, Bump Elliott returned to his alma mater as head coach in 1959.
Although he coached through 1968, the 1964 season was his best at Michigan.

deficit late in the game.

In a do-or-die effort midway through the final quarter, the Michigan offense finally got rolling after a series of fumbles and a rugged Spartan defense almost completely stymied the Blue attack.

Timberlake led the Wolverines to midfield with a pair of 11- and eight-yard passes to Sygar, and then let loose with a 29-yarder to Henderson as Michigan created its first major offensive threat.

Henderson was finally stopped at the Michigan State 21, and on the next play it was Sygar again this time getting the pitch from Timberlake on the oft-used option. He dashed to the 9-yard line before being forced out of bounds.

Two plays later, Timberlake hit Sygar on the swing pass, and the Niles, Ohio, sophomore neatly dodged a Spartan defender and jumped into the end zone. The first Wolverine touchdown of the day pushed the score to 10-9, the Spartans on top with just under seven minutes to play.

Michigan coach Bump Elliott had the choice – pass or run for two points or stick with a one-point kick that would tie it up. Elliott took one look at the clock and made up his mind – go for broke.

"We went for two after that first touchdown because we wanted to win it right here and then."

With all of jammed Spartan Stadium in a single, held breath, Timberlake rolled to the left on the option and pitched to fullback Mel Anthony going around the end. Anthony cut in, twisted, dove and ended up just short of the goal stripe.

Taking Timberlake's kickoff, the Spartans had only to hang on to the football for six minutes to take the one-point victory.

But a fired up Michigan defense, paced by big tackle Bill Yearby, stopped State in its tracks on three downs, and on the fourth Dick Rindfuss returned the punt to the Michigan State 41.

Carl Ward hit left tackle for four yards, Timberlake ran around left end for four more, and Anthony smashed for two and a Michigan first down at the Spartan 31-yard line.

There was 2:33 showing on the clock when Timberlake pitched to Sygar, who lofted Henderson the winning pass clear in the M.S.U. secondary, and Henderson romped into the end zone.

Timberlake put on the finishing touches, firing to end Steve Smith for a two-point conversion.

Earlier in the game it was a different story. Michigan received the opening kickoff and immediately fumbled the football. On the second play from scrimmage Anthony fumbled a Timberlake pitchout and Spartan Ed Macuga pounced on the loose ball at the Michigan 17.

It was only a matter of minutes before State made the most of the break. A key pass from quarterback Steve Juday to quarterback-playing-flanker Dave McCormick set the ball at the 4, and Juday followed two plays later with a sneak from the 1 for the touchdown.

Halfback Jim Detwiler fumbled the kickoff after State's first touchdown, but Ward recovered. Then on the first play Ward fumbled and recovered again.

Timberlake passed 29 yards to Smith for a first down, but after the Wolverine drive moved the ball to the Michigan State 18, Detwiler fumbled again and the ever-wary Spartans jumped on the ball.

State showed off its new spectacular pass-catching end Gene Washington, a glue-fingered sophomore, on the next series as Washington outstretched Rindfuss on a 43-yard pass play that sent the Spartans deep to the Michigan 15.

The fumbles weren't all Wolverine, though, as Juday, hit hard by red-dogging-linebacker Tom Cecchini, fumbled on the next play and Yearby recovered for Michigan.

The Wolverines got their first big chance to get some points on the scoreboard in the middle of the second quarter when a 16-yard dash around right end by Anthony and a pass interference call pushed the Wolverines to the M.S.U. 14 and a first down. When three plays fizzled, Timberlake's 22-yard field goal attempt went wide to the right.

Returning to Spartan territory just before the half, Timberlake's pass for Ward went incomplete, but a second pass interference call gave Michigan the ball at State's 35. The veteran quarterback again went to the air lanes, and with just seconds to go before the intermission hit Henderson, who stepped out of bounds at the 13.

Timberlake then swung his foot through a 29-yard field goal and three points on the last play of the half to cut the Spartans' lead to 7-3.

The intermission wasn't rest enough on the kick-off. Ward lost the ball on a hard tackle and once again the Spartans recovered, gaining possession at the Michigan 18.

This time the Wolverine defense held and on fourth down from the 14 State's barefoot field goal kicker Dick Kenney misfired on the first of two attempts.

The second one came half a period later when the Hawaiian import's boot went wide to the left on a kick from the 34.

State knocked on the Michigan end zone door at the beginning of the fourth period when McCormick engineered a drive that was halted at the Wolverine 9-yard line. It was two strikes and you're out for Kenney. On fourth and 5, M.S.U. coach Duffy Daugherty sent in sophomore Larry Lukasik to boot the field goal that gave the Spartan's a 10-3 lead.

The Wolverines held M.S.U.'s leading ground-gainer, Clinton Jones, to a minus two yards rushing and allowed the Spartans only four completions in 12 pass tries. Timberlake hit home on nine of 18 attempts through the air, and Anthony was Michigan's big man on the ground with 70 yards in 21 carries.

Daughtery pointed to injuries as a big factor in the last minutes of the game."The hitting was hard out there and we got banged up quite a bit."

Duffy added that "I felt our boys played real hard all the way but it was that passing late in the game that really hurt."

Elliott said it "just feels real good" to beat Duffy.

SCORE BY PERIODS

MICHIGAN..........0	3	0	14	—	17
M.S.U. 7	0	0	3	—	10

All-America quarterback Bob Timberlake (28) kicked the field goal in the final period to put the game away for U-M's 10-0 win.

U-M BLANKS BUCKEYES, EARN ROSE BOWL BID

BY GARY WYNER
Special to The Michigan Daily

COLUMBUS, Nov. 21, 1964 - Singing "California Here We Come," the Michigan Wolverines ran from the field here following their title-clinching 10-0 victory over arch-rival Ohio State before a record crowd of 84,685.

Michigan coach Bump Elliott, who played on U-M's championship team of 1947, said in the locker room, "This is my happiest moment in football."

The victory gave Michigan its first Big Ten title and trip to the Rose Bowl since the 1950 season, when it downed the Buckeyes, 9-3, in the famous "Snow Bowl" game. The Wolverines finished the 1964 season with an 8-1 record, 5-1 in the conference. The Buckeyes are now second in the final league standings at 5-1, and 7-2 overall.

Sophomore defensive back Rick Volk intercepted two Buckeye passes and knocked down another to stop three separate Buckeye drives deep in Michigan territory in the fourth period. Bill Yearby also

Jim Detwiler scored the Wolverines' first touchdown on Bob Timberlake's 17-yard pass in the second quarter.

batted down a fourth-down desperation aerial in the final quarter as the Michigan defense stopped the Buckeyes' gambling pass attack.

In the final minute of play of the first half Michigan senior quarterback Bob Timberlake fired a 17-yard touchdown pass to halfback Jim Detwiler and booted the conversion point to give the eventual victors a 7-0 halftime lead.

The touchdown play was set up by a 50-yard Stan Kemp punt, which was bobbled by Buckeye halfback Bo Rein and recovered by the Wolverines' John Henderson on the O.S.U. 20.

Timberlake ran for three yards and then fired to Detwiler, who snagged the ball on the 2-yard stripe and dragged two defenders into the end zone. Elliott said after the game that this play had not been used all season.

The Wolverines final points came on a 17-yard field goal by Timberlake in the opening minutes of the final period.

The field goal was set up after Volk took a Steve Dreffer punt and returned the pigskin 27 yards to the Ohio State 24. Michigan picked up quick yardage with fullback Mel Anthony carrying 12 and three yards on the first two plays. But the Buckeye defense held on the 10, so Elliott decided to go for the three-pointer.

Much of the credit for the victory goes to the Michigan defensive unit which played probably its best game of the season. Elliott said that "the defense played a great game and has been grossly underestimated all year."

With Michigan notching its third shutout of the year, defensive line coach Bob Hollway remarked, "Friday night we decided we were going to shut them out, and that's just what we did."

Billed as a defensive contest, this 61st meeting between the two football powerhouses turned out to be just that as Ohio State held Michigan's nation-leading ground attack to 115 yards. The Wolverines picked up another five yards through the air, marking its lowest offensive performance this year.

The Buckeyes outgained the victors in total offense with 180 yards. When the chips were down, the Wolverine defense refused to budge and consistently thwarted the Ohio State power plays which have

been Buckeye coach Woody Hayes' main weapon against Michigan on many other occasions.

Hayes said his defense "was absolutely fabulous." He summed up the game by saying: "Each team got the breaks, but Michigan took advantage of them and we didn't."

After a scoreless first quarter, Tom Kiefuss recovered a Timberlake fumble on the Michigan 29, but the Bucks were held for three plays. Hayes sent Bob Funk in to attempt a field goal, but his try was unsuccessful. Ohio State then downed the ball on the Michigan 1-yard line on the kick, and the Wolverines were unable to move from there.

Kemp's punt was returned to the Michigan 33, but Ohio State once again was unable to advance.

Although it snowed here yesterday it had no impact on the game such as the famous 1950 "Snow Bowl" game when Michigan last qualified for the Rose Bowl. However, the factors of wind and cold did have an effect on the game. The temperature was 20 degrees.

Elliott commented that "the wind was certainly a factor in the game. It was hard to throw against it." Timberlake completed only three of nine passes, while the Buckeyes had seven completions in 21 attempts.

The wind was blowing out of the south when the Buckeyes won the toss at the start of the game and decided to defend the south goal so they would have the wind at their backs.

Timberlake kicked a field goal 27 yards, despite the wind being against him in the fourth quarter.

In the third period, Timberlake had attempted a 32-yard field goal with the wind but it was wide to the left.

Wolverine punter Stan Kemp kicked his team out of trouble several times with a 40-yard average in nine kicks. Three of these kicks went 50 yards. One of these 50-yarders was fumbled by Buckeye halfback Bo Rein on the Ohio State 20-yard line and recovered by John Henderson.

Michigan scored its only touchdown of the game two plays later.

Kemp, however, narrowly avoided tragedy several times as some of his kicks were almost blocked. Elliott attributed this to a "very hard Ohio State

rush." Hayes said that the weather conditions being what they were, his players were purposely rushing Kemp hard in case of a faulty snap which would give them a good chance to block the punt.

Center Brian Patchen didn't hike the ball on any of the punts because of a bad shoulder.

Instead, linebacker Tom Cecchini took care of the centering job in punting situations.

Elliott praised the defensive backfield for the key plays that were made. Dick Rindfuss, Rick Sygar and Rick Volk handled the job without substitution until the final minutes of the game when victory was assured.

Rindfuss had a cast for his sprained leg taken off last Sunday after missing the Iowa game.

He had practiced with the team since Tuesday. Elliott said that before the game, "we didn't know how much Dick could play, but we knew he could play some."

Volk intercepted two passes to halt threatening Ohio State drives in the fourth quarter.

Elliott said the first interception at the Michigan 8-yard line early in the fourth quarter was the key play.

Later Volk picked off another pass at the Wolverine 28-yard line to stop a second O.S.U. drive. Volk had another opportunity to intercept a pass in the closing minutes of the game. He knocked down the pass on a fourth-down situation so the Wolverines could take over at the Buckeye 43-yard line instead of in Michigan territory.

Elliott, looking back over the season, said that after the Purdue defeat "the team just tried to climb a ladder. They had to battle up from the bottom. We felt we could give anyone a fight in a ball game. We felt we could still win the championship and every week this became a little more realistic."

Michigan had its own version of Woody Hayes in offensive line coach Tony Mason. In the fourth quarter, Mason took off his jacket and from a distance was a replica of Hayes in his baseball cap and short-sleeved white shirt. Hayes was in his short-sleeved shirt all through the game despite the low temperature.

SCORE BY PERIODS

MICHIGAN	0	7	0	3 —	10
OHIO STATE	0	0	0	0 —	0

CHAPTER 33

MICHIGAN ROUTS OREGON STATE, 34-7

By Bob Pille

Special to The Detroit Free Press

Pasadena, Calif., Jan. 1, 1965 - Michigan's return to the Rose Bowl after 14 years was just what the folks are accustomed to in the big saucer.

The Wolverines ran over their usual sacrifice from the Pacific slopes – this time Oregon State by 34-7.

They had been saying all along that the Beavers didn't belong in the Rose Bowl, and it was proved that they didn't belong there against Michigan anyway.

Whether Southern California, the team they wanted in these parts, would have looked much better is doubtful.

Sure, the Trojans had that keyed-up afternoon against Notre Dame, but they also had previous losses to Michigan State and Ohio State, two teams the Wolverines beat on the road here.

The Wolverines had everything in the 55-degree sunshine against Oregon State and they topped it off with the finest football afternoon that Mel Anthony ever enjoyed.

The 206-pound fullback from Cincinnati slammed to three touchdowns and 123 yards and was voted most valuable player of the game.

Anthony's first touchdown, an 84-yard run that brought Michigan from a 7-0 deficit midway in the second quarter, was the longest run from scrimmage in Rose Bowl history.

His two later scores, coming on bursts of one yard and seven yards, gave him the three that matched the bowl record set by Notre Dame's Elmer Layden against Stanford in 1925, and tied by another U-M fullback, Jack Weisenburger, in that 49-0 rout of Southern Cal in 1948.

Michigan also whacked Stanford, 49-0, in 1902, and pushed past California, 14-6, in 1951 in previous trips here.

Halfback Carl Ward got the touchdown that put the Wolverines in front with a 43-yard dash late in the first half, and all-America quarterback Bob Timberlake got the last one on a 24-yard thrust.

While becoming the first Big Ten team to win four times out here, Michigan rolled up 415 yards – 332 of these on the ground as befits the team standing third in the nation in rushing games – but it won't improve the Wolverines' No. 4 ranking in the national polls, but they deserve better.

Except for that 21-20 loss to Purdue, they probably would have the No. 1 status.

Certainly Oregon State, rated No. 8, won't dispute that.

The Beavers got a touchdown five plays into the second period on a five-yard flip from quarterback Paul Brothers to end Doug McGougal, and that was it.

Until they pushed to the U-M 5 in the fading moments with Bump Elliott's bench already in the game for seven minutes, the Beavers weren't outside their own territory again after they scored.

The Wolverines dominated in every department and when they were stopped early in the game, they were stopping themselves with mistakes, as they did occasionally last fall.

Even the Oregon State touchdown had a Michigan contribution, with a thoughtless clipping penalty by Dick Rindfuss keeping the Beavers in possession after they had punted.

The Wolverines almost scored first, getting the ball at the Oregon State 41 in the opening minutes when Arnold Simkus hooked the arm of halfback Charlie Shaw and linebacker Tom Cecchini recov-

Mel Anthony earned M.V.P. honors in the 1965 Rose Bowl after rushing for three touchdowns, including a Rose Bowl-record 84-yard scoring romp in the first half.

ered the fumble.

But after a first down, Michigan stalled at the 23 and Timberlake's 40-yard field goal attempt fell short.

Once Michigan got rolling, the rout followed.

The ground yards were short of the 415 Iowa used in trampling California six years ago but four U-M backs – Anthony (13 for 123), Ward (10-for-88), Timberlake (12-for-57), and No. 2 fullback Dave Fisher (5-for-30) – each rushed for more yards than Oregon State's best runner.

Michigan's linemen provided the blocking and the mad dog defense of Oregon State, headed by Mad Dog O'Billovich, hardly even nipped anybody all afternoon.

The Beavers actually had the ball for six more plays than U-M but the Wolverine defense limited them to short chunks. And Oregon State didn't have anybody running as well as Anthony.

On his 84-yard run, Anthony took the option pitch from Timberlake, shook loose over the right side behind blocks from Ward and end John Henderson, and was away.

The only player close to Anthony as he crossed the goal line was halfback Jim Detwiler, another white-shirted U-M player.

The run erased the old Rose Bowl record, a 81-yarder by Iowa's Bob Jeter against Cal in 1959.

Timberlake, after 20 attempts without a miss, was wide on the conversion kick to leave Michigan in arrears, 7-6, but that was about the only thing the Wolverines did wrong all afternoon, and the deficit was temporary.

Less than four minutes and only seven Michigan plays later, it was Ward's turn with his 43-yarder.

The quick sophomore, Anthony's fellow townsman from Cincinnati, also took a pitchout going to the right, pulled free as he was almost pinned at the sidelines, sliced back to the left and was away. This time Timberlake's pass for the two-point conversion was batted incomplete.

The Wolverines sealed things midway in the third period when sophomore guard Bob Mielke blocked a Beaver punt, with Anthony recovering at the Oregon State 15.

The Beavers were stubborn and it took a half-dozen plays.

Detwiler set it up with two blasts, and then Anthony got the final yard for a touchdown over Brian Patchen and Dave Butler. Timberlake tried running this two-point conversion and got it.

Next time the Wolverines had possession they rolled 78 yards in eight plays.

Timberlake passed 30 yards to Anthony along the way, then handed to Anthony for the last seven through the left side, then kicked the conversion.

The last touchdown that made it 34-7 with 9:56 remaining in the game was all Timberlake.

Starting at his own 46, he ran for nine yards, ran for 15 yards, rested while Detwiler ran for seven, then kept the ball on the option play around the left side and banged 24 yards to score.

It was the final Wolverine play for the much honored quarterback.

He trotted off the field with a 134-yard day in total offense, and the finest yardage total in a season for a Michigan player.

Timberlake's first 15 yards of the afternoon broke Bob Chappuis' old record from 1947.

Throughout the afternoon, Timberlake was 7-for-10 on his passing for 77 yards to go with 57 rushing yards, and for the season he had 631 yards running, 814 throwing.

Brothers (89 yards) and Gordon Queen (90) each passed for slightly more yardage than Timberlake, but Brothers didn't complete a throw except for the seven straight in the touchdown push and Queen hit late when the decision was long settled.

Through the afternoon, both Beaver quarterbacks often made the unhappy acquaintance of Michigan linemen but Timberlake was thrown for a notable loss only once.

Really, it was just like being back in Ann Arbor with a stadium holding more than 100,000 – to be exact 100,423 – and the Michigan band playing a victory concert after the game.

The only difference was that in 30 seconds after the final gun they had the goalposts demolished and that doesn't happen to Fritz Crisler's home goalposts.

SCORE BY PERIODS

MICHIGAN	0	12	15	7	— 34
OREGON STATE	0	7	0	0	— 7

CHAPTER 34

AT LAST, WOLVERINES WHIP M.S.U.

By Curt Sylvester
Special to The Detroit Free Press

Ann Arbor, Oct. 12, 1968 - If there has been a sweeter time in Michigan Stadium it hasn't been in the past three years. That's for sure.

If Bump Elliott has taken a sweeter ride than the one atop his Michigan Wolverines at 4:01 p.m. Saturday, it was somewhere in the distant past. The days between have been hazy, misty, dark days of Michigan State domination.

The Wolverines ended three years of frustration in front of 102,785 fans by dropping the proud Spartans, 28-14 and giving Elliott his second victory over Michigan State in 10 years of coaching here.

The game was probably the most even and hardest fought since the 7-7 tie in 1963, but the difference turned out to be the clutch defensive job by the Wolverines and the offensive prowess of quarterback Dennis Brown and tailback Ron Johnson.

The statistics didn't show a Michigan domination of the game, but the Wolverines, obviously sky-high for the match, just wouldn't give up.

Johnson scored on the fifth play of the game and Brown passed to John Gabler for another touchdown sandwiched around a Spartan touchdown by flanker Charley Wedemeyer. And when they got around to scoring again two quarters later, the Wolverines responded by putting the game out of reach.

Brown, on a broken play, passed 53 yards to Jim Mandich for the go-ahead touchdown and fullback Garvie Craw added the clincher with a 25-yard scoring run as the clock ran down to 2:11 to play.

Michigan State lost the game because of untapped scoring opportunities. But the Wolverines forced the mistakes with fierce play in their defensive front. It wasn't a game Michigan State lost; it was a game Michigan won.

In the victory, third straight after an opening loss and the first of the Big Ten season for Michigan, the Wolverines scored more points than they had in the last three years. During that span they had lost three games by a cumulative score of 78-14.

And maybe, just maybe, the 34-0 rout the Wolverines suffered in front of the same home crowd last year had something to do with their determination to win this one.

Michigan State moved freely at midfield and four times moved to Michigan's 25-yard line or better without scoring as the Wolverines belted them back or forced mistakes. The loss was the first after three victories for the Spartans and evened their conference mark at 1-1.

The difference in total offense was insignificant. Michigan had 420 yards and State had 356, including 295 on the ground. But State gained its yards with 90 plays while winning Michigan controlled the ball for only 55 plays.

"It's a funny game, when you have the ball for 90 plays and lose," Daugherty said.

"You can't miss scoring opportunities like we did and expect to win the ball game.

"Michigan played a very fine game. It deserved to win. It played a very spirited game."

The spirit may have been the difference in the game but Johnson's 152 yards rushing, and Brown's 49 yards rushing and 177 yards passing didn't hurt either.

The Wolverines got the first break of the game on the kickoff. It went to their speedster, George Hoey, and he ran it back to midfield. If he had cut to the inside, getting behind a blocker, the Wolverines wouldn't have had to wait four plays for a

All-America halfback Ron Johnson (40) gave Michigan fans a spectacular performance against arch-rival Michigan State. Johnson finished the day with 152 yards rushing in 19 carries and one touchdown.

Dennis Brown (22) led the Wolverines' second-half comeback with a 53-yard touchdown pass to Jim Mandich.

touchdown. Hoey would have had it himself.

As it was, the Wolverines felt out the Michigan State line with four running plays for a first down and then sprung Johnson off tackle and he went roaring 38 yards for the touchdown.

Tim Killan converted and Michigan led, 7-0, after only 1:56 of the game.

State scored in just as startling fashion about four minutes later. Fullback Dick Berlinski got a big 13-yard gain when he took a pitchback on a third-and-10 situation and went six more yards after Tommy

Love had gone for nine.

Two plays later, Wedemeyer left his flanker position on a reverse – the second time he handled the ball all season – and went 37 yards down the right side, diving into the corner for the touchdown. Gary Boyce's extra point kick was wide and Michigan led, 7-6.

Brown cushioned that lead before the first quarter was over, hitting Mandich for 38 yards and then throwing to Gabler in the end zone, 33 yards away, making it Michigan, 13-6, when Killian missed the conversion kick.

The Spartans' frustration began midway in the second quarter when they ground their way from their 43-yard line to the Michigan 14, twice plunging the ball forward on fourth down plays.

But on the 14 the Wolverines jarred William Feraco for a fumble, which guard Ron Saul saved for the Spartans. Love was caught for a five-yard loss and Berlinski was tripped by defensive end Phil Seymour for a one-yard loss.

The Spartans had to try for a field goal from 36 yards, but it failed and the halftime score remained 13-6.

The Spartans took the second-half kick and went straight down the field with Don Highsmith running four straight plays for 32 yards. But when they got to the Michigan 26, a penalty for unsportsmanlike conduct pushed them back 15 yards and they couldn't get it back.

The Spartans then punted.

Still Michigan State would not stop running. The Spartans stopped Michigan, gained two quick first downs and Highsmith carried to the Michigan 19, but he was hit hard and fumbled with Hoey recovering for the Wolverines. Another drive thwarted.

The Spartans finally broke through with Highsmith and sophomore Earl Anderson grinding out the yardage on the ground. Al Brenner took a pass from Feraco on the third play of the fourth quarter for 14 yards to the Michigan six. Two plays later, Anderson stepped over the goal line.

Trailing, 13-12, State had the choice of kicking the extra point and tying or running a play or passing for two points. They chose to pass, and on a fake kick Wedemeyer passed to Frank Foreman to give State the lead, 14-13, with most of the quarter yet to play.

The turning play of the game came when the Spartans put a rush on Brown, but he escaped. Just before being forced out of bounds, he tossed a pass to Mandich, who roared down the right side of the field for a 53-yard touchdown play.

The Spartans then had to play catchup ball and Feraco's pass, intended for Gordon Bowdell, was intercepted by Tom Curtis at the Michigan 17.

Craw scored the final touchdown of the day on a draw play. The hard-running fullback broke two tackles, suddenly found daylight and trudged into the end zone.

Just like that the three years of waiting were over.

SCORE BY PERIODS

MICHIGAN..........13	0	0	15	— 28
M.S.U. 6	0	0	8	— 14

Michigan captain Jim Mandich (88) and Ohio State's captains enter the field just moments before the kickoff of the greatest game in Michigan's storied football history.

INSPIRED MICHIGAN UPSETS #1 BUCKEYES

BY CURT SYLVESTER
Special to The Detroit Free Press

ANN ARBOR, Nov. 22, 1969 - Call it a miracle or just call Michigan the new super team of the Big Ten.

Either is just fine, thank you.

The Wolverines defeated the best college football team in the country, Ohio State, 24-12, Saturday in one of the proudest moments in Michigan's long and bitter rivalry with the Buckeyes.

The victory, in front of a record 103,588 in Michigan Stadium and millions on television, gave Michigan the Rose Bowl trip, a tie for the Big Ten title with the Buckeyes and avenged last season's disastrous 50-14 loss at Ohio State.

The Big Ten athletic directors made it official a few hours after Saturday's result by naming the Wolverines to represent the conference in Pasadena on Jan. 1.

The Wolverines will meet Southern Cal in the grand-daddy of bowls. U.S.C. rallied to beat U.C.L.A.,

14-12, Saturday and qualified for an unprecedented fourth straight visit to the Rose Bowl.

The Buckeyes came to Michigan with a 22-game winning streak, 17 straight Big Ten wins and the title of "best college team ever."

But the Wolverines, led by tough little Barry Pierson and unshakable Don Moorhead, simply beat it out of them – the winning streaks, the No. 1 ranking and the undisputed Big Ten title.

Pierson made three interceptions at defensive halfback and returned an Ohio State punt 60 yards to set up the touchdown that broke the game open for Michigan in the first half.

Moorhead completed 10 of 20 passes, gained 67 yards rushing and looked more like Rex Kern than Rex Kern himself as he directed the inspired Wolverines to victory.

Michigan fell behind twice in the first half as the Bucks scored on a one-yard run by fullback Jim Otis and a 22-yard pass from Kern to Jan White.

But the Wolverines came back with a pair of touchdowns by their own hard-hitting fullback, Garvie Craw, on runs of three and one yards, a two-yard burst by Moorhead and a 25-yard field goal by Tim Killian.

There were other contributors: sophomore tailback Billy Taylor with 84 yards, including a beautiful 28-yard run that helped Michigan come from behind for the last time; Craw, who gained 56 of the hardest yards in the game, through the middle of the Ohio State line; flanker John Gabler and tailback Glenn Doughty who showed the Bucks some speed in the fourth quarter.

What the Wolverines did was to beat the Buckeyes at Woody Hayes' own game. They simply overpowered him and they simply out-defensed him.

That, probably, is not too surprising. Michigan coach Bo Schembechler learned a lot of his football under Hayes a few years ago and he obviously learned it very well.

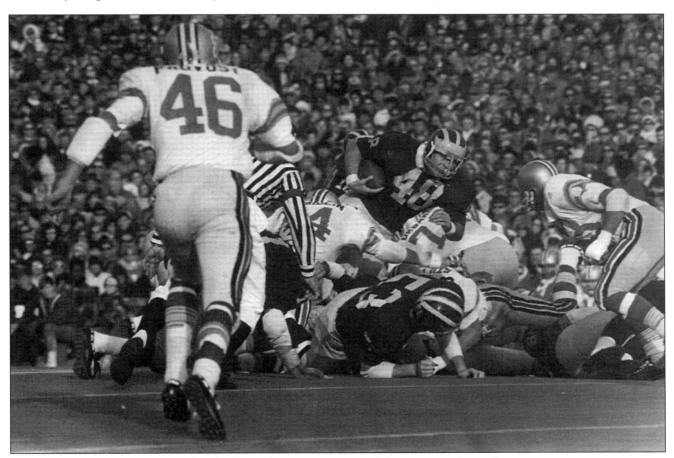

Garvie Craw (48) bursts up the middle for the Wolverines' opening touchdown against the Buckeyes.

Jim Mandich (88) turns upfield against the Buckeyes.

Schembechler took Michigan into the game knowing it could not make a mistake and hope to win. The Wolverines made mistakes, but not until they had a two-touchdown lead in the first half and they forced Ohio State to make more.

Instead of Ohio State forcing mistakes as they had all season against weaker opposition, Michigan was forcing mistakes on Ohio State.

The Wolverines intercepted six Ohio State passes but Moorhead had only one pass intercepted. Ohio State fumbled twice and lost one. Michigan didn't fumble.

"We knew we were going to win from the very beginning," said Schembechler. "We said after Iowa we were going to win."

And that they did. The only disappointment for the Michigan fans was that the Wolverines didn't score a touchdown in the final minutes of the game so they could have gone for two points as Hayes did in last year's game.

But the 24 points of the first half were all the Michigan defenders needed. The guys up front – middle guard Henry Hill, tackle Pete Newell and linebacker Marty Huff – kept Otis under control, although the O.S.U. bulldozer finished the game with 144 yards.

The defensive ends – Cecil Pryer and Kill Keller – kept the pressure on Kern and then his replacement, Ron Maciejowski. And the defensive backs had a field day.

"Pierson's performance was one of the greatest I have ever seen," Schembechler raved.

The little 175-pounder made three interceptions, four unassisted tackles, helped out on another tack-

Dan Dierdorf cleared many of the holes for Garvie Craw, Billy Taylor and the other Michigan backs to rip for big yardage against the Buckeyes.

le and treated the charging Otis with scorn, knocking his feet out from under him in the open field once and then pulling him down by the head on another occasion.

Tom Curtis, the Wolverines' senior safety, intercepted two passes and broke the N.C.A.A. record on interception return yardage, bringing his three-year total to 431 yards on 25 interceptions and erasing the old national mark of 410 held by Michigan State's Lynn Chadnois.

Wolfman Thom Darden also made an interception and linebacker Mike Taylor broke up a pass.

When the game started it looked like Ohio State might be on its way to another easy victory, much like the first eight of this season.

Kern ran for 25 yards on the first play of the game and Otis went seven on the second.

But the Wolverines stopped the drive on their own 10-yard line.

The Bucks did score on their next series after Larry Zelina returned a Michigan punt 36 yards to the Wolverines' 16. Kern hit White for a 13-yard gain and Otis crashed over on his third bolt into the line.

O.S.U.'s Stan White missed the extra point and the Wolverines began to work.

Doughty took the kickoff and returned it 30 yards to the Wolverines' 45. Moorhead put the drive in motion with an eight-yard pass to split end Mike Oldham and a seven-yarder to Jim Mandich.

The Michigan quarterback hit Mandich again for nine yards and then Gabler ran for 11 yards on a counter play. Moorhead ran for six and then Craw went over from the one.

Frank Titas' extra point kick put Michigan on top, 7-6, with 3:35 left in the first quarter.

The Bucks began moving again, but now it was primarily on the passing of Kern instead of the running of Otis. Michigan was called for pass interference once, then Kern hit White for 28 yards and again on a 22-yard TD pass.

Little did Hayes, as usual attired in his short shirt-sleeves, realize that would be the last touchdown his team would score.

Doughty again got the Wolverines going, this time with a 31-yard kickoff return.

Moorhead followed with a pass to Billy Harris for nine yards, Gabler ran for seven and Moorhead hit Mandich for nine, giving Michigan the ball on O.S.U.'s 33.

Taylor then made one of his patented broken field runs, shaking off linebacker Phil Strickland, halfback Ted Provost and safetyman Mike Sensibaugh as he rattled 28 yards to the Bucks' 5-yard line.

Craw got four yards on his first try and one on his second, putting him over the goal line with 11:54 left in the half. Titas' kick gave Michigan the lead, 14-12.

The Bucks couldn't move the ball on their next try, and when they punted, Pierson made the catch and bucked the Buckeyes for 60 yards with stiff arms and footwork as he gave Michigan the ball on Ohio State's 3-yard line.

Craw went for one yard and then Moorhead dived around right end for a touchdown, Titas kicked the point-after and suddenly Michigan was in command, 21-12.

The Wolverines scored again before the half ended as Killian hit a 25-yard field goal.

Curtis made two interceptions in the final minutes of the half as Kern tried desperately to get another TD.

Michigan also had one touchdown taken away. Moorhead hit Mandich in the end zone, but the Wolverines were charged with illegal procedure and Killian had to kick his field goal.

Michigan might have scored several touchdowns in the last half but the Buckeyes were still tough and they gave away nothing.

The key to the victory was the ability of Michi-gan to contain the O.S.U. offense during the last half of play. Otis continued to gain yards, but more often than not Newell, Huff and Hill were ready for him at the center of the line.

Kern was under tremendous pressure and yielded to Maciejowski in the final quarter.

Behind Maciejowski the Bucks finally crossed midfield but Pierson intercepted a pass and that ended the drive.

The victory left Michigan, the 17-point underdog, and Ohio State, the invincible, with identical 6-1 Big Ten records atop the conference standings.

SCORE BY PERIODS

MICHIGAN	7	17	0	0	— 24
OHIO STATE	6	6	0	0	— 12

Wolverine fullback Fritz Seyferth (32) plunges over the Stanford goal line to give Michigan a 10-3 lead in the final quarter. The Indians, however, would come back to win, 13-12, in the closing seconds.

STANFORD JOLTS U-M IN FINAL MOMENTS, 13-12

BY CURT SYLVESTER
Special to The Detroit Free Press

PASADENA, Calif., Jan. 1, 1972 - Two years of frustration and agony ended for the University of Michigan in the Rose Bowl Saturday to be replaced by new frustration and new agony.

Unlike two years ago, when injuries and illness cut down both the Wolverines and their coach, Bo Schembechler, there were no excuses unless Stanford quarterback Don Bunce can be considered an excuse.

Bunce's superb passing, plus a trick play in a punting situation, and the field goal kicking of little Rod

Garcia, were good for a last-gasp, 13-12 victory for Stanford over Michigan in the 58th Rose Bowl game.

Bunce completed five consecutive passes in the last two minutes and, with just 12 seconds left on the clock, Garcia stepped up to kick the game-winning field goal from the 21-yard line.

The Wolverines had time for only one more play – a long, incomplete pass – which was the same way the 10-3 loss to Southern California ended here two years ago.

"This was the best offensive team we've faced," said Schembechler. "We lost the game because of our failure to move the ball consistently."

It wasn't that the Wolverines couldn't move the football. They punched it for 264 yards through the stubborn Stanford defense, but U-M was stopped twice on fourth-down plays that might have led to scores.

And every time the Wolverines would get the lead, which happened three times, Bunce would just settle back and start throwing.

Nothing spectacular, just enough for one first down and then another and another.

By the time the gun sounded and the ecstatic Stanford fans came pouring onto the field, Bunce had put the ball in the air 44 times (just four short on Ron Vanderkelen's record of 48 attempts in 1963) and completed 24 of them for 290 yards.

Yet, if it hadn't been for the fake-punt play, which Stanford coach John Ralston loves to throw into his game, the Indians would never have been able to end Michigan's 11-game season-long winning streak.

It was midway in the fourth quarter with Stanford trailing, 10-3, and the ball on the Indians' own 33-yard line, that Ralston threw the play in.

With fourth down and 10 yards to go, the center snapped, Murray's leg swung up and the ball was nowhere to be found.

It had been snapped to the deep back – the blocking back – who handed it to fleet-footed Jackie Brown, who went 31 yards down the field before the Wolverines' Bruce Elliott ran him out of bounds.

"That fake punt was a key play," said Schembechler. But he admitted the play did not come as a surprise. "We ran against it all week."

Bunce fired a 12-yard pass to Bill Scott and moments later Brown broke past the line of scrimmage into the wide-open spaces of the Michigan defensive backfield and raced 24 yards for the touchdown. Garcia's conversion tied the score, 10-10.

A few minutes later, Ed Shuttlesworth raced downfield to cover on Barry Dotzauer's punt and caught punt-return man Jim Ferguson by the waist on the 6-yard line and hurled him down in the end zone.

With the safety, a 12-10 lead and only three minutes and 18 seconds left in the game, it looked as if the fourth-ranked Wolverines would escape with a win.

But they hadn't counted on Bunce's clutch passing. The senior quarterback, who was a redshirt when Stanford upset Ohio State in the Rose Bowl last year, began hitting short passes.

A 12-yarder to Scott, a 16-yarder to John Winesberry, an 11-yarder to Miles Moore, a 14-yarder to Reggie Sanderson and a 12-yarder back to Winesberry.

That put the ball on the 21-yard line and that was close enough for Garcia – who had missed five tries in a one-point loss to San Jose State this season – to kick the game-winning field goal.

The Wolverines had two chances to pull the game out – two dim chances. Kickoff return man Bo Rather couldn't escape on his return and second-string quarterback Larry Cipa couldn't connect on his bomb attempt to Rather going down the sideline.

With that, a good part of the non-record 103,154 fans poured down on the upset heroes of Stanford and the Wolverines filed silently off the field.

It was the first time this season the Wolverines had not been able to take the football and drive it down their opponent's throat.

Still, the Wolverines drove it. Billy Taylor had 82 yards, Shuttlesworth had 62 and Glen Doughty had 56. They just couldn't get it down Stanford's throat.

It seemed that every time a critical third- or fourth-down call came along, there was a Pete Lazetich or a Greg Sampson or a Jeff Simeon there to jam up the play.

Stanford stopped the Wolverines twice on fourth-down plays. The last time it happened, Michigan had marched from its own 39-yard line to Stanford's 1, where Taylor was piled up on a power sweep.

"Stanford deserved to win," said Schembechler. "We didn't get first downs when we needed them."

After a slow start, the Wolverines seemed to be gradually taking control of the game with their time-consuming ground game.

With Shuttlesworth, Doughty and Taylor moving the ball, Michigan moved from its own 29-yard line to Stanford's 7. The Wolverines had to settle for a 30-yard field goal by Dana Coin and a 3-0 lead at the half.

When the Indians stopped Michigan on the 1-yard line on the first drive of the second half, it apparently breathed some life into them.

Bunce hit four straight passes in the ensuing drive and Garcia tied the game, 3-3, with a 42-yard field goal.

It was then that Michigan had its only sustained touchdown drive of the day, with the option play going for big chunks of yardage and Taylor and Doughty getting the rest.

The only pass in the 71-yard drive was a five-yarder from Slade to Doughty on the 1-yard line, setting up Fritz Seyferth's one-yard plunge for a TD.

Coin's extra-point kick gave Michigan the lead, 10-3. But, unfortunately for the Wolverines that only succeeded in getting Stanford riled up for its game-winning, last-quarter efforts.

SCORE BY PERIODS

MICHIGAN..........0	3	0	9	—	12
STANFORD..........0	0	3	10	—	13

Dennis Franklin's 4th-quarter injury following his touchdown in Michigan's 10-10 tie with Ohio State pushed the Big Ten athletic directors to vote to send Ohio State to the 1974 Rose Bowl.

U-M TIES BUCKEYES, FORCES ROSE BOWL DILEMMA

BY CURT SYLVESTER
Special to The Detroit Free Press

ANN ARBOR, Nov. 24, 1973 - With an utter disregard for the tradition, the legend and the general mayhem of this 76-year-old rivalry, mighty Michigan and awesome Ohio State performed the unthinkable Saturday.

The Wolverines and Buckeyes battled to a 10-10 standoff before a Michigan Stadium-record crowd of 105,223 in a game that was intended to decide the Big Ten title, a possible national championship and the Rose Bowl berth.

What it did, on this damp and dreary day was give U-M and O.S.U. an equal share of the conference title, jar the Buckeyes loose from any national championship hopes and leave the bowl bid hanging until Sunday afternoon.

For the Wolverines, the bowl bid may be hanging precariously, however, because they lost star quarterback Dennis Franklin with a broken collarbone late in the fourth quarter after he had brought them from a 10-0 halftime deficit into the tie.

U-M trainer Lindsay McLean confirmed Franklin's broken collarbone, but said, "Our team doctors won't rule him out of the Rose Bowl. Some people simply heal quicker than others."

The Wolverines finished their schedule with a 10-0-1 record and the Bucks wrapped it up with a 9-0-1 mark. In the Big Ten, they both have identical 7-0-1 records.

And, who do you blame for the tie?

Coach Woody Hayes, docile on the sidelines all afternoon, had his second-string quarterback Greg Hare (the best of O.S.U.'s passers) throwing from deep in his own territory the last four times he had the ball.

And U-M coach Bo Schembechler had his ace kicker Mike Lantry booming away from 58 and 44 yards out in a pair of desperation field-goal tries in the last minute and six seconds of the game.

"I'm really disappointed in the tie," said Schembechler after about 15 minutes with his players. "But I'm extremely proud of the way our players came back. That took a lot of character and a lot of pride.

"I'll tell you this," he added quickly. "We didn't settle for a tie. We would have done anything to win that game."

And what about Woody?

"I don't think he wanted to settle for a tie, either," laughed Bo.

The two halves of the contest could have been two entirely different games.

The Buckeyes, moving on the legs of their unstoppable tailback, Archie Griffin, controlled the first half and the Wolverines, perked up by fullback Ed Shuttlesworth's powerful inside running, dominated the second half.

If the Bucks had the look of No. 1 in the first half, the Wolverines had it in the second.

The Bucks got a 31-yard field goal from Blair Conway and a five-yard TD run by freshman fullback Pete Johnson in the first half.

The Wolverines got a 30-yard field goal from Lantry and a nine-yard TD run by Franklin in the second half.

And, tradition be damned, neither team was about to give up another touchdown, field goal or safety the rest of the afternoon. A tie it was to be.

To come back from their 10-0 halftime deficit, Michigan's defense had to buckle Griffin for 64 second-half yards (after 99 in a devastating opening half) and limited elusive O.S.U. quarterback Cornelius Greene to 20 yards (after 12 in the first half).

The rest depended on Franklin's execution, his occasional passes to wingback Clint Haslerig or tight end Paul Seal, and Shuttleworth running behind the blocking of his front five: center Dennis Franks, guards Mike Hoban and Dave Metz, and tackles Jim Coode and Curtis Tucker.

The Wolverines showed their intentions from the moment they took the second-half kickoff, driving from their own 28 to the O.S.U. 32 before a Franklin toss into the end zone was picked off by Buckeye defensive back Neal Colzie.

But the Bucks weren't going anywhere against the U-M defense, led by linebackers Carl Russ and Steve Strinko, and safety Dave Brown.

When U-M stopped Greene on fourth and 2 at the Michigan 43, Franklin got them moving again.

Haslerig caught an 11-yard pass for a first down. Shuttlesworth knocked off 11 yards in two carries and then 12 in two more. That's the way it went. Shuttlesworth time and time, until the Bucks halted the drive at their own 13-yard line, forcing Lantry's field goal from the 20.

After a short O.S.U. punt moments later, U-M had it at midfield. A 35-yarder from Franklin to Seal got Michigan within range.

And on fourth down and inches at the 10-yard line, Franklin faked to the big fullback at the middle, then cut neatly inside the O.S.U. defensive end to score the TD.

The Wolverines were moving again late in the game from their own 11 to the Ohio State 49, with Franklin passing a pair of 14-yarders to Haslerig and a seven-yarder to Shuttlesworth.

Then it happened. Franklin was hit as he threw

Dennis Franklin rolls out, looking for a Wolverine receiver downfield.

to Shuttlesworth and went down hard, landing on his right shoulder and suffering a broken collar bone.

After two plays behind second-string quarterback Larry Cipa, the Wolverines faced a fourth-and-2 situation.

Lantry then attempted a field goal from the 48-yard line – and the boot had the distance – but it ended less than 24 inches to the left of the upright.

Hare came in to throw, but his first pass was intercepted by U-M defensive back Tom Drake at the O.S.U. 33. Moments later, with less than 30 seconds to play, Lantry's field goal try went wide to the right.

The Bucks got their big plays from Griffin in ringing up their first 10 points. Six carries for 59 yards set up Conway's 30-yarder early in the second quarter and 41 yards in another five tries set up Johnson's scoring run.

In between, the Wolverines missed their best scoring chance of the first half when a clipping call brought back Gil Chapman's kickoff return from the O.S.U. 28-yard line to the U-M 12 – a 60-yard penalty, in effect.

A score there might have made the difference. But it wasn't to be this time. Instead, the two clubs settled for their first tie game since 1949 and only the fifth in the 70-game history.

SCORE BY PERIODS

MICHIGAN..........0   0   0   10 — 10
OHIO STATE......0   10   0   0 — 10

No Rose Bowl trip for U-M

BY CURT SYLVESTER
Special to The Detroit Free Press

ANN ARBOR, Nov. 25, 1973 - A shocked and angry Bo Schembechler lashed out at Big Ten officials and athletic directors Sunday for denying his unbeaten University of Michigan team the opportunity to play in the Rose Bowl, and instead voting to send the Ohio State Buckeyes.

"There's no question about it, I'm very bitter," snapped the U-M coach after learning that Ohio State had been selected as the Big Ten representative. "I resent it. It's a tragic thing for Big Ten football.

"I'm very disappointed in the administration of the Big Ten," he said. "It hasn't been very forceful and it hasn't been very good."

The athletic directors were polled by telephone Sunday morning through the Big Ten office in Chicago. Commissioner Wayne Duke called U-M athletic director Don Canham with their decision early in the afternoon.

"I couldn't believe it," said Canham. "It's just unbelievable." He had predicted Saturday that U-M would be the choice, possibly 9-1.

The final count and the votes of the individual athletic directors were not announced by the Big Ten. But Schembechler, in Detroit to film his weekly TV show when he learned of the vote, had his suspicions.

"It was engineered by some guys and I'd like to know how those schools voted, and particularly how our sister institution (Michigan State) voted," said Bo.

M.S.U. athletic director Burt Smith told The Free Press on Saturday that Dennis Franklin's broken collarbone, suffered late in the fourth quarter of the 10-10 tie with Ohio State, might affect the athletic directors' decision.

"If it's true that he said that, I resent it," stormed Schembechler.

"I think that was a little unethical on his part to make such a public statement," added Canham.

There was little doubt in Schembechler's mind, however, that the injury to his first-string quarterback threw the vote to O.S.U.

"I think that had everything to do with it," he said. "There were petty jealousies involved and they used the injury to Dennis Franklin as a scapegoat.

"I feel bad for Dennis Franklin and for the 30 seniors on this team," Bo said, with his voice quivering.

"Those guys were there as sophomores and they wanted to go back. I'm an old coach. I'll get another chance to go, but they won't get that chance. And if you took a vote of the Ohio State players right now I'm not so sure they'd want to go."

So frustrated was Schembechler that he even said he'd be willing to go to another bowl game.

"If it were a major bowl, yes, I'd go," he said. "We deserve to go. We came back in the second half against Ohio State and outplayed them."

Canham also was irked by the fact that his colleagues had deserted him on an issue that many felt was only a formality, since the two teams had tied in their head-on meeting and Ohio State had been the Rose Bowl representative last season.

"The issue was Franklin but who is deeper in quarterbacks than we are?" asked Canham.

"Didn't Larry Cipa step in and beat Ohio State two years ago? Didn't he fill in for Franklin and win a game for us this year?

"How about Tom Slade? Didn't he take us through an unbeaten season and miss winning the Rose Bowl by a single point? I don't think these are bad quarterbacks.

"I don't think the loss of Franklin would have hurt us all that much," said Canham. "We'd have had to change our game plan maybe – maybe throw a little more."

The consensus among the athletic directors was something else, obviously, although one of them –

Iowa's Bump Elliott – said the decision shouldn't have been decided by one player's injury.

"Let me just say that Franklin's injury should have made no difference in the voting," said Elliott.

Franklin's injury was the key, I believe," said Purdue's George King.

"I felt the vote should have gone that way (to O.S.U.)," said Cecil Coleman of Illinois. "Franklin's injury was the big factor. If either team had lost its quarterback, I wouldn't vote for that team."

Smith, the first-year athletic director at Michigan State, reaffirmed his feeling that Franklin's injury was an important factor.

"Naturally, Franklin's injury would have something to do with the decision," said Smith.

"That's only natural. But I don't appreciate Canham's remark about me being unethical.

"It's nobody's business how I vote," he added. "I didn't talk to anyone about it. I did what I felt was best for the conference.

"I have to agree with the decision because it's a conference decision," he said. "How could I influence anybody's voting?" asked Smith. "I certainly didn't pressure anybody. Remember, I'm the rookie athletic director. You think those other men are going to listen to me?"

As far as Canham and Schembechler are concerned, there is little action they can take now.

"I'm not going to protest," said Canham. "I didn't politic and I'm not going to protest. It wouldn't do any good anyway."

"I don't know what I'm going to do," said Schembechler. "This is the lowest day of my career as a player and a coach. I'm very resentful at the way this thing was handled."

CHAPTER 38

Fullback Russell Davis posted two touchdowns for the Wolverines in their explosive second half.

STUBBORN WOLVERINES STORM PAST BUCKEYES, 22-0

By Curt Sylvester
Special to The Detroit Free Press

COLUMBUS, Nov. 20, 1976 - Goodby, Ohio State jinx, hello Rose Bowl.

After four years of agonizing and mind-bending failures, the University of Michigan finally got the job done on Ohio State Saturday.

Not with flying footballs and heart-stopping field goals as the seconds slipped off the scoreboard clock.

The Wolverines did it their way – with an unstop-pable running game and an unfailing defense – as they shoved Ohio State aside, 22-0, to grab a share of the Big Ten title and earn their first Rose Bowl trip since the 1971 season.

Ohio State gained a measure of consolation by accepting a bid to the Orange Bowl – the same bowl that Michigan went to as runner-up a year ago – against the Big Eight representative, yet to be deter-mined.

Led by the rushing of senior Rob Lytle, the Wolverines broke up a scoreless halftime tie with

All-America halfback Rob Lytle rambles for big yardage against the Buckeyes.

Rob Lytle scores Michigan's third touchdown, in the fourth quarter. He finished the day with 165 yards on 29 carries.

three second-half touchdown drives that never left the outcome in doubt.

No need for a tie-breaking touchdown, no need for a vote of the Big Ten athletic directors, no need to second-guess the play on fourth and one at the Ohio State goal line.

Those were the things that had spoiled it for Michigan for the last four years but they couldn't spoil it this time.

"We have always played well against them (O.S.U.), but the missed field goals or something have always held us back," exclaimed U-M coach Bo Schembechler. "But I felt going into this game we weren't going to be stopped."

And once the Wolverines got the Buckeyes loosened up in the second half – springing Lytle on option pitches, cutting quarterback Rick Leach inside and running fullback Russell Davis up the middle – the Wolverines weren't about to be stopped.

Davis scored twice on three-yard runs in the third quarter and Lytle burst across from the same dis-

tance in the fourth.

Bobby Wood kicked two extra points and Jerry Zuver, the holder on extra points, ran a two-point conversion in the closest thing to razzle-dazzle you can expect to see from Michigan for a long time.

All that was left to be done was the defensive mop-up and those hustling guys up front – Greg Morton, John Hennessey, Steve Graves, Tom Seabron and the rest – made it easy.

They pressured Ohio State quarterback Jim Pacenta relentlessly all afternoon and, except for a 24-yard run by Pacenta and a 21-yarder by tailback Jeff Logan, they were there to cut off the Buckeye running game.

The result was the first Ohio State shutout in 12 years, since Michigan turned the trick – 10-0 on the way to Pasadena in 1964.

It couldn't help but impress the 88,250 Ohio Stadium fans, who started wandering home after Michigan's final TD midway in the third period. Not to mention those millions who turned in on television that is, if they stayed awake through the first half.

As the coaches say, the first half was hard-nosed, defensive football; translated, that's a heck of a lot of bumps, bruises and punts.

Eleven times during the first half the punters had to exercise their skills. O.S.U.'s Tom Skladany booting six times for a 51-yard average and U-M's John Anderson kicked five for an average of 41 yards, as the teams traded field position and ran at each other's mid-sections.

"We didn't play a real good offensive game in the first half," explained Schembechler afterward, "We made mistakes, we didn't do what we wanted to do."

But the second half was another story.

Instead of going to the passing game as so many thought they'd have to, the Wolverines stuck to their ground game. But they livened it up with more of the option plays they had been using all season and it worked.

Michigan used up the first six minutes and 11 seconds of the second half on an 80-yard drive, with Leach running 20 yards on a broken play and cleverly drawing O.S.U. offsides with a long count to set up Davis' touchdown.

Not a pass was thrown in the drive, but U-M led, 7-0.

The TD succeeded in getting Woody Hayes mad, but even that couldn't get the Bucks going.

Hayes felt U-M tackle Billy Dufek Jr. had moved prematurely on the scoring play so he flailed the air momentarily. To no avail.

The TV replay indicated that Hayes might have been justified, but Dufek explained with a grin: "I was just getting off the ball quick."

Ohio State got off three plays and a punt, and once again Michigan was marching. This time the drive began at the U-M 48. A big 16-yard reverse by wingback Jim Smith and another 16-yard jaunt by Lytle, who finished the day with 165 yards, set up Davis' second TD run.

Again, not a pass was thrown and when Zuver finished his scamper into the end zone it was 15-0 for U-M with less than two minutes left in the third quarter.

"We felt 14 points weren't enough in this game," Schembechler said. "We couldn't go (to the Rose Bowl) with a tie, so we had to go for two. We put that play in just this week. The only question was whether we'd do it after the first or second touchdown."

The Wolverines were moving again early in the fourth quarter until Leach's only pass of the half was intercepted by O.S.U.'s Tom Roche on the Buckeye 13.

But Zuver came right back to intercept Pacenta's first toss and U-M was set up on the 16-yard line of O.S.U., ready to go for its convincing third TD.

The closest the Bucks came to scoring was late in the first half after Pacenta and Logan had escaped the U-M defenders, but Pacenta put the ball into the air in the end zone and defensive back Jim Pickens made the interception.

It was obvious from the celebration in the Wolverines' locker room how much it meant to beat the Buckeyes for the first time in five years, especially in Columbus with the stakes as high as they were.

"This has to rank with the great ones we've had," said Bo, "you'd have to go back to the 1969 game. We really won't feel the impact of this game until we get home with our friends."

But nobody could have doubted it. It was a celebration that many had waited years for.

And nobody was going to miss out.

SCORE BY PERIODS

MICHIGAN	0	0	15	7 —	22
OHIO STATE	0	0	0	0 —	0

The scoreboard tells the final story.

Bo's finest moment: He did it his way

Buckeye coach Woody Hayes and Bo before the game.

BY JOE FALLS
Special to The Detroit Free Press

If he coaches until he's a hundred years old and with that new heart, who knows?—Bo Schembechler will never experience a more satisfying moment than the one in Ohio Stadium Saturday afternoon.

Man, he did it all.

He ended all the jinxes, put to rest all the hexes, and proved he can win the big ones and win them his way.

Stubborn? Sure, he's stubborn. You saw that tug of war in the first 30 minutes. The whole stadium was yawning at intermission. The commercials were the most exciting thing on TV.

But Bo wouldn't yield. No, sir. He remained firm to his purpose, resolute in his belief that his way would prevail. And it did.

He believed that his offensive line could handle Ohio State's beefy defenders, and that is exactly what happened. It took time, but Bo's iron will became the dominating factor in this game.

So what if they put them asleep in the first half? Michigan was playing the Buckeyes even.

That was good enough for Bo.

He knew that in time, it would turn for him and it did, on the very first drive of the second half. Bo opened it up, going to the plays which worked so well all season long – the pitches, the reverses, and then the inside slams when the Ohio State secondary was loosened up by Michigan's wide game.

And – probably most satisfying of all – he did it without completing a single pass.

Perhaps you can say this was hardly a vintage Ohio State team. The Buckeyes certainly didn't scare anyone as they usually do in this house of terrors.

Actually, they made only one move all day long near the end of the first half – and then they were thwarted by the inexperience of their quarterback, Jim Pacenta, who threw a ball up for grabs. The Wolverines grabbed it in the end zone.

No, these were not the Buckeyes who would strike fear into everyone just by rumbling out of their dressing room before the start of the game. But who knew that before the start of the game?

The Buckeyes missed the likes of Cornelius Greene, Archie Griffin and Brian Baschnagel, but they were still good enough to run over everyone in the Big Ten and come into the game with 278 points in the bank.

Then they got zilch against Michigan, and the Wolverines richly deserved the shutout.

They took complete control of the game in the second half until it became a complete blowout.

This was Schembechler's finest moment – even more satisfying than that 24-12 upset he pulled on Ohio State in his first year. That was a dynamic victory, but Bo was new on the job then and nobody expected anything of him.

Now he has been around for eight years and much of this time he has had to live with the taunts that he clutched in the big ones.

You can't say that this time or even hint at it. He was as relaxed as he has ever been coming into this climactic game. Once you survive open-heart surgery, what can bother you any more? Or – more likely – he knew he had the stuff to do it to his old boss this time.

It was a beautiful moment in every way for Bo, for he finally got Woody Hayes off his back. He showed the old man the off-tackle stuff, but he also flashed a quick huddle at him, a deep pitch reverse and – most stunning of all – a rollout by Jerry Zuver on an extra-point try.

In fact, that may have been the highlight of Bo's career at Michigan when his veteran wolfmen stunned everyone in the stadium by rolling right and racing in for two points following Michigan's second touchdown.

Right there, Bo was rubbing Woody's nose in it, turning an apparent 14-0 lead into what suddenly was an insurmountable and embarrassing 15-0 bulge.

The Wolverines were superbly prepared.

Even after the sluggish first half, they kept executing as they have all season long. They were pretty to watch, with quarterback Rick Leach keeping Ohio State loose with his options, Rob Lytle running magnificently through the gaping holes and Russell Davis getting the tough yards inside.

And how sweet it must have looked to Bo when the Ohio State fans – who expect so much all the time – started leaving the stadium early in the final quarter. They had seen enough and the rest would have been too much to take. Their Bucks were dead and there was no hope of a miracle this time.

The miracle is that they made it to midfield.

The truth is, Bo and Michigan needed this one very badly. They have hardly been a showcase piece on national TV. They laid an egg in the Orange Bowl last New Year's Night and usually have come up short against Ohio State.

Now they have a crisp victory, one that no amount of second guessing can take away from them. The Wolverines earned it in every way.

All that is left is to prove is that they can win the final one. If they do that, Bo could ride a crest that will carry him to greatness for years.

Tune in from Pasadena. And who said: "Throw the ball, Bo?"

It wasn't me.

CHAPTER 39

Rick Leach (7) and Roosevelt Smith (26) scored Michigan's two touchdowns in a win that earned a trip to the Rose Bowl.

GUTTY WOLVERINES STOP BUCKEYES, 14-6

BY CURT SYLVESTER
Special to The Detroit Free Press

ANN ARBOR, Nov. 19, 1977 - A more stubborn, bull-headed outfit you couldn't have found anywhere in the country Saturday.

But you just might find something very similar in the Rose Bowl next Jan. 2.

Through as much pure cussedness as anything else, the University of Michigan punched out two touchdowns and made five dramatic defensive stands to grab the Rose Bowl trip and a share of the Big Ten title with a 14-6 victory Saturday over Ohio State before a N.C.A.A. record crowd of 106,024 fans in Michigan Stadium and a national television audience.

The Buckeyes didn't come up completely empty, however. After the game, they accepted an invitation to play No. 2 Alabama, the Southeastern Conference champion, in the Sugar Bowl.

Just for those who may have forgotten, that's two straight victories over Ohio State for Michigan, two straight co-championships and two years in a row the mighty Buckeyes have not scored a touchdown against Michigan.

Not to mention the fact that the Wolverines will be making their second straight trip to the Rose Bowl, which a few years ago seemed to be reserved for Ohio State only.

It's enough to get under a man's skin, which seems to be exactly what happened to the Buckeyes' not-always-so-agreeable Woody Hayes.

With his star quarterback, Rod Gerald, sitting on the ground after fumbling away the Buckeyes' final big scoring opportunity in the closing minutes, Hayes took out his frustrations of the day by punching an ABC-TV cameraman – later identified as Mike Freedman of Los Angeles – in the stomach.

"This is by far the best game we've ever played and lost," grumbled Hayes before stalking out of his post-game press conference in a huff after he was asked about the incident with the cameraman.

As miserable a day as it was for Woody, it was a day of celebration for the Wolverines, who had been beaten once and doubted so often during the season.

"I feel great," said U-M coach Bo Schembechler, who now stands even-steven at 4-4-1 with his old boss Woody. "This football team has had to overcome more adversity than any other team I've coached, and as I told them after the game, they're the most tenacious team I've ever had. They will not lose."

Statistically, it was not the Wolverines' day. They had only 10 first downs to Ohio State's 23; they had only 141 yards rushing to O.S.U.'s 208; and Rick Leach hit only three of nine passes for 55 yards to Gerald's 13-for-16 and 144 yards.

Thanks to a defense that came up with one big play after another, the Wolverines could have cared less about the numbers.

"I've been down there when we got all the sta-tistics, but this time we've got the points," said Schembechler with a grin.

"We got two touchdowns and they got two field goals and that's all that matters."

Only twice did the Wolverines push their way into the end zone against the Buckeyes, but what could you expect? Before Saturday, Ohio State had the best record in the country in defense against the score.

Tailback Roosevelt Smith came off the bench for the still gimpy Harlan Huckleby in the second quarter, caught a 22-yard pass from Leach to set up the go-ahead (7-3) touchdown, and then scored it on a one-yard dive into the end zone.

And in the third quarter, after linebacker Ron Simpkins recovered a fumble on the O.S.U. 20, Leach ran for 11 yards and scored two plays later for the TD that wrapped up the victory.

Gregg Willner kicked both of the U-M extra points.

Defensively, the Wolverines had more heroes than anybody could count, which explains why the best the Bucks could do was a couple of field goals – a 29-yarder in the first period and a 44-yarder in the third by Vlade Janakievski.

Simpkins, a mere sophomore, had his finest day of the season, getting in on 20 tackles.

Up front, middle guard Steve Graves and tackles Dale Keltz and Curtis Greer were also at a high for the season. And it was outside linebacker John Anderson who hit Gerald at the eight-yard line with only four minutes to go, forcing the fumble that defensive halfback Derek Howard picked up to end the Bucks' final scoring threat and rouse Woody's wrath.

Considering everything, however, Gerald certainly had nothing to be embarrassed about.

He drove the Bucks from their own 23-yard line all the way to the Michigan 12 on the opening drive of the game, catching the U-M defense by surprise with his speed.

"There's no way to simulate Gerald," Schembechler explained. "His quickness just overtook us. We didn't have to change anything, we just had to react quicker."

And that's apparently what they did. Just as the

The Wolverines' rugged defense shut down Ohio State's offensive attack most of the afternoon.

television coverage returned from Tel Aviv to Ann Arbor, the Wolverines got tough and the Bucks had to settle for the field goal. So much for one drive.

Three plays and a punt later, the Bucks went at it again, this time going from their own 39-yard line to Michigan's 8. Gerald was dumped by Greer for a nine-yard loss on the next play, Gerald made a bad pitch on the next and Janakievski's attempted 42-yard field goal was wide.

So much for drive No. 2.

With six minutes to go in the half and O.S.U. still up, 3-0, Smith came into the game and promptly ran for 14 yards in three carries, caught a 22-yard pass from Leach and then scored the go-ahead score.

Simpkins' fumble recovery, after Keltz and Graves had nailed O.S.U. tailback Ron Springs at the Buckeye 16-yard line, set up the 20-yard drive for the second U-M touchdown.

Except for a fourth-quarter drive that helped use up some time, the rest of the day belonged to that stubborn U-M defense.

Immediately after Leach's TD, the Buckeyes began driving again, from their own 15 to the U-M 11. Gerald was tossed for a two-yard loss, Springs lost one on a pitch, Simpkins sacked Gerald for another 13 yards lost, and Janakievski had to kick his second field goal.

A third time, the Buckeyes had moved but couldn't score.

The Bucks got their best scoring chance of the afternoon moments later when Smith fumbled at the Wolverines' 31-yard line.

But on a third-and-one play at the U-M 22, Simpkins blitzed and dropped fullback Paul Campbell for a two-yard loss. Again, the field goal try missed and the Wolverines had made yet another big defensive stop.

There were still two left to be made, however, and the Wolverines were up to it. Linebacker Mel Owens stopped Campbell inches short of a first down at the Michigan 10 on a fourth-down play early in the fourth quarter and Anderson forced the

With the Big Ten title on the line for the sixth straight year, a record crowd of 106,024 packed Michigan Stadium on its 50th anniversary to watch the Wolverines and Ohio State meet in this epic contest.

fumble out of Gerald with four minutes to go.

The Buckeyes had to be stopped again near midfield in the final minutes. But after what had happened earlier, there wasn't a whole lot of doubt.

For the second straight year, Michigan, 10-1 for the season, had stolen a share of the title from the Buckeyes, also 10-1, in the season finale.

In the Big Ten record books, each team has a 7-1 conference record. And in the Rose Bowl, once again it will be Michigan.

SCORE BY PERIODS

MICHIGAN	0	7	7	0 —	14
OHIO STATE	3	0	3	0 —	6

Angry Woody hits TV camerman

By JIM BENAGH
Special to The Detroit Free Press

ANN ARBOR - Woody Hayes promised earlier this week that his Ohio State Buckeyes "would come out smoking" against Michigan, and they did – grabbing an early lead. But before the day ended, his team was smoldering and Woody was doing a slow burn.

A question about Hayes having his season-ending incident – this time poking ABC-TV cameraman Mike Freedman on the Ohio State sideline in the waning minutes – cut short his post-game explanation of how a quarterback-oriented game turned into a defensive struggle.

Hayes went into a mini-rage when he was asked about the incident, recreating a pet peeve he has about photographers shoving their cameras in his face. He did it by balling his fist in front of a writer's face and saying: "They stick it in your face every damn time."

Freedman was still focusing on Hayes some 20 yards from the volatile Buckeye coach, when he said, "He took a whack at me. He aimed for my stomach. I blocked it. He was all pent up. He had to take it out on somebody."

Ironically, according to an ABC spokesman, the cameraman had made peace with Woody before the game to avoid such a situation.

Then Woody told the writers to write what they want because that is what they would do anyway, made a hushed obscenity at them and stalked out.

But Hayes' post-game show came after he gave a pretty good explanation of what happened during another close, fierce struggle.

He kept referring to "the one factor being in their (Michigan's) ability to stop us when we got in scoring range."

He gave Michigan credit: "It was not by accident but by design."

"We moved the ball and our defense was as sound as it could be," he said.

Hayes had opened his remarks by saying: "Gentlemen, that was the best game we've ever played and lost."

A big factor, though Hayes did not make a big deal about it, was his admission that his standout quarterback, Rod Gerald, had been hurting for the past three weeks with tendinitis of his left leg above the ankle. Gerald's running plays make the O.S.U. option offense go.

Gerald said later he was given a shot to ease the pain before the game, but that the injection didn't take. By the end of the first quarter, he was hurting.

Hayes said the quarterback had been getting in only one good day of practice a week.

Gerald was even more befuddled than Hayes at the Buckeyes' inability to score.

"We had the stats to win," he said, "We tried to come out fast – to start fast," he said of the O.S.U. game plan, which followed Hayes' early week revelation about "smoking."

"We did what we wanted to do but we just didn't score," Gerald continued. "I don't know why we couldn't get the ball across the goal line. That's what was puzzling everybody."

The son of a Dallas, Tex., Baptist preacher, admitting the awesome bigness of Michigan Stadium turned him on said: "The Michigan game – that's our season."

But he said he'd give it his best in a bowl.

"The sign of a good team and a great individual is how many times he gets up when he's knocked down," Gerald said, looking as if he wanted to start stoking the fires again whenever Woody's ready.

CHAPTER 40

In a display of offensive fireworks, all-America quarterback Rick Leach (7) threw for three touchdowns and ran for a fourth in Michigan's 28-14 win over Notre Dame.

LEACH SPARKS WOLVERINES PAST IRISH

BY TOM HENDERSON
Special to The Detroit Free Press

SOUTH BEND, Ind., Sept. 23, 1978 - Rebounding from a horrible first half, quarterback Rick Leach passed for three touchdowns and ran for another score Saturday to lead fifth-ranked Michigan to a 28-14 victory over Notre Dame in a bruising, classic football struggle – the first game between these national powerhouses in 35 years.

Leach was merely 3-for-14 with his passes at halftime when Notre Dame led, 14-7. But the senior from Flint turned from Mr. Hyde to Dr. Jekyll in the second half, hitting on five of six passes for 89 yards and three TD's as the Wolverines simply blew out the Irish.

Notre Dame coach Dan Devine let his 14th-ranked team dress in its fabled green jerseys – they were worn just once last year in a 49-19 massacre of Southern Cal – but it was going to take more than superstition to beat the Wolverines in this game, which was heavily scouted by the major bowls.

And so the Irish, one-point favorites coming in despite their 3-0 loss to Missouri two weeks ago, now have lost their first two games at home for the first time since 1896. And Michigan has its 10th win in 12 games against the Irish, who had won the last game these teams played, 35-12, in 1943 in Ann Arbor.

"The story of the game was the second half," said U-M coach Bo Schembechler. "We didn't play well at all in the first half, but we came back and played excellent offensive football.

"I felt if we could get back in the game in the second half, the momentum would swing our way. We don't often trail at halftime like that. The thing was, to come out and keep at 'em.

"There were a lot of kids out there who played their guts out that second half. A lot. We will not wilt physically. All I know is we played Notre Dame and we won."

"Michigan beat us fair and square," said Notre Dame coach Dan Devine, who is now 1-1 against Bo. "Offensively, they came up with the big play when they needed it in the second half. We got forced out of our game plan. They just played good, strong fundamental football.

"We just broke down in the second half."

Notre Dame self-destructed. Leach, who hadn't scrimmaged during the week because of a foot injury, had plenty of help from the Irish in fashioning the U-M comeback before a sold-out crowd of 59,075 in Notre Dame Stadium and a national television audience in the millions. Notre Dame committed five turnovers, all of them in the second half, and three

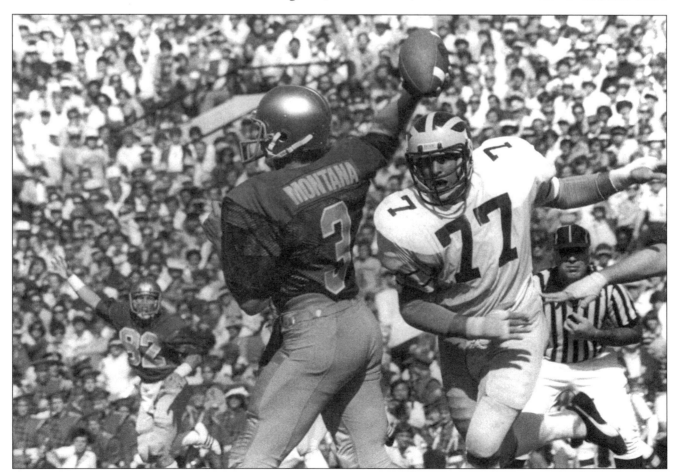

Irish quarterback Joe Montana, however, had a much more difficult day.

Rick Leach (7) led Michigan to a 10-2 record in 1978.

of them led to touchdowns.

U-M had just one turnover, but it was crucial. Russell Davis fumbled the opening play from scrimmage and Notre Dame recovered on the U-M 17. Four plays later, senior tight end Dennis Grindage caught his first varsity pass for a seven-yard score and the Irish led by seven with just 1:53 elapsed on the clock.

The first Irish fumble, on an errant pitchout on a reverse, resulted in a punt that gave Michigan the ball at the Notre Dame 49. Leach fashioned a nine-play drive, capping it himself on a dive off tackle with 9:39 to play in the half.

Notre Dame quickly followed with what was to be its last hurrah, a beautiful 75-yard, 10-play drive, that was a perfect blend of passing and running. Vagas Ferguson ran the ball in from the 4 to give the Irish the lead again, 14-7, with 5:21 to play in the half.

It was all Michigan from there. The secondary shut down Notre Dame's Heisman Trophy candidate, quarterback Joe Montana, who was seven for

10 in the first half but only nine for 19 in the second half.

Tailback Harlan Huckleby began ripping off yardage in big chunks – he led both teams with 107 yards in 22 carries. And Leach began to hit his receivers in the clear.

They had been open all day, but Leach couldn't have found them with a map in the first half. He was miserable, and when he was hitting his receivers they were dropping the ball.

But Leach found them in the second half.

He hit tight end Doug Marsh with a six-yard TD toss to tie the score at 14-14 late in the third quarter; he hit Marsh again on a 17-yard toss up the middle in the fourth quarter to put Michigan ahead, 20-14 (the extra-point kick by Gregg Wilner was blocked); and he hit flankerback Ralph Clayton on a perfectly thrown, 40-yard bomb with 9:18 to go in the game to make it 26-14.

The Wolverines added insult to injury, and two points to the scoreboard, when they tackled Montana in the end zone for a safety late in the game.

All three of U-M's touchdowns in the second half came after Notre Dame turnovers.

The Irish got the kickoff to open the second half and drove into Michigan territory. But their first turnover of the day, on a fumble by Ferguson that was recovered by Curtis Greer, gave U-M the ball at its own 29.

Michigan promptly ripped off 71 yards in 15 play, converting four of four third-down chances. The big one was a superb scrambling play by Leach on a third and 13. The pass to Marsh covered 14 yards, giving U-M a first down at the ND 35.

Five plays later, on a third and goal from the six, Leach hit Marsh in the left corner of the end zone for a 14-14 tie.

Wolverine co-captain Jerry Meter, whose dad played for Notre Dame in the win over U-M in 43, intercepted a pass by Montana on the next series and ran it back 14 yards to the ND 34.

Five plays later, on the first play of the fourth quarter, Leach found Marsh all alone at the goal line and the Blue had their first lead of the day.

The Irish took the ball on the kickoff and their fans began to roar, anticipating some luck of the Irish. They got luck – lots of it and all of it bad. The Notre Dame mystique never made an appearance.

Notre Dame made one first down with 11 minutes to go in the game, but a personal foul on receiver Kris Haines gave the Irish a first and 25. On second down, Montana served up another interception, to Mike Harden at the ND 41, and that was the game.

Leach made sure of that on the second play. Dropping straight back, he found Clayton all alone on a post pattern and the stunned, panicking Notre Dame team found itself down by a dozen when U-M's attempt at the two-point conversion failed.

Wasted for the Irish was a sensational day by linebacker Bob Golic, who was a second-string all-American in football last year and first team in wrestling. Golic had 26 tackles on the day to set an all-time Notre Dame record.

Wasted also were the 75 yards gained rushing by both Jerome Heavens and Ferguson, who were particularly effective in the first half.

"I'm not taking anything away from Michigan, but I really don't think they were that tough," said Heavens, chewing on some sour grapes.

The win was the first for U-M after four straight losses in the games they've played on real grass instead of plastic.

SCORE BY PERIODS

MICHIGAN..........0   7   7   14 — 28
NOTRE DAME 7   7   0   0 — 14

Anthony Carter (1) returned a second-half kickoff 67 yards to set up Michigan's first touchdown.

OLIVER BOOTS IRISH
TO VICTORY ON FINAL PLAY

BY MICK McCABE
Special to the Detroit Free Press

SOUTH BEND, Ind., Sept. 20, 1980 - The University of Michigan staged one of its great comebacks Saturday, but it was all for naught as Harry Oliver kicked a 51-yard field goal with four seconds left to give Notre Dame a thrilling 29-27 victory.

Oliver, a 5-foot-11 junior from Cincinnati, kicked a 51-yard field goal as the clock ran out.

"I knew right away that it was true and that he kicked it good," said Notre Dame coach Dan Devine.

"I've never seen Oliver kick one that far, but it went through today and that's all I care about."

Before Oliver did his damage, it appeared as though the 14th-ranked Wolverines (1-1) were going to come away with an upset over the No. 8 Irish (2-0).

With only 41 seconds left on the clock, U-M quarterback John Wangler passed to tailback Butch Woolfolk in the end zone. The ball bounced off Woolfolk's hands but landed in the grasp of U-M tight end Craig Dunaway to give U-M a 27-26 lead.

"The ball was supposed to go to the fullback or

John Wangler threw for three touchdowns in a contest which saw Notre Dame win, 29-27, on a last-play field goal.

the tight end," said Wangler. "They squeezed it in and I looked for somebody coming back."

Woolfolk, who did not start the game, had runs of 21 and 17 yards on the drive to set up the score.

After the TD, U-M tried for a two-point conversion but failed on an incomplete pass to Dunaway, leaving them with the one-point lead.

Notre Dame took over on its own 20 with less than a minute left, and on the first play reserve freshman quarterback Blair Kiel passed to split end Tony Hunter. The pass was incomplete but defensive back Marion Body was called for interference, moving the ball to U-M's 48-yard line.

U-M's Jeff Reeves nearly intercepted Kiel's next pass, and on the third down Kiel hit Phil Carter for a nine-yard gain.

Hunter caught a five-yard pass on fourth down and made it out of bounds to stop the clock with just four seconds left in the game, and set up the long field-goal attempt.

"This is the type of game that you win 20 times and lose 20 times," said U-M coach Bo Schembechler. "You just try and win it 21 ways. They won it one more way than we did.

"There were so many sets of circumstances where we could have won it that were unbelievable. If we would have got the two-point conversion, that would have put Notre Dame in a very precarious position. Do they go for the field goal (and a tie) or not?

"The pass interference play was a key. Without pass interference there is no field goal. If we catch the interception they are not going to score. And finally, if we keep their out-cuts in bounds, they're not going to score."

For a while it looked as though there would be no need for any last-second heroics. Notre Dame took a 14-0 lead in the first half on a six-yard run by Carter and a 10-yard pass from Mike Courey to Pete Holohan.

The U-M option game was going nowhere early in the game. Schembechler finally put in Wangler at QB with five minutes left in the first half.

Wangler responded by marching U-M 68 yards in eight plays for a TD. Lawrence Ricks gained 20 yards on a draw and Anthony Carter snared a catch for a 17-yard gain. Then Wangler passed eight yards

to Ricks for the score with 1:50 on the clock.

Body intercepted a Notre Dame pass at the Irish 27. On fourth down, the Wolverines faked a field goal as Rich Hewlett passed 12 yards to Stanley Edwards. That set up Wangler's nine-yard TD pass to Norm Betts to tie the score at the half.

U-M's Carter began the second half by returning the kickoff 67 yards to Notre Dame's 32.

Six plays later Edwards scored from two yards away and U-M had a 21-14 lead.

The U-M defense shut down Notre Dame's offense but the Irish managed a score when cornerback John Krimm picked off a Wangler pass and returned it 49 yards for a touchdown. The pass was intended for Carter, who was wide open and probably would have scored on the play.

But Oliver missed the extra point attempt, and U-M clung to a one-point lead.

The Wolverines may have been able to put the game away midway through the last quarter when they were marching down the field. But Woolfolk fumbled the ball on Notre Dame's 26 and the Irish eventually turned that into a four-yard touchdown by Carter to take the lead.

"I've made a lot of mistakes in my life but that may have been the worst," said a dejected Woolfolk.

"We were all really down," said Wangler. "Everybody played their hearts out and we thought we had the victory. This probably would have been the highlight of my career if we had won. My job is to win ball games. I'm happy with the way I played but it doesn't do any good to play this hard and lose."

The U-M defense that looked shaky last week while barely beating Northwestern had some problems stopping the Notre Dame attack.

"Sure, we have to tighten up our defense," Schembechler said. "We know where our problems are. But we don't have to apologize to anybody. We had as much right to win it as Notre Dame did. If there was a minute left (after Oliver's field goal) and they kick off to us, who knows.

"Nobody can deny it was a great game."

SCORE BY PERIODS

MICHIGAN.........0	14	7	6	— 27
NOTRE DAME ...0	14	6	9	— 29

Anthony Carter (1) scored Michigan's winning touchdown on a 13-yard pass from John Wangler.

DEFENSE THROTTLES BUCKEYES EN ROUTE TO PASADENA

BY MICK McCABE
Special to The Detroit Free Press

COLUMBUS, Nov. 22, 1980 - The amazing Michigan defense did it again.

For the fourth straight week, the Wolverines did not permit their opponent a touchdown, and as result the Wolverines will spend New Year's Day playing in the Rose Bowl.

The 10th-ranked Wolverines stymied the fifth-ranked Buckeyes here Saturday, 9-3, and gave U-M coach Bo Schembechler his ninth Big Ten championship.

Michigan may have been helped by the conservative play-calling of Ohio State coach Earle Bruce, who conceded later he may have made a mistake in continuing to pound at the unyielding U-M line. O.S.U. tailback Cal Murray, who led the Big Ten in rushing, gained only 38 yards in 14 carries.

Art Schlichter became the third Heisman Trophy candidate to look like just another quarterback against the Wolverines (9-2 overall, 8-0 in the Big Ten). Just as they did against California's Rich Campbell and Purdue's Mark Hermann, the Wolverines kept the Ohio State quarterback in check all day.

And this is virtually the same U-M defense that was giving Schembechler nightmares early in the season, when the Wolverines were only 1-2 after three games before winning their last eight.

"I'm very pleased to win this because this Michigan team exceeded all our expectations; they never gave up," said the U-M coach. "When people had given up on us they vowed to come back and win the championship. It may not have been the prettiest victory or the most explosive offensive game you wanted, but it was a great victory.

"This, in my opinion, is the best of all the championships because we won it outright. We haven't won an outright championship since 1971. You can't believe what this means to us."

A year ago, the difference in Ohio State's 18-15 win was U-M's horrible kicking game.

And the Wolverines were almost done in by the foot again as U-M's Ali Haji-Sheikh missed two field goal attempts and an extra point.

Haji-Sheikh's first miss was a 38-yarder after U-M drove from its own 20-yard line to O.S.U.'s 21.

Vlade Janakievski booted a 33-yarder to give the Buckeyes a 3-0 lead early in the second quarter before Haji-Sheikh converted a 43-yarder midway through the period. U-M could have taken a halftime lead, but Haji-Sheikh missed a 42-yarder on the first play of the second quarter.

Defensive back Marion Body got the Wolverines the ball on U-M's 44 in the third quarter when he hit Gary Williams after Williams had caught a pass over the middle and Tony Jackson recovered the fumble.

"I was watching film on him (Williams) all week and when I saw him coming across the middle I knew the ball was going to him," Body said. "I sprinted to him as fast as I could and I hit him. I don't think he saw me."

As they had throughout the first half, the Wolver-

ines marched steadily down the field.

On third and 11 from O.S.U.'s 13, John Wangler hit Anthony Carter with a pass over the middle, and the U-M sophomore caught the ball between O.S.U. linebacker Marcus Marek and safety Bob Murphy.

"I faked to the outside and went back to the post," Carter explained. "We have a play where I fake inside and go outside and I kind of feel that was the play they were looking for.

"Before the play I told Wangs that (cornerback Vince) Skillings was coming up real quick to stop the run and I could beat him."

Wangler called the TD play at the line of scrimmage.

"I saw the kind of coverage they were using and I thought A.C. could beat them to the outside," Wangler said.

"Wangler and Carter," Schembechler said with a smile. "You just knew sooner or later Anthony was going to get one."

As it turned out, the Wolverines did not need any more points. A Body interception gave the Wolverines a chance, but tailback Butch Woolfolk's option pass was intercepted in the Ohio State end zone.

Janakievski missed a 35-yard field goal attempt and U-M ran seven minutes off the fourth-quarter clock, moving to O.S.U.'s 32. But on fourth down Schembechler chose to punt instead of trying a 49-yard field goal into a slight wind.

After Schlichter scrambled for 13 yards, he missed four straight passes, three of them long bombs, and the Wolverines took over at O.S.U.'s 33.

Again, after three running plays, Schembechler elected to punt and Ohio State had one more chance, with 1:08 left to play.

"I hoped the kicking game wouldn't beat us," Schembechler explained later. "If I would have had more confidence in the kicking game, I would have kicked the field goals."

Schlichter hit Doug Donley for a 27-yard gain to U-M's 32, but the Wolverine defense tightened. On third down, Paul Girgash forced Schlichter into a 15-yard intentional-grounding penalty; and on fourth down, Robert Thompson sacked Schlichter with less than 20 seconds to play.

Ohio State spent most of the first three quarters trying to establish some sort of running attack, but it never worked.

"Perhaps, looking back, we should have passed more," said Bruce, who was booed during the game. "But so often, in a game like this, you're better off when you are able to jam it in there."

The Wolverines were the ones doing the jamming as the U-M ground game piled up 197 yards rushing in 61 attempts while Wangler hit on 11 of 22 passes for 120 yards. For the most part, the Wolverines stayed on the ground.

The Ohio State strategy was just fine with Schembechler.

"We defensed Ohio State on what they did best," he said. "Our defense must be quick because Murray is a heckuva back."

And the U-M defense is a heckuva defense.

SCORE BY PERIODS

MICHIGAN..........0	3	0	6	—	9
OHIO STATE......0	3	0	0	—	3

Anthony Carter (1) and Bo Schembechler are interviewed by NBC-TV's Merlin Olsen following a brilliant Wolverine win in the Rose Bowl.

FINALLY!
BO, U-M WIN ROSES, 23-6

BY MICK MCCABE
Special to The Detroit Free Press

PASADENA, Calif., Jan. 1, 1981 - As its fight song boasts, the Michigan football team is returning to Ann Arbor as true "Champions of the West" for the first time under Bo Schembechler.

And it was a passing attack that brought the usually running-minded Schembechler his first Rose Bowl victory.

U-M quarterback John Wangler and all-America wide receiver Anthony Carter hooked up just enough Thursday to complement the power running of tailback Butch Woolfolk and another strong defensive performance to lead U-M to a 23-6 victory over Washington.

It gave the fifth-ranked Wolverines (10-2) their first victory here since 1965 and the first after five frustrating losses under Schembechler.

"I've been here five times and five times I sat here

with my head between my legs," Schembechler said. "Now I can smoke a cigar and enjoy it."

It was the first time a Schembechler-coached U-M team finished the season with a victory and the ninth straight win for the Wolverines. And don't forget: this is the same U-M team that was 1-2 after three games.

"This football team has given us, the coaches, the fans – all of us – a great thrill the way they played," said Schembechler. "We played a great football team today. We felt going in they were a great team and they were. The thing that amazed me was that our defense still kept them out of the end zone." For the last 22 quarters, no team has managed to score a touchdown against a Michigan defense that returned

only three starters from a year ago.

While the defense did its job, the passing from Wangler to Carter got the offense going.

In the first half, Carter did not catch a single pass and carried the ball once for two yards.

But the second half was a different story, as the sophomore wide receiver caught five passes for 68 yards and a TD. He also ran with the ball three times for 31 yards.

"John (Wangler) just hadn't gone to him," Schembechler said, explaining Carter's first-half stats. "John felt if he did he would be forcing the ball. At half-time we told him to force it into him."

The Wolverines, who led, 7-6, at the half on Woolfolk's six-yard run, at first hardly resembled Big Ten

Butch Woolfolk (24) was named the Rose Bowl's M.V.P after a stellar performance of 182 yards on 26 carries and one touchdown.

champions.

"Every Rose Bowl we've played in we were down at the half," Schembechler said. "We felt if we were leading by a point and had not played well the game would eventually come our way.

"The other thing was that we let Anthony stand there alone long enough so we wanted to bring him into the ball game. When you do, things happen."

The Wolverines' defense stops Washington at the goal line.

Carter was back when he caught a 27-yard Wangler pass to put the ball at the 11-yard line of Washington on U-M's first possession of the third quarter. Four plays later Ali Haji-Sheikh booted a 25-yard field goal to make U-M's lead 10-6.

In the first half Washington quarterback Tom Flick completed 15 of 23 passes for 189 yards. But all that produced were two field goals by Chuck Nelson. In the second half the Wolverine defense limited Flick to eight of 16 attempts for 93 yards.

The Huskies came close to scoring in the first quarter when they ran four plays inside the eight-yard line. But they came up short when Toussaint Tyler was stopped inches from the goal line on fourth down.

Washington also got to U-M's 25 in the second quarter before Brian Carpenter picked off a Flick pass.

"We knew going in we would not get many

opportunities, and when you got them you had to stick points on the board," said Washington coach Don James. "Michigan has a great defense and we ran a lot of plays in the first half. They saw the plays and they reacted to them.

"They kept getting better."

On their possession after Haji-Sheikh's field goal, the Wolverines came back. Wangler passed 10 yards to Chuck Christian, 17 yards to Alan Mitchell and then 14 yards to Carter to set up the seven-yard TD pass to Carter.

Michigan sealed its win on Stan Edwards' one-yard touchdown run with 4:02 remaining. During the drive Carter carried the ball on an end around for 21 yards and caught an 18-yard Wangler pass.

Woolfolk, the only effective weapon U-M had in the first half, finished the game with 182 yards in 26 attempts. He also finished with the game's most valuable player award.

"This is the biggest game I've ever had," the junior tailback admitted. "We won the high school state championship in New Jersey and we won the Big Ten championship in my freshman year. But those can't compare to this."

Schembechler, who suffered a heart attack the morning before his first Rose Bowl game in 1970 (he later had open-heart surgery), was mobbed after the win, receiving a bloody nose from one of his own players during the celebration.

"By the time I got pounded on out there I could hardly breathe," he said with a smile.

"And I don't have the best of hearts."

He admitted he shed a few tears over his first bowl victory.

"I'm on top of the world in every respect," he said.

SCORE BY PERIODS

MICHIGAN.........0	7	10	6 — 23
WASHINGTON....0	6	0	0 — 6

All-America defensive back Garland Rivers (13) made life difficult for the Irish.

WOLVERINES PLUCK IRISH LUCK

BY TOMMY GEORGE
Special to The Detroit Free Press

SOUTH BEND, Ind., Sept. 13, 1986 - Michigan took the gifts Notre Dame offered – three turnovers inside the U-M 15 – and muscled its way to a 24-23 win Saturday at Notre Dame Stadium.

And then with 1:33 left, amid a potential game-ending drive and after a turnover-free three quar-

ters, the Wolverines returned the favor. Bob Perryman fumbled at the Notre Dame 26 and linebacker Wes Pritchett recovered. Irish quarterback Steve Beuerlein then completed 33- and 16-yard passes to move Notre Dame to Michigan's 28. Seventeen seconds were left. Finally, in trotted Irish kicker John Carney.

"I turned to Mike Reinhold on the sidelines and said, 'Mike.. he's going to make it,' " said U-M quar-

All-America quarterback Jim Harbaugh outdueled Notre Dame's Steve Beuerlein in an aerial battle that the Wolverines barely managed to win, 24-23.

Wolverine assistant coach Gary Moeller and Bo on the sidelines.

terback Jim Harbaugh. "He said, 'Hey, suck in that stomach, Jimmy. No way. No way.' "

Carney's 45-yard kick had the distance but drifted left with 13 seconds left, and the thrilling finish kept the score intact – Michigan 24, Notre Dame 23 – before a capacity crowd of 59,075 and a national TV audience.

It was Notre Dame's 16th consecutive sellout and 113th of the last 114th games.

There were big plays and bigger controversies, but it wound up a season-opening victory for U-M, a crushing debut loss for Irish coach Lou Holtz.

"There are an awful lot of sad young men in our locker room right now," Holtz said. "We never seemed to have anything bounce our way the entire day. But hopefully this game will serve as a strong foundation."

Notre Dame's foundation would have been much surer had Carney's kick sailed more to the right, had he not earlier missed an extra point or had tight end Joel Williams been ruled inbounds on his apparent

touchdown catch deep in the end zone with 4:26 left that would have given Notre Dame a 26-24 lead.

However, as Harbaugh said, "Good luck is the byproduct of hard work." And Irish turnovers on this day were their first steps to defeat.

Notre Dame made four of them:

• The first, two minutes into the second half when flanker Reggie Ward fumbled at U-M's 7. Safety Tony Gant recovered.

• The second, with 8:57 remaining in the third quarter, when the Irish did not pounce on a high, short Michigan kickoff and U-M safety Doug Mallory did, at Notre Dame's 27.

• The third, with a minute left in the third quarter, when fullback Pernell Taylor fumbled at Michigan's 15, recovered by Mallory.

• And the fourth, with 10:54 to play, when Beuerlein's eight-yard toss into the end zone was intercepted by cornerback David Arnold.

The crucial miscues were the interception and the flubbed kickoff. Especially the kickoff, because

Michigan had just erased Notre Dame's 14-10 half-time lead by taking the second-half kickoff, driving 78 yards and scoring on Jamie Morris' one-yard run. Mallory then recovered the kickoff. Harbaugh needed only six seconds to find Morris for a 27-yard touchdown and a 24-10 U-M lead.

The game's final points came on Williams' two-yard catch with 3:10 left in the third quarter (after which Carney missed the extra point) and Carney's 25-yard field goal with 4:26 remaining (after Williams was ruled out of bounds on his catch).

Notre Dame didn't punt once in nine possessions. It produced 455 yards, averaged 6.3 yards a play, had 27 first downs, and was eight-for-12 on third-down conversions. It was enough to make Michigan coach Bo Schembechler rub his eyes afterward in despair.

"I expect a better question than that," he said when asked about his defense. "But Lou Holtz is a very diverse offensive coach, and he kept us off balance with so many different formations. We were in hostile territory. We came out with a victory. I don't care how you come out with them."

Harbaugh, scrambling and passing on a variety of rollout plays, was 15-of-23 for 239 yards and a touchdown, and Morris rushed for a game-high 77 yards and caught three passes for 31 yards.

"I've never caught a ball that far downfield," Morris said of his touchdown grab. "It was a throw-back play, where the back just runs downfield down the sideline. That was a big thrill."

Notre Dame took advantage of a shanked punt and its swarming goal-line defense to lead at half-time, 14-10.

Michigan's offense controlled the ball for nearly 19 minutes of the half. Harbaugh was 7-of-9 passing for 101 yards, and his scrambling and roll-out passing helped Michigan to 203 yards, 11 first downs and three drives that covered at least 60 yards.

After Pat Moons missed a 42-yard field goal, Notre Dame drove 75 yards, with Tim Brown scoring on a three-yard run. Michigan needed only 33 seconds to answer, however, as Morris shook three Irish tacklers on an eight-yard scoring run.

Two minutes into the second quarter, Irish flanker Reggie Ward fumbled and safety Tony Gant recovered at the Michigan 7. But Monte Robbins' shanked punt of 21 yards gave the ball right back to Notre Dame, at the Michigan 26.

Eight plays later, Mark Green dived one yard for a touchdown and a 14-7 Irish lead with 8:08 left.

Moon's 23-yard field goal made it 14-10 at the half.

SCORE BY PERIODS

MICHIGAN	7	3	14	0 —	24
NOTRE DAME	7	7	6	3 —	23

Mike Gillette's game-winning field goal on the final play avenged a loss against the Hawkeyes from 1985.

SWEET REVENGE FOR WOLVERINES

BY TOMMY GEORGE
Special to The Detroit Free Press

ANN ARBOR, Oct. 18, 1986 - It was as if he were home again in St. Joseph in his backyard, booting Campbell's soup cans and pretending the game was on the line. Oh, how many countless times as a child had Mike Gillette played game-winning scenarios over and over with his cans.

And Saturday afternoon, he found make-believe can become ecstatic reality.

Gillette's 34-yard field goal as time expired lifted fourth-ranked Michigan to a heart-thumping, 20-17 victory over eighth-ranked Iowa before 105,879 at Michigan Stadium and a national TV audience.

It was redemption for Michigan. Redemption for Gillette.

The shoe was on the other foot for Iowa, which beat Michigan, 12-10, last season on Rob Houghtlin's game ending 29-yard field goal in Iowa City. This time, it was the Wolverines fans who swarmed the field in wild celebration. This time, it was Houghtlin and Iowa coach Hayden Fry and the rest of the Hawkeyes who walked off the field with that sickening feeling, with the shock and trauma of losing as – on the game's last play – the ball sailed cleanly between the uprights.

"We're even now," said Fry, who later sat alone in the first row of Iowa's team bus and, behind those dark glasses, pensively contemplated this one that slipped away.

For Gillette, it was the final, giant leap back from an up-and-down freshman season in 1985. He set the Michigan season record for field goals (16) only to lose his starting job to Pat Moons when Gillette was suspended for the Ohio State game for disciplinary reasons. He kicked a U-M record 53-yard field goal in the first quarter Saturday, and then punched the winning kick that made Michigan 6-0 (3-0 in the Big Ten). Iowa is 5-1 (2-1 in the Big Ten).

"What a day, huh?" Gillette said. "I didn't think about anything but hitting the ball like an extra point. All I had to do was hit the ball straight."

After U-M called a time-out with five seconds left, the ball at the Iowa 17, and summoned Gillette, Iowa called another time-out.

"He (Gillette) came over," Michigan coach Bo Schembechler said, "and I said, 'They're trying to psyche you out. They're trying to ice you.' He said, 'Yeah, yeah, yeah.' This is the last guy that would be flustered. He's the cockiest guy that ever lived."

And grateful he got another chance.

"It was a long time coming," Gillette said. "I couldn't ask for more."

Nor could Michigan, especially when it was given new life with 1:57 remaining and the game tied at 17.

Moons had missed a 27-yard field goal with 5:10 remaining. Iowa then took possession and drove from its 20 to the Michigan 43. On third and 1, quarterback Mark Vlasic's option pitch to fullback Richard Bass squirted loose, and U-M linebacker Andy Moeller recovered at the Michigan 49.

Michigan then took advantage of Iowa's heavy blitzing with screen passes and a nifty third-and-five run of five yards by tailback Jamie Morris to the

Iowa 27 that helped set up Gillette's game-winner.

"After Pat missed," Gillette said, "Coach (Alex) Agase told me they were going with me if we got the chance."

Vlasic, who replaced starter Tom Poholsky in the second half, said of the critical fumble:

"It was just a poorly executed play. It was a mistake on our part and we paid for it. I had every reason to believe we would have gone down there and scored.

Fry said: "It was a good pitch. He (Bass) just fumbled it."

Fry was disappointed that his team squandered so many scoring opportunities in the first half although it led, 10-3, at halftime.

Bass scored on a one-yard run and Houghtlin kicked a 29-yard field goal for Iowa's first-half points. But on three second-quarter possessions, Iowa drove to the Michigan 45, 44 and 18 and didn't score.

The drive that stalled at the U-M 18 was killed by safety Erik Campbell's interception of Poholsky in the end zone on a second-and-one pass. And early in the fourth quarter, Iowa had the ball at U-M's 19. On fourth and 1, tailback Rick Bayless was crunched for a one-yard loss by middle guard Billy Harris.

"That's a ball game we never should have lost," Fry said. "We missed excellent scoring opportunities in the first half and it should have been at least 17-3. We just made some critical mistakes."

Michigan did, too.

Quarterback Jim Harbaugh was intercepted twice and fumbled twice. After Michigan played a flawless third quarter – Gerald White made bruising runs, carrying tacklers with him for the final three yards on both his 25-yard touchdown catch and 10-yard scoring run that gave Michigan a 17-10 lead – Harbaugh was intercepted by Hawkeye safety Dwight Sistrunk at the Michigan 40 with 12:44 to play.

Sistrunk grabbed the pass as it bounced off split end Ken Higgins' hands and raced to the Michigan 19. Three plays later, Vlasic tied the score at 17 on a 15-yard strike to Robert Smith.

"We were struggling in the first half and got it together in the third quarter," Harbaugh said. (Michigan now has outscored opponents in the third quarter, 55-9.) "Bo was going up and down the locker room and ripping offensive guys individually and as a group. He kind of cleaned our cobwebs.

"I had a feeling we would get the ball back and get a chance at the end. Even if they had scored, I felt we'd get it back and have a chance. Last year just couldn't happen to us again."

Harbaugh completed 17 of 28 for 225 yards. Poholsky was five-of-15 for 99 yards and two interceptions and Vlasic completed four of four for 64 yards.

SCORE BY PERIODS

MICHIGAN	3	0	14	3 —	20
IOWA	7	3	7	0 —	17

After falling behind, 14-3, an inspired Jim Harbaugh (4) rallied the Wolverines to a 26-17 lead in the final period. The eventual win gave Michigan the Big Ten title and a Rose Bowl berth.

A MICHIGAN-BUCKEYE CLASSIC

BY TOMMY GEORGE
Special to The Detroit Free Press

COLUMBUS, Ohio, Nov. 22, 1986 - Michigan had been there before – no, not in quite the same setting or for such tremendous stakes, but this scenario was all too familiar. Precious seconds left. The ball floating toward the goalposts on a game-deciding field goal.

For Michigan, the Big Ten co-championship appeared to be slipping away.

The roses were wilting.

But in the five seconds it took Ohio State's Matt Frantz to attempt a 45-yard field goal that drifted left with 61 seconds left, several Wolverines experienced memories both sweet and sour. Oh, how sweet Saturday afternoon's recollection will be for Michigan, which beat Ohio State, 26-24, before an Ohio Stadium record crowd of 90,674 and a national television audience.

Michigan (10-1) and Ohio State (9-3) share the Big Ten championship with 7-1 records, but the Wolverines will go to the Rose Bowl against Arizona State in Pasadena, Calif., on New Year's Day because they won this classic battle. Ohio State accepted a Cotton Bowl berth in Dallas.

In the end, U-M's destiny was decided by one kick. Again for the Wolverines, in the final seconds. Hit or miss?

They had been there before.

"I've been there a lot in 24 years of coaching," said Michigan coach Bo Schembechler, who got the game ball after becoming U-M's all-time leader in coaching victories with 166, passing Fielding H. Yost.

Schembechler, of course, vividly remembers Michigan's recent games decided by late kicks, beginning with the game-ending loss by a field goal, 12-10, at Iowa last season and the game-ending miss by Chris White that left U-M and Illinois tied, 3-3, at Champaign.

Then came Notre Dame's final-seconds miss by John Carney in this year's season opener, a 24-23 U-M win; the last-second boot that beat Iowa, 20-17, at Michigan Stadium; and Minnesota's game-ending kick last weekend that ruined U-M's perfect season, 20-17.

"We have been there before," U-M quarterback Jim Harbaugh said. "We've seen it happen against us and for us. I was getting ready over there, if it went through, to try and drive us to get a field goal to win it."

Cornerback Garland Rivers was on the field during Frantz's kick, lining up deep and running and leaping for the block.

"I tried not to think about all the times before this has happened to us, but just tried to knock the ball down, and I almost got it," Rivers said. "I dove and looked back. And what did I see? I saw victory."

What Rivers and U-M's defense saw in O.S.U.'s first two offensive series was a punishing attack that looked as if it would give Michigan more than it could handle. The Buckeyes covered 125 yards in 13 plays on those two drives en route to a 14-6 halftime lead.

But Michigan rebounded in the second half and finished with 529 yards in offense (268 rushing and 261 passing). U-M made 27 first downs, averaged 6.5 yards a play and led in possession time, 35:39 to 24:21.

Harbaugh and tailback Jamie Morris were the catalysts.

Harbaugh backed his guarantee of victory by completing 19 of 29 passes for 261 yards.

Morris ran all over the Buckeyes with 210 yards on 29 carries and two touchdowns.

"Bo told us Thursday that he wanted us to run and play our best game ever, to play like we never have before, and then he came to my room last night and said there would be some creases and holes," Morris said. "We just had to find them." Morris did.

But Frantz knew he could make up for Morris and all of Michigan's punch. Especially when tailback Thomas Wilcher fumbled at O.S.U.'s 37 with 3:17 left, setting up the Buckeyes' potential game-winning drive.

"I thought it would be good," Frantz said. "I just knew it would be good. It felt good when I kicked it. I can't believe it."

O.S.U. coach Earle Bruce said: "If you saw it, there was nothing wrong with the kick. He kicked it hard and far, but sometimes you hook it, which is what happened.

"I felt one of the keys in this game was the third time we had the ball, when we had an opportunity to make a field goal and didn't (Frantz's 43-yard attempt was short). Another key was the fact they ran the ball effectively and kept the ball in the second half. This is a tough game to lose, especially in Ohio Stadium. It's going to take awhile to get over this one."

Ohio State scored on its first possession, with Jim Karsatos passing four yards to Cris Carter. After Michigan's Mike Gillette kicked a 32-yard field goal, O.S.U. tailback Vince Workman ran 46 yards for a touchdown on an option pitch. Gillette kicked another field goal from 34 yards with 6:47 left in second quarter, completing the first-half scoring, 14-6.

Harbaugh, who was intercepted by safety David Brown in the first quarter, had a pass swiped by linebacker Michael Kee at O.S.U.'s 4-yard line with 40 seconds left in the half. Also in the first half, U-M freshman flanker Greg McMurtry, possibly distracted by the sun's glare, dropped a 43-yard pass in the end zone.

Morris scored on a bruising eight-yard run with 3:53 left in the third quarter, putting Michigan ahead for the first time, 19-17. But U-M's two-point conversion try failed, prompting Schembechler to com-

Against Ohio State, junior tailback Jamie Morris (23) led Michigan's powerful ground attack with 210 yards rushing on 29 carries and two touchdowns.

plain vehemently to the officials that Ohio State was guilty of pass interference.

The Wolverines soon made up for that when Wilcher scored from seven yards early in the fourth quarter for a 26-17 lead.

Karsatos and Carter hooked up again, however, this time from 17 yards out with 9:42 left, making it 26-24. The teams traded punts until Wilcher's fumble, recovered by safety Sonny Gordon.

Ohio State drove to Michigan's 28, and on fourth and 2 Bruce sent in Frantz.

"It was a tough decision," Bruce said. "You have to take that chance. He had been kicking the ball from that distance well in practice and before the game."

But Frantz didn't in the final seconds. The roses, after all, were glimmering for Michigan.

SCORE BY PERIODS

MICHIGAN	3	3	13	7 —	26
OHIO STATE	14	0	3	7 —	24

Michigan quarterback Michael Taylor (9) put on a spectacular offensive performance, including 3 touchdown passes, but the Wolverines lost to the Hurricanes in the final minute.

WOLVERINES' DREAM KICKED AWAY

BY STEVE KORNACKI
Special to The Detroit Free Press

ANN ARBOR, Sept. 17, 1988 - How quickly can a dream game turn into a nightmare?

How quiet can 105,834 fans become?

Miami answered those questions for Michigan in a 31-30 victory Saturday. The No. 1 Hurricanes scored 17 points in the final 5:23 to run their winning streak to 14 games.

Again, it was a field goal from a nondescript walk-

on kicker that sealed the Wolverines' disappointment.

Carlos Huerta's 29-yard kick with 43 seconds left provided the winning points. Last Saturday, Notre Dame's Reggie Ho beat U-M on a 26-yard field goal with 73 seconds remaining.

Coach Bo Schembechler and several players complained that two pass-interference calls weren't made on the Wolverines' attempt to move into field-goal range in the final seconds.

Miami strong safety Bobby Harden agreed that

his bump of Chris Calloway was a penalty.

"It was definitely pass interference," said Harden.

"Jimmy Johnson did a great job of officiating," said Schembechler, pointing to the Miami coach. "He was officiating the game over there for those dumb guys."

Wolverines flanker John Kolesar was on his knees near the Hurricanes' 30 when time ran out, waiting for the call that didn't come. The U-M players were experiencing a variety of emotions.

Michael Taylor, who had completed 16 of 24 passes for 214 yards and three touchdowns, limped into the tunnel with cramps and a sick feeling.

"We should have won and I hated to look up there and see we hadn't," said Taylor. "All I knew was that the final score was 31-30 and they won."

Free safety Vada Murray had two interceptions but no solace after the defensive collapse.

"I sat on the bench watching the scoreboard," said Murray. "I was really hurt. It was so unfortunate."

Defensive end Mark Messner pressured Steve Walsh (24-of-45 for 335 yards and three touchdowns) in the five-step drop but never caught him. He let out his frustrations.

"I was screaming at the officials at the end," said Messner. "We had the No. 1 team and blew it. All that hoopla going on in their locker room should have been ours. But it was so quiet on our side that all you could hear were the showers."

U-M dropped to 0-2 for the first time since 1959; Miami is 2-0. The Hurricanes won with a sequence of big plays Schembechler termed "ungodly."

Huerta had set up his own heroics moments before the winning field goal. His onsides kick was recovered by Harden at the Wolverines' 47 to give

Tony Boles had 129 yards on 33 carries against Miami.

the Hurricanes one last shot at victory.

Walsh completed a 14-yard pass to Andre Brown, and Cleveland Gary bullied his way for 18 yards to put Miami in field-goal range. Gary caught nine passes for 162 yards, rushed for 44 yards and scored three touchdowns (two receiving).

The Hurricanes made it 30-28 with 2:58 left on a 48-yard pass from Walsh to Gary.

Walsh's two-point conversion pass was intercepted by David Arnold.

The teams had traded fourth-quarter touchdown passes earlier, and it was 30-22 with 5:23 remaining. Miami scored on a seven-yard pass from Walsh to tight end Rob Chudzinski of Toledo.

Walsh's two-point conversion pass to Dale Dawkins put the Hurricanes within range of a tie.

Little did they know.

Taylor had completed a 16-yard touchdown pass to Calloway to put U-M up, 30-14, with 10:32 left to play.

The Wolverines had several missed opportunities early in the first half, but scored twice within 33 seconds in the final minute for a 20-14 halftime lead.

Taylor returned after missing one play to throw a five-yard touchdown pass to tight end Jeff Brown with 57 seconds left. Demetrius Brown, who replaced Taylor for one play after Taylor was shaken up, handed off to Tony Boles (129 yards on 33 carries).

A time-out was called and Taylor returned. Boles executed a dive fake up the middle and Taylor faded right to find Brown open behind the coverage. However, the Wolverines quarterback was sacked by Greg Mark on the two-point conversion attempt.

Darryl Spencer fumbled the ensuring kickoff, which U-M's Rusty Fichtner recovered at the Miami 35 with 51 seconds left.

Taylor opened the drive with a 13-yard pass to Calloway. He found Kolesar open for an 18-yard touchdown pass on third and 6.

Kolesar ran his route up the middle and gained a step on Harden with a quick fake left.

He then cut right and sprinted to the corner of the end zone for a diving catch with 24 seconds left.

Chris Horn sprinted to the right to score on the two-point conversion. It was his fourth career carry for U-M and his first point contribution.

The Wolverines added to their lead with a 29-yard Mike Gillette field goal late in the third quarter.

U-M scored first on a 22-yard Gillette field goal. Gillette was wide on 47- and 34-yard attempts later in the first quarter, and the Hurricanes had a 7-3 lead entering the second period.

Gary's 49-yard touchdown on a short pass by Walsh was the Hurricanes' big break in the first half. As in breaking tackles, Gary caught the ball over his left shoulder and powered through defensive backs Anthony Mitchell and Arnold.

Both Wolverines had opportunities to stop the fullback short of a first down. But the 226-pounder powered past them and raced down the sideline for the score.

Gary vaulted in from one yard out to give Miami a 14-6 lead with 3:36 left in the half.

Wide receiver Doyle Aaron went 34 yards after taking the hike on a fake punt play on fourth and 5 to set up the score.

SCORE BY PERIODS

MICHIGAN 3	17	3	7	— 30
MIAMI 7	7	0	17	— 31

Leroy Hoard (33) added two of the Wolverines' touchdowns and earned the Rose Bowl's M.V.P.

A THUNDERING HOARD

BY STEVE KORNACKI
Special to The Detroit Free Press

PASADENA, Calif., Jan. 2, 1989 - The Rose Bowl is close enough to Hollywood, thought Leroy Hoard. Why not watch film of Butch Woolfolk's most valuable player performance in the 1981 Rose Bowl and do a remake?

So he did.

Hoard ran 19 times for 142 yards and the clinching touchdown against Southern Cal, sparking Michi-

gan's come-from-behind, 22-14 victory before 101,688 fans.

"I go to the film room back at Michigan and watch the 1981 Rose Bowl all the time," Hoard said. "It's an inspiration to me. It gave me something to dream of."

Monday the dream came true. Hoard, a redshirt sophomore from New Orleans, came close to Woolfolk's 182-yard effort and was awarded the m.v.p. cup.

"It meant a lot to me," Hoard said. "I want to

give a piece of the award to all the seniors, who got me through the hard times. But that's not possible. So I'm giving it to my mother."

Hoard surpassed 100 yards in four of the last five games he played this season, finishing with 752.

Michigan looked like a goner at halftime. The Wolverines trailed, 14-3, and showed few signs of the excitement to come. Coach Bo Schembechler walked to the locker room, fuming and wondering.

Not again. Not another loss in the Rose Bowl.

But the Wolverines were a changed team in the second half, scoring 19 points. It was a reversal of their last appearance here. U-M led Arizona State, 15-3 at halftime, only to lose, 22-15, in 1987.

"You're not playing like yourselves!" Schembechler shouted at his team at halftime.

"You're not playing like Michigan!"

Defensive tackle Brent White said, "That teed us off. It made us mad. We wanted to go out and play like Michigan, and we did."

Southern Cal was shut out in the second half. White sacked Rodney Peete and the defense broke him down. The Trojans ran for 107 yards in the first half, but managed just 31 yards on 16 carries in the second half.

"We finally played our gap-control defense," said defensive tackle Mark Messner. "We applied pressure to all the gaps and built our wall."

It was Schembechler's first Rose Bowl win against the Trojans, who accounted for three of his seven defeats here. This was Schembechler's second win in Pasadena, the first coming in 1981 against Washington.

The U-M victory, coupled with last year's Michigan State win over Southern Cal, gave the Big Ten its first back-to-back Rose Bowl victories since 1964 and 1965.

Schembechler was carried off the field on the shoulders of his players, both arms extended.

"It tears your heart out," he said. "And I don't have a very good one. I'm elated. That's the word I'm looking for."

Hoard was the second-half impetus, breaking 32- and 61-yard runs to become the first running back to rush for more than 100 yards against the Trojans this season.

Southern Cal was second in the nation in rushing defense this year, allowing 76.6 yards per game.

Hoard's shortest run, a one-yard touchdown with 1:52 left, meant the most. It came on fourth down, and put U-M in position to finish with no less than a tie.

"When the trap play was called for me," Hoard said, "I whispered to myself, 'You have to do it.' I got the handoff and made it to the corner of the end zone."

A shower of Rose Bowl seat cushions poured out of the stands at that point, delaying the game. Hoard picked one up and fired it off the field.

Hoard gained 128 yards rushing against Indiana, and had big games against Illinois (137 yards) and Ohio State (158) in the stretch drive. He was suspended after the Indiana game for skipping two classes, and did not play against Northwestern.

Mike Gillette's extra point supplied an eight-point lead. Peete drove U.S.C. to the U-M 27, but inside linebacker John Milligan's first career interception sealed the outcome.

"I'd never made a big play here before," said Milligan, a sophomore from Trenton. "I've always dreamed of it. I don't have to any more.

"Peete had been rolling right and throwing back to the other side. I expected it and he did it again. It was all mine. My first interception."

The Wolverines scored their first touchdown on a six-yard pass from Demtrius Brown to Chris Calloway in the third quarter. Brown was hit by outside linebacker Cordell Sweeney upon release, and Calloway beat single coverage by safety Mark Carrier with a diving catch.

Hoard's two-point conversion run was stopped, and Schembechler argued in vain that defensive tackle Tim Ryan was offsides on the play.

Hoard's first one-yard touchdown run put the Wolverines up, 15-14. But Brown's two-point conversion pass was incomplete.

Brown completed 11 of 24 passes for 144 yards and a touchdown. Peete, the Heisman Trophy runner-up, completed 15 of 21 for 158 yards and two interceptions.

Brown threw 84 passes this year without an interception. "I'd like to talk to Tracy Butts, their defen-

Wolverine quarterback Demetrius Brown (7) hit Chris Calloway for one touchdown in Michigan's second-half comeback rally.

sive back who said they'd pick off four," said Brown. "I understood the offense better and made better defensive reads this year. I guess he didn't know it."

Michigan's first-half offense moved as if it never got out of the traffic jams outside the Rose Bowl. The Wolverines rushed for 37 yards on 19 carries and passed for 85 yards before intermission. "I told them that if they cut out the mistakes, we would win," Schembechler said.

"But it was important to take that opening kickoff and go down and score, and we did."

The Wolverines also scored the first time they had the ball in the first half. A 49-yard Gillette field goal put them on the board quickly, but the offense sputtered after that.

Gillette's kick was the longest field goal for U-M in a bowl game. But his 34-yard attempt at the end of the half went wide right, keeping the Trojans ahead, 14-3. Gillette missed a 22-yarder in the third quarter, his first miss from 30 yards or less in 14 attempts this season.

Southern Cal didn't drive into U-M territory until the second quarter. That's when tailback Aaron Emanuel, benched by Trojan coach Larry Smith because of poor practice attitude, entered the game. He carried for 52 yards in the second quarter, taking the pressure off Rodney Peete. Emanuel finished with 55 yards.

With the U-M defense forced to respect Emanuel's inside and outside running ability, the Trojans quarterback had more room to maneuver.

Peete scored two touchdowns in the second quarter.

Emanuel lost a fumble at the Wolverines 16, but Tony Boles lost the ball on the next play, setting up U.S.C.'s first score. U-M free safety Tripp Welborne and Trojans linebacker Scott Ross made the key tackles on the turnovers.

Ross, who entered the game with a team-high 131 tackles, suffered an injury to his right leg later in the half and never returned.

Peete ran right on his one-yard score, receiving the key block from flanker John Jackson, who nailed cornerback David Key. Welborne, coming from behind and Arnold, approaching, couldn't catch him.

The next drive was a Peete highlight film. He eluded Messner to avoid a sack and later broke containment for a 23-yard run, his longest of the season. Milligan was no match for his 4.5-second speed over 40 yards and allowed Peete to break outside.

Peete scored a four-yard touchdown on third and 4 by freezing Wellborne at the line of scrimmage. Wellborne, respecting Peete's ability to turn the corner, was caught flat-footed as Peete cut inside for the score.

SCORE BY PERIODS

MICHIGAN	3	0	6	13	— 22
U.S.C.	0	14	0	0	— 14

Wolverine halfback Leroy Hoard (33) dives for paydirt against Ohio State. Hoard turned in a sizzling 152 yards on 21 carries in the 28-18 victory.

WOLVERINES WIN 2D STRAIGHT BIG TEN TITLE FOR BO

BY STEVE KORNACKI
Special to The Detroit Free Press

ANN ARBOR, Nov. 25, 1989 - It was outright joy for Michigan.

Coach Bo Schembechler got up on a chair in the locker room Saturday after the Wolverines beat Ohio State, 28-18, and shouted, "This is one of the great victories for Michigan!

"You made history and you should cherish it."

Everyone cheered. The history Schembechler cited was his first back-to-back outright Big Ten titles, and the first by any team since Michigan State in 1966.

The No. 3 Wolverines (10-1, 8-0 in the Big Ten) had their first perfect conference record since 1980, and will face No. 12 Southern Cal (8-2-1) on Jan. 1 in the Rose Bowl. They will attempt to become the first Big Ten team to win back-to-back Rose Bowls.

But U-M had more reasons for joy than team

Bo Schembechler's final appearance at Michigan Stadium wrapped up the Wolverines' 13th Big Ten title in 21 seasons.

accomplishments.

Schembechler said free safety Vada Murray, carried off the field late in the game after colliding with teammate Todd Plate, was fine and resting in University of Michigan Hospital.

Murray was knocked out but regained consciousness. Team trainer Russ Miller said there was no indication of a serious neck injury.

Cornerback Plate and tailback Leroy Hoard were understudies who found stars on their doors after the game. Hoard (152 yards rushing) started in place of Tony Boles, and Plate filled Lance Dottin's shoes. Both were out with injuries.

Plate made his first two career interceptions and broke up a touchdown pass. The former walk-on from Brooklyn (Mich.) Columbia Central was asked if he ever heard of Barry Pierson, the Wolverines cornerback who made three interceptions in the 1969 Ohio State game.

"No, I haven't," said Plate, who will join Pierson in the lore of this rivalry. "This hasn't set in yet and it's hard to put into words. Was it a case of in my wildest dreams? Yep."

Hoard gained more than 100 yards against Ohio State for the second straight year, getting 158 in 1988. Hoard limped off with a sprained left ankle after his 40-yard run early in the fourth quarter.

Most of the 106,137 fans in Michigan Stadium chanted, "Lee-roy! Lee-roy!"

Schembechler said the injury was minor and expected him at 100 percent for the Rose Bowl.

Hoard carried a rose out of the locker room. "I'm going to take it home and stick it up on the wall next to the one from last year," Hoard said. "It's a little rotten, but it's still up there."

Michigan also hung in there this year, winning 10 straight after opening with a loss to Notre Dame.

"We had a great attitude," Plate said. "We were optimistic because we felt we had the talent to come through." And the depth.

After Hoard put the Wolverines on the 4 and was injured, fullback Jarrod Bunch became the go-to back. Michael Taylor threw him a five-yard touchdown pass, making it 21-12.

Cornerback Vinnie Clark, who had Bunch in his grasp, pounded the ground. It was early in the fourth

Jarrod Bunch (32) replaced Leroy Hoard and scored one touchdown.

quarter, and Hall of Fame Bowl-bound Ohio State (8-3, 6-2 in the Big Ten) was again down by more than a touchdown.

U-M had four chances to score in the first half, but fumbled away two opportunities.

"We should have been up, 28-0," Wolverines offensive coordinator Gary Moeller said.

Schembechler was pleased with the running game (310 yards) but was disappointed in the passing (100 yards) and noted that Michael Taylor's arm might have been less than healthy. The three turnovers also drew his ire.

The two fumbles came deep in Buckeyes territory in the first half.

Hoard was hit in the air by cornerback David Brown; nose guard Pat Thomas recovered it at the O.S.U. 22. It was his fourth fumble of the year.

Taylor broke up the middle and fumbled after a hit by inside linebacker Derek Isaman. Brown fielded the bouncing ball at the O.S.U. 16.

The Wolverines did sustain two drives for a 14-0 lead.

Hoard scored in the first quarter on third and goal from the 1. He cut right and scored easily as wishbone backs Bunch and Allen Jefferson parted Buckeye defenders.

Jefferson then scooted left for a two-yard touchdown that capped a 13-play bulldozer drive. U-M didn't pass and Taylor picked up 10 yards on third and 3 to avert settling for a short field goal attempt.

That's all the Buckeyes could salvage from a sharp two-minute drill that featured Greg Frey completions for 19 and 23 yards and a 22-yard Scottie Graham run. O.S.U. had goal-to-go at the 4, but two Graham runs failed and Plate broke up a pass to Jeff Graham.

Plate said it was his favorite play of the day because it kept points off the board.

Pat O'Morrow's 20-yard field goal with 25 seconds left made it 14-3 at the half.

O'Morrow added a 22-yarder on the first drive of the second half, which came about after Clark intercepted Taylor at the O.S.U. 45.

Middle guard Mike Teeter batted down the third-and-four pass by Frey (14-25, 220 yards) and the Wolverines stopped the Buckeyes inside the 5 for the second time.

The Buckeyes finally cracked the end zone on Scottie Graham's three-yard run with 4:03 left in the third quarter. Graham gained 133 yards on 28 carries.

That made it 14-12, and Frey fumbled the exchange on the two-point conversion play, keeping the Wolverines ahead.

Bunch's touchdown gave U-M some padding it would need. Graham's four-yard touchdown with 7:04 left made it 21-18 and Tripp Welborne's block of O'Morrow's point-after was the Wolverines' second block. Murray, leaping high up the middle as did Welborne, blocked O'Morrow's 42-yard field goal attempt in the second quarter.

SCORE BY PERIODS

MICHIGAN..........7	7	0	14	—	28
OHIO STATE......0	3	9	6	—	18

CHAPTER 50

Bo Schembechler explains his strategy to Alan Mitchell on the sidelines.

Bo says good-bye

BY MITCH ALBOM
Special to The Detroit Free Press

ANN ARBOR, Nov. 13, 1989 - He began his legacy by driving down the wrong street, getting lost, and having to call the football office from a pay phone. "Uh, this is Bo Schembechler, the new coach," he said to a rather confused secretary. "Where the heck are you?"

Twenty-one years later, on a cold winter evening, he was saying good-bye. This time the room was stuffed with reporters, tight-lipped coaches, former players and a million memories.

This time, it was the University that felt lost.

"The hardest thing I've ever had to do," said Bo Schembechler, 60, choking back tears as he announced his retirement, "is give up my football team, but I'm doing it because I think I've run my luck about as far as I can take it."

There goes a legend. What will Michigan do without Bo? Who will win all those games?

Who will pace the sidelines on Saturday afternoons, who will scream at the referees, who will waddle through an army of apple-cheeked freshmen every August as they squat on the playing field. "GENTLEMEN, THIS IS MICHIGAN!" he would say. "AND AT MICHIGAN WE DO THINGS ONE WAY."

His way.

It was always his way. Oh, maybe not this retirement part. He had wanted to tell his team first, but when he woke up Wednesday, the story had leaked. That upset him. So did these questions about the athletic director position – a job he can't possibly keep, not if you know his personality.

Here walks the ultimate coach. On his first day of practice, 21 autumns ago, he sucked a mouthful of air and blew into a whistle – only to find the whistle was broken. So? He just screamed, "GATHER ROUND," and began a remarkable era of college football, one that would span countless big games and Big Ten titles and Rose Bowls and star players and never, never a losing season. Nor the hint of scandal. His way. Always his way. He beat Ohio State, he beat U.S.C., U.C.L.A., Notre Dame. He beat the Big Ten knotheads, he beat the doctors. He beat everything they could throw at him; he just couldn't beat himself. Finally, after a lifetime of pushing the outer envelope of his existence, he said, "All right, you win. I'll slow down. I will live."

"Something told me after the last Ohio State game I would not be back again," he said Wednesday. Truth is, he knew sooner than that. The thing that was telling him was his own voice.

And there is no mistaking that voice.

"This has been the greatest job I've ever had," he said. And he will miss it. Big time.

This, after all, is the last of the one-name coaches: Woody, Bear, Bo. You know how some men seem born for their occupations? Check out that walk, that frumpy coat, that crooked smile, those booming vocal cords. A football coach. "That's all I am," he would always say. As of Jan. 2 – after his final game, the Rose Bowl against U.S.C. – he will be one no more. Gary Moeller, his long-time assistant, will take over. Bo's Wolverine days, at least the active ones, will be finished.

Oh sure, he said he "might stay on" as athletic director, the position he has held the last year. I don't buy it. Not for a second. He will be gone when the

football is over. Let's face it.

Bo is never one for office work. He was never one for watching. I once sat next to him in the stands, and he nearly punched a hole in my arm. And that was basketball!

No, a football coach should coach football, not play executive. Bo never really liked the role of athletic director, he really took it on because of university pressure and his desire to keep the football team away from any evil new bosses. Once he hands over the whistle on Jan. 2, he will find a new challenge, something closer to home, something with fewer airplanes, something in sports. I promise you this: He will not go gentle into that good night.

He never has.

This, after all, is a man who once destroyed an office when the Big Ten sent Ohio State to the Rose Bowl instead of Michigan. A man who got so mad once at halftime, he kicked an entire tray of Coca-Colas into the air. A man who stood in the middle of practice and got blind-sided by a speeding receiver, knocking him down, making his entire body throb with pain. You know what he did? He looked up, saw his team gathered in a circle, and rose to his feet. "That," he said, dusting himself off, "would have *killed* a mortal man."

That's Bo. Ask any of his former players to tell you a story and they will inevitably launch into an impersonation, some bark, some holler, some magic words that have stayed with them years after Schembechler has forgotten them.

Think of what he has done. When he first arrived, the program was merely average, in the shadow of national champion Ohio State and his one-time mentor Woody Hayes.

"GENTLEMEN," Bo said to his skeptical players, "THOSE WHO STAY WILL BE CHAMPIONS!" That November, his Wolverines shocked the nation by upsetting Ohio State in the biggest game to be played here this century.

He kept his word.

When he first arrived the coaches' "locker room" was five hooks on the wall.

"GENTLEMEN," he told his staff, "THERE WILL BE SOME CHANGES AROUND HERE!"

Today, they are building the new Center of Cham-

Bo and President Gerald Ford, a Michigan football player from 1932-34, visit during a Wolverine practice.

pions, a state-of-the-art athletic facility that costs $12 million. Bo raised every penny from contributors and threw in a healthy chunk of his own money to boot.

He kept his word.

Throughout his time here, there were scandals across the nation, other coaches were buying players, changing grades, handing out sports cars, cheating. "GENTLEMEN," he announced. "WE WILL RUN A CLEAN PROGRAM!" They never wavered. Once, in his first year at Michigan, an overzealous booster called to complain about the use of a player. Bo ignored him.

"You don't understand," said the man. "I'm a very influential member of the M Club."

"Not anymore, you're not," said Bo. He kept his word.

So it should be no surprise that he is keeping his

word now. He promised himself and his wife, Millie, who had stood there that morning two years ago as the doctors gooped his chest and prepared to slice him open, that he would not push things beyond human limits. On Wednesday, Millie stood in the corner of the crowded press conference, her lips tightly clenched.

"Did you cry?" someone asked her.

"All day," she confessed.

She met him on a blind date in St. Louis, back when nobody knew his name. Bo who?

How do you spell that? They went for a ride in a Missouri riverboat. He played with her children. He seemed so happy. Three months later they were married.

And by the following winter, their lives had changed forever. He was suddenly coach of the Michigan Wolverines. Who knew what fame that

Always a great teacher, Bo makes sure his players understand what is expected of them if the Wolverines are to win.

would bring? Who could foresee the success – all those Big Ten titles, the coach-of-the-year awards, the banquets, the speeches.

Who might predict that students would one day chant, "Bo is God!"

Nobody. So in the margins around football, Bo and Millie tried to build a normal life. It hasn't really been normal. "You work 14 or 15 hours a day, you get to bed late, you get up early, you eat on the run, you don't have time to exercise," said Schembechler, listing the perils of coaching. After awhile you say, "It's time to stop."

The time has come.

Health concerns him now, he admits it. Oh, once upon a time, he laughed at it. He suffered a heart attack the morning of his first Rose Bowl, and as they pushed him down on the operating table he said, "Hey doc, I've got a game to coach today."

Now, health is not so funny. Despite an image to the contrary, Schembechler does not wish to be buried on the sidelines. There were moments this season when the travel left him exhausted. Another airplane. Another bus. Another press conference. Last month, when someone tried to coerce him into yet another commitment, he exploded. "I can't! I can't do it!" he yelled. "I don't want to die, OK."

His doctors told him he was pushing his luck. Two heart attacks? Two open-heart surgeries? Sixty years old? Yeah. You could call that pushing your luck.

But let this be known: What he did Wednesday was not because of some X-ray or medical chart. It was not because a collapse was imminent. On the contrary. He wants to walk away while he still can.

"I'm not sick, make sure you write that," he admonished one reporter.

OK. He's not sick.

But he is gone. This is for real. And the feeling is like losing an old friend, a favorite teacher, and, for the players – a father figure. True to form, he announced his retirement now rather than go recruiting when he knew he wouldn't coach the kids he attracted.

"That wouldn't be right," he said. And that was reason enough to say good-bye.

That man who will replace him, Moeller, his offensive coordinator, is his hand-chosen successor. Moeller not only thinks like Bo, reacts like Bo, and has a rhyming nickname (Bo, Mo), but he was in that car 21 years ago when Schembechler took the wrong turn and wound up cruising Ann Arbor like a general in search of his army.

"Yep, a green Toronado," Moeller said Wednesday. "I can still remember that car."

Good. Tradition should count for something.

It has counted for 21 years. We were lucky to have Schembechler all this time. So were his players. So were his coaches. So were the mothers and fathers whose living rooms he graced, from mansions in California to a rundown tenement in Detroit, where Bo once visited a promising player and found his mother huddled around a fire rock that was the only heat in the house.

"We've got to do something about that," he told his assistant when they left. "And we've got to get that kid into Michigan."

He came. He graduated. He is on his way to becoming a teacher.

You want to know the true Schembechler legacy? That's it right there. Kids you won't see in the N.F.L., but who have their degree and a nice job and a family, thanks largely to the stumpy, grinning tough guy who wore the blue cap and the black shoes.

There goes a legend.

"Would you like to be a sportswriter next?" someone jokingly asked. Schembechler laughed. "No, because I'd be too much of a homer. I'd always come down in favor of the coach."

You know what, Bo? That hasn't been so hard to do. As Moeller spoke of the future and reporters scribbled away, someone saddled up to Schembechler and asked if he would be available the next morning.

"Hey man," said Bo. "I got some film to look at. I got one more game to coach here, you know."

And with that, he left his farewell party. What becomes a legend most? In this case, just being himself. Really, now. What more could you want?

CHAPTER 51

Desmond Howard makes one of the greatest catches in Michigan football history.

WOLVERINES ROLL IN CLOVER

BY DAVE DYE
Special to The Detroit News

ANN ARBOR, Sept. 14, 1991 - Instead of waiting for the luck of the Irish to strike again, Michigan coach Gary Moeller decided to put fate in his own hands.

Better yet, he put it in the hands of Desmond Howard.

A bold fourth-down call in the fourth quarter Saturday helped the Wolverines end a four-game losing streak to Notre Dame. U-M led, 17-14, and was faced with a fourth and 1 from the Irish 25-yard line.

Quarterback Elvis Grbac took a short drop and lofted a pass deep into the end zone.

Howard, despite being double-covered, made a spectacular diving catch for a touchdown with 9:02 remaining.

The third-ranked Wolverines, who had nearly blown a 17-0 lead, finished off a 24-14 victory before 106,138 at Michigan Stadium.

"God was on our side this time," said Grbac, who completed 20-of-22 for 195 yards with no interceptions.

It was Howard's second touchdown of the day, and his sixth in two games. He also scored on a 29-yard reverse in the second quarter. Ricky Powers, who had 164 yards on 38 carries, added a 16-yard

Gary Moeller, the heir to the Wolverine legacy, chats with Irish coach Lou Holtz before the 1991 Michigan-Notre Dame game.

touchdown run late in the first half.

"I guess I'm popular with a lot of people right now," Moeller said when asked about ending the Notre Dame losing streak. "You know it's not a jinx. But you still say to yourself, 'Is it there or isn't it?'

"I don't think our kids thought that they couldn't beat Notre Dame, but you have to break that thing."

But it wasn't broken until the gutsy fourth-down call.

"I can hear him now," Moeller said of his predecessor, Bo Schembechler. "He was probably saying, You crazy son-of-a-gun. What are you doing?'

"It takes a guy like Elvis to put it out there and a guy like Desmond to run under it to make the coach look good."

Moeller said he was willing to take the gamble because he had confidence U-M's defense could hold the Irish in case the pass failed.

The defense did just that after the touchdown. Three consecutive incomplete passes near midfield

forced Notre Dame to punt with 6:30 remaining. The Wolverines kept the ball on the ground and ran out the clock.

Linebacker Erick Anderson, a fifth-year senior, led the Wolverines with nine tackles. He also made a touchdown-saving tackle on a reception by tight end Derek Brown in the second quarter. Two plays later, he recovered a fumble deep in Michigan territory.

"I've never felt so good since I've been here," Anderson said. "It's a big relief to know I'm not going to leave this place without beating Notre Dame. That would have been hard to take."

The seventh-ranked Irish (1-1) scored on their final drive of the first half and first drive of the second half to cut Michigan's lead to 17-14.

The Wolverines (2-0) got the ball first in the second half, but they got conservative on third and 3 from Notre Dame's 36 and Powers was stopped for a 1-yard loss.

Elvis Grbac's offense was finely tuned to give the Wolverines a wonderful offensive fireworks show against the Irish.

Notre Dame scored on Rick Mirer's 35-yard pass to Tony Smith as Smith beat cornerback Lance Dottin down the left sideline to make it a three-point spread.

The Wolverines had dominated most of the first half, but Notre Dame came to life with a clutch drive that was capped by Mirer's 3-yard touchdown pass to fullback Jerome Bettis with 17 seconds left in the half.

The Irish had a lot of problems early, though. On the second play, Mirer had no pressure on him in the pocket, but he threw a terrible pass that was intercepted by Dottin. Michigan started at the Notre Dame 42, but settled for J.D. Carlson's 23-yard field goal and a 3-0 lead.

"The turnover on the second play got Michigan's crowd into it and put us in a bad situation," Notre Dame coach Lou Holtz said. "Michigan played about as perfect a game as they can play. We had every reason to go in the tank (after trailing, 17-0) and we didn't. I thought we really hung in there."

The Wolverines took control with two impressive second-quarter touchdown drives.

The first one was a 82-yard drive in 11 plays. U-M mixed it up well on this series. On the touchdown, Powers ran left and gave the ball to Howard, who came back to the right side.

Howard made a fake on cornerback Rod Smith at the 25-yard line and then used tackle Rob Doherty's block to cruise into the end zone.

Michigan later moved 80 yards in 14 plays to go ahead, 17-0, on Powers' touchdown.

Grbac continued to make all the right reads, completing three third-down passes on the drive.

SCORE BY PERIODS

MICHIGAN	3	14	0	7 —	24
NOTRE DAME	0	7	7	0 —	14

Bernie Legette leaps for a 1-yard touchdown. The Wolverines would score early and often in their 31-3 rout of Ohio State.

WOLVERINES TAKE FOURTH STRAIGHT FROM COOPER & CO.

BY DAVE DYE
Special to The Detroit News

ANN ARBOR, Nov. 23, 1991 - With a trip to Pasadena, Calif., already secure, Michigan put the final touches on an outright Big Ten championship Saturday with a 31-3 victory over Ohio State before 106,156 at Michigan Stadium.

"We worked so hard, why share it with Iowa?" linebacker Brian Townsend said of Michigan's 36th

Big Ten title and 14th outright. "We beat Iowa (43-24 in the Big Ten opener). We felt they didn't deserve to share it."

Desmond Howard scored his 23d touchdown, on a 93-yard punt return that gave Michigan a 24-3 halftime lead. Howard also had three receptions for 96 yards, but he was shut out on a TD catch for the first time all season.

Burnie Legette, Jesse Johnson and Tyrone Wheatley also scored touchdowns for U-M, which now will play the Washington Huskies in the Rose Bowl on New Year's Day.

"I would think it would be frustrating to lose four years to Michigan," Ohio State coach John Cooper said.

Cooper should know. The Buckeyes are 0-4 against U-M since hiring Cooper, who was given a three-year contract extension through 1995 before the game.

The 28-point victory was the biggest for Michigan against Ohio State since a 58-6 final in 1946.

The fourth-ranked Wolverines (10-1 overall, 8-0 in the Big Ten) have allowed only 23 points in the last five games, including shutouts against Purdue and Illinois.

"Defensively, you couldn't ask for anyone to play as well as we have the last couple of weeks," linebacker Erick Anderson said. "To hold Illinois and Ohio State to that many points, not too many teams can say that."

The Buckeyes had the edge in time of possession (33 minutes, 54 seconds to 26:06) and ran 25 more offensive plays than U-M, but they made some costly turnovers that kept the game from being lost. An interception and a fumble deep in Ohio State territory led to 10 points by Michigan in the second quarter.

The Buckeyes' best opportunity was wasted when Carlos Snow fumbled on a first-and-goal play at the Michigan 1-yard line in the fourth quarter.

"We got a couple breaks early and, as I've told you before, I coach that man (Howard) to run those punts back like that," Michigan coach Gary Moeller said, laughing.

"I guess if you're 10-1, you've got to be happy, and I'm happy. I've got as fine a group of kids any could ever want to coach. They all work hard, and that's why we've had a good season. I feel honored I'm the coach at Michigan."

The Wolverines moved 76 yards on the game's

Elvis Grbac & Co. celebrate in the end zone.

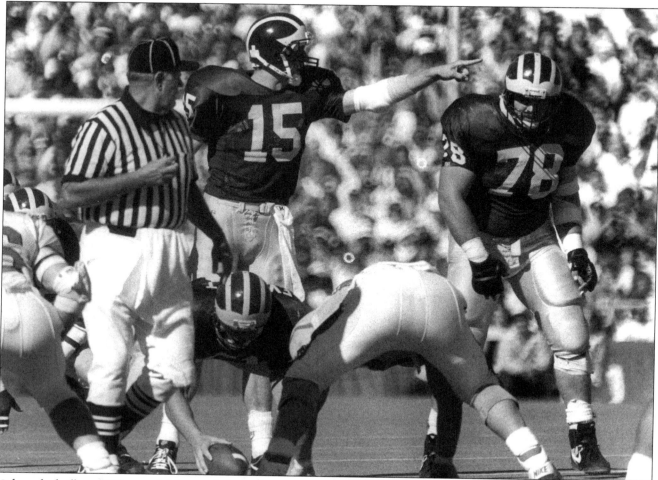

Grbac, the brilliant Wolverine field general, directs his offense.

first possession to take the lead on fullback Legette's 1-yard dive. The Wolverines had lined up for a field-goal attempt on fourth and 2 from the 3. But they faked it with holder Ken Sollom, also the third-string quarterback, making a shovel pass to fullback Greg McThomas for a 2-yard gain.

The Ohio State players started to celebrate when they saw McThomas was tackled short of the end zone, but they were quickly disappointed to find out it was first and goal.

Tim Williams' 50-yard field goal cut the lead to 7-3 early in the second quarter but the Michigan defense forced turnovers on consecutive plays to help break the game open.

Lance Dottin intercepted Kent Graham's over-thrown pass and returned it 18 yards to the O.S.U. 12 to set up Johnson's 1-yard TD run.

On Ohio State's next play, Snow fumbled with strong safety Otis Williams making the recovery at the Buckeyes' 21. J.D. Carlson kicked a 37-yard field goal for a 17-3 lead.

Howard had been relatively quiet to this point. That wasn't likely going to last, and it didn't.

His big play, with 4:15 left in the half, was the longest punt return for a TD in Michigan history, surpassing Dave Brown's 88-yarder against Colorado in 1974. Howard stepped around an attempted tackle by Brent Johnson after catching the punt at the 7-yard line. He got a block upfield from Dwayne Ware to break loose down the left sideline, and celebrated in the end zone in front of a section of Ohio State fans by breaking into a Heisman Trophy-like pose.

SCORE BY PERIODS

MICHIGAN..........	7	17	7	0	— 31
OHIO STATE......	0	3	0	0	— 3

Hail to Howard

BY JOE FALLS
Special to The Detroit News

Anthony Carter or Desmond Howard?

Is it OK if I change my mind?

Until this season, I never saw a college football player quite like Anthony Carter, No. 1.

He was a water bug who never stopped skipping across the pond. Skip, skip, skip, swoosh!

Nobody could touch him. Nobody could catch him. He had a tough hide, too. You could knock him down, flatten him; but he always got up.

Amazing for one with such skinny legs.

But now, as this 1991 season ends with the Wolverines scoring a solid 31-3 victory over Ohio State, I must change my opinion. The greatest Michigan player I have ever seen is No. 21, Desmond Howard.

Both Carter and Howard were spectacular – almost breathtaking beyond belief. But the choice has to be Howard because not only has he done it brilliantly, he also has done it more consistently.

Not once did he let us down this season. Not once did he fail to make the big plays, even when the scoreboard was against the Wolverines. Not once did he fail to thrill us, as he did one final time Saturday in the gloom of the big stadium.

Punt return: 93 yards.

Catch: 50 yards.

Catch: 42 yards.

This is almost unbelievable because we all wait for it to happen and it happens. He comes through for us.

Carter was a tremendous performer but the edge – and it is only a slight edge – goes to Howard because he could do so many things. He could catch the ball, return kickoffs, return punts and run the reverse like few players in history of the game.

I saw Tom Harmon only as a newsreel runner in the theaters, though he seemed to be on the screen every Saturday. He also made it in Life magazine, which was big in those days.

He was the best until I saw Ron Kramer play

Desmond Howard strikes a Heisman pose after a touchdown against Ohio State.

tight end for the Wolverines – a two-way player in the 1950's – and I put him at the head of the list.

Now it must be: 1-Howard, 2-Carter, 3-Kramer, 4-Harmon.

As this game unfolded, I thought about the most skilled players at Michigan and came up with Elvis Grbac or Harry Newman at quarterback, Harmon and Jamie Morris as the runners, Howard and Carter as the wide receivers and the hulking Kramer at tight end.

Howard, though, is the eye-popper of all of them and if I owned a TV station, I would rack up his 23 touchdowns and show them from now until New Year's Day, no comments needed, no comments necessary.

This season the young man was what every kid who ever touched a football in his back yard dreamed about. Remember? Wasn't every play a touchdown, a blazing run across the field, leaving tacklers in your wake, pulling away to the roar of the crowd.

That's what he gave us, and I personally thank him and if the Heisman people are smart, they can save themselves some stamp money by calling off the vote and declaring him the winner by acclamation.

Let me ask you this: If you have a ballot, who are you going to vote for? Also know this:

Howard won't get all the votes because that's how it goes in any free election. You always have to factor in the matter of prejudice. Some Southwest voters will vote for Southwest players and so on around the country, and what the officials should do is make all the ballots public.

As for the game with the Buckeyes, it wasn't much of a game. The Wolverines were sluggish on offense but got some breaks and were never in any trouble. The defense, meanwhile, was a swarm, and this was one of the best signs of the season.

It showed the defense was improving, but even more important, it showed the old bend-but-don't-break philosophy of the Bo Schembechler days may be on the way out. Nothing wrong with Bo's ways but he never won the national title with them, and the fact is you have to gamble a little on defense just as on offense to reach the top in this modern-day game in which so many of the teams are equal.

I gave up my Heisman ballot years ago because I refused to be part of a system that honored only offensive players, and, generally, only one position, but here is a write-in vote for Desmond Howard.

A familiar sight: Desmond Howard stretching to gather in a touchdown pass.

CHAPTER 53

Howard, with his Heisman award, poses for the press after winning the 57th Heisman Memorial Trophy at The Downtown Athletic Club in New York City.

Howard wraps up Heisman Trophy

BY MALCOLM MORAN
Special to The New York Times

NEW YORK, Dec. 14, 1991 - Back in mid-September, when the leaves were still green and Desmond Howard's football season at the University of Michigan was just one game and four touchdowns old, he sat in a restaurant in Ann Arbor, Mich., and listened to a question that seemed as much of a courtesy as anything else.

What do you think of your chances of winning the Heisman Trophy?

Howard's response seemed more genuine than political. He felt his chances were slim and none. Anthony Carter, Michigan's record-setting receiver from 1979-82, had never come close.

How could Howard expect anything more?

This is how Howard made it his, a week at a

Desmond Howard's stunning performance against Notre Dame made him the leading Heisman candidate during the 1991 season.

time, hanging on to footballs by his fingertips, often while parallel to the ground. By early yesterday evening, Howard's grip was firm and everlasting. He was named the 57th Heisman Award winner by a margin of 1,574 points – the second largest in the history of the award – over Casey Weldon of Florida State.

But there were fewer electors than voted for O.J. Simpson of Southern California over Purdue's Leroy Keyes in 1968. Howard won 85 percent of the first-place votes, 3 percent more than Simpson.

Howard, a 5-foot-9-inch, 174-pound junior who is scheduled to graduate in May, has one remaining year of eligibility because he did not play as a freshman. When asked about a reported offer to play in the Canadian Football league, Howard said he intended to return to Michigan as a graduate student for a final season.

"As of now, my thought process is to get a degree at Michigan, beat Washington in the Rose Bowl, and at least start on my Ph.D. in social work."

Howard became Michigan's first Heisman winner since Tom Harmon, Old 98, won the award 51 years ago. He was the 11th winner from the Big Ten Conference, and the first since Archie Griffin of Ohio State won his second consecutive trophy in 1975. Howard and Notre Dame's Tim Brown, the 1987 winner, are the only wide receivers to win.

He is the 11th junior to win and the fourth in as many years, following Barry Sanders of Oklahoma State, Andre Ware of Houston and Ty Detmer of Brigham Young. Detmer, who was brought to The Downtown Athletic Club, finished third, with 445 points. Weldon and defensive tackle Steve Emtman of Washington, who finished fourth, were also at the ceremony.

And the nationally televised presentation became the culmination of a process that began when Howard entered St. Joseph High School on the outer edges of Cleveland. "He looked like a sixth grader," said Bill Gutbrod, Howard's coach there.

Howard was a high school sophomore when he began at St. Joseph, making a three-bus trip that would last at least an hour each way. He was a running back and a defensive back, used within the offense much the way Raghib Ismail would later be used at Notre Dame.

"We didn't throw to him that much," Gutbrod said, "Because every time we put him out in a slot as a wide receiver, half the team would go with him."

So Howard spent most of his time lining up as a tailback, behind Elvis Grbac, who would become his quarterback at Michigan. At St. Joseph, the two combined for one touchdown pass; Howard had more interceptions (10) than receptions (7) in his senior season.

But at Michigan, with Howard a wide receiver, the two combined for 19 touchdown passes this season and 31 over the past three seasons, N.C.A.A. records for the same passer and receiver. Howard caught 61 passes for 950 yards. His 23 touchdowns included two rushes, one punt return and a kickoff return.

The Heisman questions grew more serious after Howard's fourth-quarter, fourth-down, 25-yard catch against Notre Dame. His team's lead down to 3 points, with 9 minutes 2 seconds to play and the Irish threatening to come from behind for a fifth consecutive victory over Michigan, Howard and Grbac produced their best-remembered touchdown catch.

Less than two hours before his time would come in the Heisman Room, as invited guests were sipping cocktails elsewhere in the club, Howard found a television that was tuned to the Duke-Michigan basketball game.

At halftime of the basketball game, when the Heisman Award was being discussed, the young face on the screen was talking about how he came up with The Pose, his memorable imitation of the trophy after he scored a touchdown against Ohio State.

Howard's statement began a celebration. Just as Tom Harmon's performance against the Buckeyes had helped secure a Heisman – and earned a rare standing ovation for a Michigan man in Columbus – Howard eliminated any doubt.

After he weaved through the Buckeyes for a 93-yard punt return touchdown, the longest in school history, Howard made his smiling statement in the end zone, imitating the 13-inch high bronze trophy.

CHAPTER 54

THIS TY'S A KEEPER

BY STEVE KORNACKI
Special to The Detroit Free Press

PASADENA, Calif., Jan. 1, 1993 - Michigan found itself going to the well without its bucket. Tailback Tyrone Wheatley had rushed for 235 yards and three touchdowns, but was sidelined with lower-back spasms in the fourth quarter.

Leading receiver Derrick Alexander also was out with a pulled left hamstring with the game tied, 31-31, entering the final quarter.

The Wolverines' 38-31 victory over Washington seemed improbable at that point. They were the Lakers without Magic and Kareem, right?

But U-M leaned on the passing combination of Elvis Grbac to Tony McGee. And the defense posted a fourth-quarter shutout, finally harnessing quarterback Mark Brunell.

"What meant the most," Wolverines strong safety Corwin (Flakes) Brown said, "was that nobody thought we could win in the fourth quarter. Now people can judge us as a great team. We never lost a game."

The No. 7 Wolverines finished 9-0-3, going undefeated for the first time since the 1973 team was 10-0-1.

McGee caught the winning, 12-yard touchdown pass from Grbac with 5:29 to play. The defense

braced for two more Huskies charges into its territory before the victors finally sang "The Victors" before what was left of 94,236 fans at the Rose Bowl.

"I kept asking the team, 'What did we come here for?' " coach Gary Moeller said.

"What did we come here for? To sing 'The Victors' in Pasadena, and we did it."

When the final gun sounded Moeller had his first Rose Bowl victory and a Gatorade shower, and the Wolverines were the celebrants.

Center Steve Everitt thrust his arms high. Last year, he played only briefly in a 34-14 loss because of a sprained left knee and ankle.

"That moment when I lifted my arms," Everitt said, "was 365 days of hell being let go. I knew I would never have to think about last year again."

The Wolverines rolled to 483 yards, an average of 7.3 per play. The line had spent extra hours running through plays with assistants Les Miles and Mike DeBord. They did so wearing street clothes in the Huntington Beach parking lot across from the team hotel.

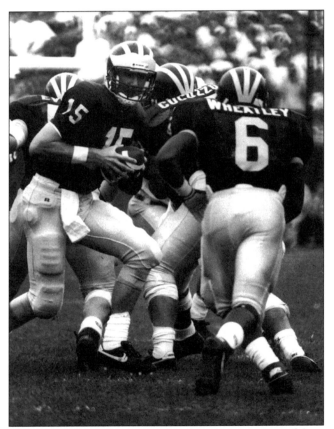

Elvis Grbac (15) and Tyrone Wheatley (6) were a powerful combination in 1992.

"The extra work helped," Miles said. "These guys were grinding their teeth for this game."

Grbac completed 17 of 30 passes for 175 yards, two touchdowns and no interceptions.

"This goes to show I can play in a big game,"

Michigan sophomore tailback Tyrone Wheatley was named the Rose Bowl's M.V.P. after remarkable touchdown runs of 56, 88 and 24 yards.

Grbac said after the contest.

He glowed.

It was U-M's first Rose Bowl win since 1989, and gave the fifth-year seniors a 2-2 record in the game.

Heroes abounded.

McGee caught six passes for 117 yards and two touchdowns, including a 49-yarder that caught linebackers and safeties cheating on a play-action fake.

"We won with versatility," McGee said. "Last year, 40 percent of our offense was Desmond Howard, and they shut us down. Now, a lot of us can score. I looked up as the final seconds disappeared and said, 'Thank God!' "

And then he cleared his throat.

The entire team sang "The Victors" with the U-M Band, and then the fifth-year seniors led the team in another locker-room chorus. Most of them broke down in tears.

But without the defense, the Maize and Blue might have been singing the blues again. It's normally hard to hand a hero's hat to a defense that allowed 31 points. But three key stops in the fourth quarter assured that Brunell would not pull out a high-scoring Rose Bowl as he had two years ago against Iowa, winning, 46-34.

Before McGee's score, the Wolverines faced first and goal at the 5. Strong safety Shonte Peoples made all three tackles, and Travis Hanson missed a 22-yard field goal attempt.

"I was focused and was not going to make a mistake," Peoples said. "I wasn't giving them an inch."

After McGee scored on a leaping catch and dive into the end zone, Washington drove to the Michigan 25.

But middle guard Tony Henderson dropped Brunell for a one-yard loss and Brunell threw two incompletions. Brunell's nine-yard scramble was two yards short on fourth down.

"We decided to make him scramble inside and not let him get outside," defensive tackle Chris Hutchinson said. "He wasn't comfortable in the pocket."

The reverse psychology worked.

But David Kilpatrick blocked Chris Stapleton's punt minutes later, and the Huskies had only 44 yards to cover in 1:03. However, four incomplete passes represented the final air blowing out of the Washington balloon. Its comeback hopes had gone flat.

The biggest knock on the Rose Bowl was that it had no national ramifications. But it might have had a huge effect on the 1993 Heisman Trophy race.

Wheatley took his place among the front-runners for the nation's top individual award by breaking away for TD runs of 56, 88 and 24 yards.

The game became a battle of one-upmanship between him and Brunell. Brunell completed 18 of 30 passes for 308 yards and two touchdowns.

Brunell achieved three Rose Bowl career passing records. He finished with 38 completions, 61 passes, 560 yards and five TD's in the last three Rose Bowls.

That broke the 452-yard standard set by Michigan's Rick Leach, 1977-79. It equaled the five touchdown passes by Southern Cal's Jim Hardy, 1944-45. The completions were one more than the record set by Southern Cal's Rodney Peete, 1988-89.

But the only statistics that counted were on the scoreboard, and for once Michigan wasn't left shaking its head at those numbers.

SCORE BY PERIODS

MICHIGAN	10	7	14	7 —	38
WASHINGTON	7	14	10	0 —	31

CHAPTER 55

Tyrone Wheatley (6) scampers for big yardage against the Buckeyes.

A BLACK EYE FOR THE BUCKEYES

By ANGELIQUE S. CHENGELIS
Special to The Detroit News

ANN ARBOR, Nov. 20, 1993 - Michigan's players and coaches will tell you they were not surprised by the lopsided victory. They will also tell you this was the Michigan team that could have made similar appearances each week.

When it counted most, with their integrity and a bowl bid on the line, the unranked Wolverines gave a soldout performance that was deserving of several curtain calls. In by far their best showing of the season, they upset No. 5 Ohio State, 28-0, before 106,867 at Michigan Stadium on Saturday.

With the victory, the Wolverines appear destined for a warm-weather bowl, most likely the Hall of Fame on New Year's Day in Tampa.

"We played like we should have all year," said Michigan coach Gary Moeller, who was carried off the field by his players. "Emotionally, we were at a higher pitch. We just set sail today."

The Wolverines sailed off with three straight victories to close out the regular season 7-4 overall and 5-3 in the Big Ten. Ohio State maintains its Big Ten lead with a 6-1-1 record, 9-1-1 overall, but must await Wisconsin's final game against Michigan State in Tokyo on Dec. 5 to find out if the Buckeyes are headed to the Rose Bowl.

"This is one of the most embarrassing games I've ever been associated with since I've been in college football," said O.S.U. coach John Cooper, who is 0-5-1 against the Wolverines.

"They made all the plays. They blitzed us. Our pass protection wasn't very good. I know one thing, it's certainly frustrating not being able to beat them – about as frustrating as it gets."

Nothing could have been more indicative of O.S.U.'s frustration than the fourth quarter, when the Buckeyes managed only four plays, including a punt.

Of course their inability to rush was perhaps even more frustrating. Ohio State, which had averaged nearly 200 yards rushing all season, gained only 58 yards on 28 carries.

And the Buckeyes' four interceptions, two fumbles and four sacks allowed were hardly as inspirational as the victory was for U-M.

"This win set us up spiritually wise," said senior cornerback Alfie Burch, who had four tackles. "It

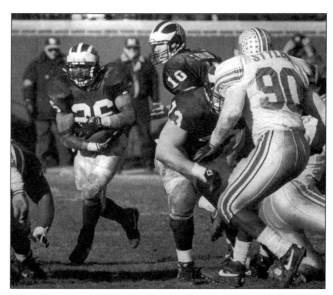

Ed Davis (26) spots an opening in the Ohio State defense and heads upfield. Davis would later score a 5-yard touchdown in Michigan's 28-0 shutout of the Buckeyes.

makes us feel better."

Michigan's defense set the tone, and its offense took it from there from the onset, as the Wolverines carried a 21-0 lead at halftime.

Bolstered by junior tailback Tyrone Wheatley's 105 yards, U-M finished with 281 yards rushing on 56 carries. Sophomore Ed Davis had 96 yards, and a 5-yard touchdown run in the third quarter. Todd Collins completed 14 or 20 pass attempts for 150 yards, including two touchdowns.

On their second possession of the game, the Wolverines proved their big-play potential.

Wheatley set up the scoring drive with a 43-yard run to the O.S.U. 30. Three plays later, Mercury Hayes reached over O.S.U.'s Walter Taylor to grab a 25-yard touchdown pass in the end zone.

"I looked out there and saw man coverage," Collins said. "Their guy was playing Mercury inside, and as I threw, I was getting hit. I knew if I could get the ball up there, he would catch it."

With the ball in the air and appearing a bit miscalculated, Moeller was ready to lose his headset until he saw the outcome.

"That was unbelievable," said Moeller, who is 3-0-1 against the Buckeyes. "I almost hit my clipboard, because I knew the ball was too far up inside him."

Michigan's big plays also came defensively through the first half, as the Wolverines pressured constantly. O.S.U. starting quarterback Bobby Hoying was sacked twice and intercepted once, and the Buckeyes' other QB, Bret Powers, was intercepted three times, all in the first half.

"I think we were too confident playing Michigan," Cooper said. "They got the turnovers early in the game. That was the difference; no question about it."

There was no question that the Buckeyes were deflated even more during their first possession of the second half. Unable to drive out of their territory, O.S.U. was forced to punt on fourth down, but punter Tim Williams took a low snap, his knee touched the ground and was credited with a 15-yard loss.

"We got out of sync," Cooper said. "Once we got down 21-0 at halftime, we thought we'd come out and make a run in the second half and make a cou-

Michigan quarterback Todd Collins (10) audibles a play at the line of scrimmage.

ple plays, and the next thing you know, we get a bad snap."

Michigan scored on the following drive, which included a 50-yard completion from Collins to Derrick Alexander with a 1-yard run by Jon Ritchie to go ahead, 14-0.

It couldn't have gotten any worse for O.S.U., which gained only 11 yards rushing in the second half. In their final three possessions, they punted twice and had a fourth-down conversion attempt broken up by Ty Law. And premier receiver Joey Galloway, with 880 receiving yards heading into the game, was held to only three catches for 47 yards.

"We had a great game plan," said Law, who had two interceptions and four in the last two games. "We were good up front, and we knew we could hold the receivers once we contained the run.

"I had a pretty good read on the receivers because I watched a lot of film. I pretty much knew what route they were coming to. I just read the ball."

It seemed U-M knew what O.S.U. was going to do all day.

"I had a good feeling about this game," fifth-year senior center Marc Milia said.

"Everything was going in our favor and Ohio State was starting to falter a little bit. When you have a situation where one team is on its rise and the other team is either plateauing or a little bit on a fall, the favor is going to be in our corner.

"We were playing at home, and we had a lot more to prove than they did. They had already secured the Big Ten championship and I think that maybe they didn't expect as good a team to show up as we were."

SCORE BY PERIODS

MICHIGAN........	7	14	7	0	— 28
OHIO STATE.....	0	0	0	0	— 0

Mercury Hayes made the game-winning catch against Virginia with no time left on the clock.

HAIL HAYES!

BY ANGELIQUE S. CHENGELIS
Special to The Detroit News

ANN ARBOR, AUG. 26, 1995 - Call it a classic, because Scott Dreisbach and the Michigan Wolverines made it one never to forget.

With the Wolverines trailing, 17-0, and just less than 13 minutes remaining, Dreisbach, a redshirt freshman making his first start at quarterback, orchestrated three scoring drives Saturday to pull off an 18-17 victory over Virginia in the Pigskin Classic before 101,444 at Michigan Stadium.

Dreisbach, who was booed early in the game after the 14th-ranked Wolverines failed to score through three quarters, looked like a veteran on the final drive, which began on the Michigan 20 with 2:35 to play.

On the 16th play, he found Mercury Hayes in the right corner of the north end zone for a 15-yard touchdown with no time remaining, giving Michigan its biggest comeback victory ever.

"(Hayes) was wide open," said Dreisbach, who was 12 of 23 for 236 yards in the fourth quarter. "I knew he'd do his part. My part was keeping it inbounds. If the ball was inbounds, I knew we'd win the game."

Dreisbach completed 27 of 52 for 372 yards and

two touchdowns, with two interceptions. He set a school record for attempts and yardage.

Hayes said he was ecstatic when he saw the referee extend his arms after a pause that seemed an eternity.

"I was basically concentrating on the ball and keeping my feet in bounds," said Hayes, who caught seven passes for 179 yards, including two touchdowns. "I'm turning around looking at the ref. He pointed down and put up his arms. I was ecstatic ... feeling good. Then everybody swarmed me at one time."

Virginia coach George Welsh said he wasn't so sure about whether Hayes was inbounds.

"I thought I saw it," Welsh said. "I thought it was out. It looked close."

It was a play that nearly didn't happen. With eight seconds left, Dreisbach threw short to Tyrone Butterfield, who dropped the pass intentionally. Had he caught it short of the end zone, the game would have been over.

"Yes, I did," Butterfield said when asked if he dropped the pass on purpose. "I tried to knock it down, but I made a mistake and tipped it up. I looked up and thought maybe somebody might catch it. I tried to wave (Dreisbach) off to not throw the ball."

Butterfield said that in the final huddle, Hayes demanded the ball.

"That last play, we knew we were going to win," Butterfield said. "Mercury looked at him and said, 'I want the ball ... I want the ball.' "

Lloyd Carr, in his debut as Michigan's head coach, never got to see the reception from his vantage point on the sideline.

"I saw the ball go up (and) I saw it come down," Carr said. "I lost my view of the play. It seemed like an eternity. The way the fans reacted, I knew we had scored."

Carr and most of the Wolverines heard the fan reaction throughout, as they marched scoreless through three quarters.

After Dreisbach's second interception, he started to hear the booing. And it was hard not to notice backup Brian Griese starting to warm up. Dreisbach said he never feared he would be replaced, especially after his teammates began to rally around him. He also had assurances from Carr.

"They were booing?" Carr said. "I thought they were booing me. I never thought about taking him out all week. All week I told him, 'Don't look over your shoulder, there won't be anybody there.' "

Said offensive lineman Joe Marinaro: "People were booing Scott but in essence, they were booing Coach Carr for not taking him out. I was happy he didn't. Griese hadn't played, either, and coming in down 17-0 is tough on anybody."

After both teams went scoreless in the first quarter, the Cavaliers scored in each of the final three quarters and led, 17-0, with 12:55 remaining. Their biggest play was Tiki Barber's 81-yard touchdown run, which put Michigan down, 14-0, and in the hole. The Wolverines were facing their first shutout since Iowa won, 26-0, in 1984.

"I never envisioned being down 14-0 ... 17-0? No," Carr said. "Our kids never lost their poise. They were down 17-0 and hung in there. I think Virginia got tired late in the game. It was a game of attrition."

Dreisbach, heralded for his strong arm and quick feet, set the tone on the second play of the Wolverines' first scoring drive with a 41-yard pass to Hayes to the Virginia 35. He recovered after being thrown for a 10-yard loss. Two plays later, Ed Davis scored on a 2-yard run. Davis also scored the first touchdown of the season for Michigan last year. Remy Hamilton missed the extra point, leaving it 17-6.

"After those six points, Coach Carr said we were going to win," Marinaro said. "He said, 'Remember what we said. We've got to have pride in the Big House.' He said it was going to come down to the two-minute drill, and he was right."

During the Wolverines' next possession after their first score, Dreisbach guided a six-play (all passes) scoring drive, culminating with a 31-yard touchdown pass to Hayes. A failed two-point conversion kept Michigan behind, 17-12.

If there was anything that surprised Dreisbach more than the touchdown pass, it was the fact he was actually passing ... and passing a lot.

Michigan gained only 52 yards rushing on 27 attempts, and Virginia gained 157 yards. The Wolverines had 424 yards in total offense to the Cavaliers' 348.

New Wolverine coach Lloyd Carr and Virginia's George Welsh visit prior to kickoff of the 1995 Pigskin Classic.

"I thought we'd run the ball all game," Dreisbach said. "With our offensive line, I thought we'd dominate it and be ahead because of our running game."

But thanks to the arm of a redshirt freshman, the Wolverines have the first victory of the college football season.

SCORE BY PERIODS

MICHIGAN 0   0   0   18 — 18
VIRGINIA 0   7   7   3   — 17

MICHIGAN FOOTBALL
ALL-TIME TEAM – EARLY ERA
1879 – 1945

Position	Name	Year
End	Neil Snow	1901
	Stanfield Wells	1911
	Paul Goebel	1922
	Bennie Oosterbaan	1927
Tackle	John Curtis	1906
	Tom Edwards	1925
	Francis Wistert	1933
	Albert Wistert	1942
Guard	Dan McGugin	1902
	Albert Benbrook	1910
	Butch Slaughter	1924
	Merv Pregulman	1943
Center	Germany Schulz	1908
	Chuck Bernard	1933
Quarterback	Boss Weeks	1902
	Benny Friedman	1926
	Harry Newman	1932
	Forest Evashevski	1940
Halfback	Albert Herrnstein	1902
	Willie Heston	1904
	Jim Craig	1913
	Johnny Maulbetsch	1916
	Harry Kipke	1923
	Tom Harmon	1940
Fullback	Bob Westfall	1941
	Bill Daley	1943
Placekicker	Dave Allerdice	1909
	Harry Newman	1932
Punter	John Garrels	1906
	Harry Kipke	1923

Editor's note: Player listings are chronological by position with final varsity season indicated.

MICHIGAN FOOTBALL
ALL-TIME TEAM – MODERN ERA
1946 - 1995

Offense	Name	Year	Defense	Name	Year
End	Dick Rifenburg	1948	End	Len Ford	1947
	Jim Mandich	1969		Ron Kramer	1956
				Mike Keller	1971
Tackle	Tom Mack	1965		Robert Thompson	1982
	Dan Dierdorf	1970			
	Ed Muransky	1981	Lineman	Alvin Wistert	1949
	Greg Strepenak	1991		Bill Yearby	1965
				Curtis Greer	1979
Guard	Reggie McKenzie	1971		Mark Hammerstein	1985
	Mark Donahue	1977		Mark Messner	1988
	Kurt Becker	1981		Chris Hutchinson	1992
	Dean Dingman	1990			
			Linebacker	Dick Kempthorn	1949
Center	Tom Dixon	1983		Ron Simpkins	1979
	John Vitale	1988		Mike Mallory	1985
				Erick Anderson	1991
Flanker	Jack Clancy	1966			
	Jim Smith	1976	Back	Bump Elliott	1947
	Anthony Carter	1982		Gene Derricotte	1948
	Desmond Howard	1991		Terry Barr	1956
				Rick Volk	1966
Quarterback	Bob Timberlake	1964		Tom Curtis	1969
	Rick Leach	1978		Thom Darden	1971
	Jim Harbaugh	1986		Dave Brown	1974
	Elvis Grbac	1992		Tripp Welborne	1989
Halfback	Bob Chappuis	1947	Punter	Don Bracken	1983
	Chuck Ortmann	1950		Monte Robbins	1987
	Ron Johnson	1968			
	Rob Lytle	1976			
	Butch Woolfolk	1981			
	Tyrone Wheatley	1994			

ALL-TIME HEAD COACHES

Fullback	Ed Shuttlesworth	1973	Fielding Yost	1901-23, 25-26
	Russell Davis	1978	Fritz Crisler	1938-1947
			Bo Schembechler	1969-1989
Placekicker	Jim Brieske	1947		
	J.D. Carlson	1990		

Editor's note: Player listings are chronological by position with final varsity season indicated.

University of Michigan's
101 Greatest Football Games
1879 ~ 1995

	Date	Opponent	Place	Result	Score
1.	May 30, 1879	Racine	Chicago, Ill.	Won	1-0
2.	Nov. 24, 1898	Chicago	Chicago, Ill.	Won	12-11
3.	Jan. 1, 1902	Stanford	Pasadena, Calif.	Won	49-0
4	Nov. 15, 1902	Chicago	Chicago, Ill.	Won	21-0
5.	Nov. 27, 1902	Minnesota	Ann Arbor, Mich.	Won	23-6
6.	Oct. 31, 1903	Minnesota	Minneapolis, Minn.	Tied	6-6
7.	Nov. 26, 1903	Chicago	Chicago, Ill.	Won	28-0
8.	Nov. 12, 1904	Chicago	Ann Arbor, Mich.	Won	22-12
9.	Nov. 18, 1905	Wisconsin	Ann Arbor, Mich.	Won	12-0
10.	Nov. 30, 1905	Chicago	Chicago, Ill.	Lost	0-2
11.	Nov. 20, 1909	Minnesota	Minneapolis, Minn.	Won	15-6
12.	Nov. 19, 1910	Minnesota	Ann Arbor, Mich.	Won	6-0
13.	Nov. 18, 1911	Pennsylvania	Ann Arbor, Mich	Won	11-9
14.	Nov. 9, 1912	Pennsylvania	Philadelphia, Pa.	Lost	21-27
15.	Oct. 31, 1914	Harvard	Cambridge, Mass.	Lost	0-7
16.	Oct. 21, 1922	Ohio State	Columbus, Ohio	Won	19-0
17.	Nov. 24, 1923	Minnesota	Ann Arbor, Mich.	Won	10-0
18.	Oct. 18, 1924	Illinois	Champaign, Ill.	Lost	14-39
19.	Oct. 25, 1925	Illinois	Champaign, Ill.	Won	3-0
20.	Nov. 13, 1926	Ohio State	Columbus, Ohio	Won	17-16
21.	Nov. 20, 1926	Minnesota	Minneapolis, Minn.	Won	7-6
22.	Nov. 3, 1928	Illinois	Ann Arbor, Mich.	Won	3-0
23.	Oct. 13, 1930	Purdue	Ann Arbor, Mich.	Won	14- 13
24.	Nov. 21, 1931	Minnesota	Ann Arbor, Mich.	Won	6-0
25.	Nov. 19, 1932	Minnesota	Minneapolis, Minn.	Won	3-0
26.	Oct. 21, 1933	Ohio State	Ann Arbor, Mich.	Won	13-0
27.	Oct. 14, 1939	Iowa	Ann Arbor, Mich.	Won	27-7
28.	Nov. 18, 1939	Pennsylvania	Philadelphia, Pa	Won	19-17
29.	Nov. 9, 1940	Minnesota	Minneapolis, Minn.	Lost	6-7
30.	Nov. 23, 1940	Ohio State	Columbus, Ohio	Won	40-0
31.	Sept. 26, 1942	Great Lakes	Ann Arbor, Mich.	Won	9-0
32.	Nov. 14, 1942	Notre Dame	South Bend, Ind	Won	32-20
33.	Nov. 25, 1944	Ohio State	Columbus, Ohio	Lost	14-18
34.	Oct. 13, 1945	Army	New York, N.Y.	Lost	7-28
35.	Oct. 12, 1946	Army	Ann Arbor, Mich.	Lost	13-20
36.	Sept. 27, 1947	Michigan St.	Ann Arbor, Mich.	Won	55-0
37.	Nov. 15, 1947	Wisconsin	Madison, Wis.	Won	40-6
38.	Jan. 1, 1948	U.S.C.	Pasadena, Calif.	Won	49-0
39.	Sept. 25, 1948	Michigan St.	East Lansing, Mich.	Won	13-7
40.	Oct. 8, 1949	Army	Ann Arbor, Mich.	Lost	7-21
41.	Oct. 22, 1949	Minnesota	Ann Arbor, Mich.	Won	14-7
42.	Nov. 19, 1949	Ohio State	Ann Arbor, Mich.	Tied	7-7
43.	Nov. 25, 1950	Ohio State	Columbus, Ohio	Won	9-3
44.	Jan. 1, 1951	California	Pasadena, Calif.	Won	14-6
45.	Oct. 1, 1955	Michigan St.	Ann Arbor, Mich.	Won	14-7
46.	Oct. 29, 1955	Iowa	Ann Arbor, Mich.	Won	33-21
47.	Oct. 13, 1956	Army	Ann Arbor, Mich.	Won	48-14
48.	Nov. 3, 1956	Iowa	Iowa City, Iowa	Won	17-14
49.	Nov. 2, 1957	Iowa	Ann Arbor, Mich.	Tied	21-21
50.	Nov. 18, 1961	Iowa	Ann Arbor, Mich.	Won	23-14

UNIVERSITY OF MICHIGAN'S
101 GREATEST FOOTBALL GAMES
1879 - 1995

	Date	Opponent	Place	Result	Score
51.	Oct. 10, 1964	Michigan State	East Lansing, Mich.	Won	17-10
52.	Nov. 21, 1964	Ohio State	Columbus, Ohio	Won	10-0
53.	Jan. 1, 1965	Oregon State	Pasadena, Calif.	Won	34-7
54.	Oct. 12, 1968	Michigan State	Ann Arbor, Mich.	Won	28-14
55.	Nov. 16, 1968	Wisconsin	Ann Arbor, Mich.	Won	34-9
56.	Nov. 22, 1969	Ohio State	Ann Arbor, Mich.	Won	24-12
57.	Nov. 20, 1971	Ohio State	Ann Arbor, Mich.	Won	10-7
58.	Jan. 1, 1972	Stanford	Pasadena, Calif.	Lost	12-13
59.	Nov. 18, 1972	Purdue	Ann Arbor, Mich.	Won	9-6
60.	Nov. 24, 1973	Ohio State	Ann Arbor, Mich.	Tied	10-10
61.	Nov. 23, 1974	Ohio State	Columbus, Ohio	Lost	10-12
62.	Oct. 4, 1975	Missouri	Ann Arbor, Mich.	Won	31-7
63.	Nov. 20, 1976	Ohio State	Columbus, Ohio	Won	22-0
64.	Oct. 1, 1977	Texas A&M	Ann Arbor, Mich.	Won	41-3
65.	Nov. 19, 1977	Ohio State	Ann Arbor, Mich.	Won	14-6
66.	Jan. 2, 1978	Washington	Pasadena, Calif.	Lost	20-27
67.	Nov. 23, 1978	Notre Dame	South Bend, Ind.	Won	28-14
68.	Nov. 18, 1978	Purdue	Ann Arbor, Mich.	Won	24-6
69.	Nov. 25, 1978	Ohio State	Columbus, Ohio	Won	14-3
70.	Jan. 1, 1979	U.S.C.	Pasadena, Calif.	Lost	10-17
71.	Oct. 27, 1979	Indiana	Ann Arbor, Mich.	Won	27-21
72.	Sept. 20, 1980	Notre Dame	South Bend, Ind.	Lost	27-29
73.	Nov. 15, 1980	Purdue	Ann Arbor, Mich.	Won	26-0
74.	Nov. 22, 1980	Ohio State	Columbus, Ohio	Won	9-3
75.	Jan. 1, 1981	Washington	Pasadena, Calif.	Won	23-6
76.	Nov. 7, 1981	Illinois	Ann Arbor, Mich.	Won	70-21
77.	Nov. 6, 1982	Illinois	Champaign, Ill.	Won	16-10
78.	Oct. 22, 1983	Iowa	Ann Arbor, Mich.	Won	16-13
79.	Nov. 19, 1983	Ohio State	Ann Arbor, Mich.	Won	24-21
80.	Sept. 8, 1984	Miami (Fla.)	Ann Arbor, Mich.	Won	22-14
81.	Oct. 19, 1985	Iowa	Iowa City, Iowa	Lost	10-12
82.	Nov. 23, 1985	Ohio State	Ann Arbor, Mich.	Won	27-17
83.	Jan. 1, 1986	Nebraska	Tempe, Ariz.	Won	27-23
84.	Sept. 13, 1986	Notre Dame	South Bend, Ind.	Won	24-23
85.	Oct. 18, 1986	Iowa	Ann Arbor, Mich.	Won	20-17
86.	Nov. 22, 1986	Ohio State	Columbus, Ohio	Won	26-24
87.	Jan. 2, 1988	Alabama	Tampa, Fla.	Won	28-24
88.	Sept. 10, 1988	Notre Dame	South Bend, Ind.	Lost	17-19
89.	Sept. 17, 1988	Miami (Fla.)	Ann Arbor, Mich.	Lost	30-31
90.	Jan. 2, 1989	U.S.C.	Pasadena, Calif.	Won	22-14
91.	Nov. 25, 1989	Ohio State	Ann Arbor, Mich.	Won	28-18
92.	Nov. 11, 1989	Illinois	Champaign, Ill.	Won	24-10
93.	Nov. 24, 1990	Ohio State	Columbus, Ohio	Won	16-13
94.	Sept. 14, 1991	Notre Dame	Ann Arbor, Mich.	Won	24-14
95.	Nov. 23, 1991	Ohio State	Ann Arbor, Mich.	Won	31-3
96.	Jan. 1, 1993	Washington	Pasadena, Calif.	Won	38-31
97.	Oct. 16, 1993	Penn State	State College, Pa.	Won	21-13
98.	Nov. 20, 1993	Ohio State	Ann Arbor, Mich.	Won	28-0
99.	Sept. 10, 1994	Notre Dame	South Bend, Ind.	Won	26-24
100.	Sept. 24, 1994	Colorado	Ann Arbor, Mich.	Lost	26-27
101.	Aug. 26, 1995	Virginia	Ann Arbor, Mich.	Won	18-17

ABOUT THE EDITORS

FRANCIS J. FITZGERALD, a noted editor, is one of college football's best sports researchers.

Fitzgerald previously edited *A Dynasty in Blue: 25 Years of Michigan Football Glory (1969-1994)* and *The Glory of Purple: A Scrapbook History of the Kansas State Wildcats' Memorable 1993 and 1994 Seasons.* He also co-edited *Devaney: A Dynasty Remembered* with former all-America Nebraska quarterback Jerry Tagge.

He resides in Northern Virginia.

•

BOB ROSIEK is perhaps the most knowledgeable source of information on the University of Michigan's rich football history.

As a student in the late 1960's at U-M, Rosiek first began to catalog the dates, scores and game accounts of the Wolverines' early football years by researching through newspapers of the late 1800's and early 1900's. Today, he maintains an extensive computerized library which contains vital information on all Michigan football games from 1879 to the present. He also has one of the most thorough collections of Michigan football game programs.

A 1970 graduate of the University of Michigan, Rosiek makes his living as an advertising executive. He is Senior Vice President and Chief Financial Officer for Young & Rubicam in Detroit, Michigan. Bob and his wife, Carol, also a U-M graduate, reside in Dearborn, Michigan.

Photo Credits

Ann Arbor News: 126, 186

Bentley Library, University of Michigan: Cover (Harmon), 1, 5, 6, 7, 8, 9-top, 9-bottom, 10, 11, 12, 13, 14, 15, 16, 17, 19, 20, 21, 22, 23, 24, 25, 27, 30, 32, 33, 35, 36, 38, 39, 41, 43, 44, 45, 46, 47, 48, 49, 51, 52, 53, 54, 56, 57, 58, 60, 61, 63, 65, 66, 67, 69, 70, 72, 73, 76, 78, 80, 83, 91, 93, 103, 106, 113, 134

Detroit News: Cover (Yost, Crisler, Howard), 89

Bob Kalmbach: 138, 139, 142, 150, 151, 157, 167, 173, 174, 180, 183, 189, 190, 191, 192, 193, 194, 196, 198, 200, 203, 204, 205, 206, 208

Ohio State University Archives: 22, 96, 98, 143

Andrew Pearch: 121

Pete Stanger: 181

Time Inc.: 71, 79

University of Michigan Athletic Dept.: vii, ix, 37, 82, 84, 85, 86, 88, 90, 100, 104, 109, 110, 114, 118, 122, 124, 127, 129, 140, 145, 147, 148, 152, 154, 155, 160, 161, 162, 163, 164, 165, 170, 172, 176, 178, 184, 187, 195, 197, 201

World Wide Photo: Cover (Schembechler), 125